Q-Birds

American Manned Aircraft as Drones

Q-Birds

American Manned Aircraft as Drones

Frederick A Johnsen

Edited by Tony Holmes
Colour profile artwork by Jim Laurier

Front cover top: B-17G drones, newly out of a surplus park, stand ready for duty in Operation *Crossroads* at Eniwetok in the summer of 1946. The B-17 drones collected radioactive airborne samples and performed other tasks too dangerous for human crews. *USAAF/Gene Furnish collection*

Front cover bottom: This QT-33 at Point Mugu in January 1978 had a functional front seat for piloted flights. The rear ejection seat was removed and additional gear placed in that area. *Frederick A Johnsen*

Back cover top: C Flight's shiny new *Crossroads* drones undertake a piloted cross-country jaunt to Roswell for staging before heading to the Pacific for the 1946 nuclear shots. *AFHRA*

Back cover middle left: This red F6F-5K drone met a watery end. While drone controllers worked to keep their aircraft operable for multiple missions, the nature of a drone's service was hazardous, and ultimately destruction was likely. *GSLASM/Gerald Balzer collection*

Back cover middle centre: B-17F 42-30595 *GREMLIN GUS* II was one of the original ten Flying Fortresses converted into BQ-7s for *Aphrodite*. The aircraft was fitted with the Double Azon guidance system during the conversion to pilotless flight. *USAAF*

Back cover middle right: The distant and grainy demise of a PQM-102 Delta Dagger is a spectacle that validates the effectiveness of the missile fired at it. *USAF*

Back cover bottom: The low-angle sun behind a QF-16 at Holloman casts long shadows past a special crew stand which screens the large jet inlet and accommodates a pilot or maintainer who start the drone and then safely depart while it is running. *USAF*

Half title page: F6F-5K BuNo 77633 was part of a small force of Hellcat drones used in combat strikes during the Korean War. The Hellcat drones, each armed with a single finless 1000lb or 2000lb bomb, were launched from USS *Boxer* (CV-21) whilst it sailed off the coast of North Korea in August–September 1952.

Page 3 top: This combat-worn B-17F became a BQ-7 drone for the *Aphrodite* project. 42-30353, formerly called *TEN KNIGHTS in a BAR ROOM*, had served with the 95th BG prior to being expended along with another BQ-7 on the ill-fated *Aphrodite* mission to the railway marshalling yards at Herford on 5 December 1944. *USAF*

Page 3 bottom: A QF-4E performs the 82nd ATRS's last Phantom II NOLO take off, in afterburner, from Tyndall on 27 May 2015. This marked the end of almost 20 years of Phantom II drone operations from the Florida base. *USAF*

First published in 2024 by Crécy Publishing

ISBN 9781800352797

Printed in India by Replika Press Pvt. Ltd.

Crécy Publishing Limited
1a Ringway Trading Estate, Shadowmoss Rd, Manchester M22 5LH
www.crecy.co.uk

Contents

Preface

The repurposing of piloted aircraft to become unmanned drones is an old goal that has evolved in capabilities and purposes since radios became practical for aircraft.

Depending on one's perspective, the use and likely destruction of formerly frontline combat aircraft as unmanned drones can seem frugal or fantastically extravagant. This volume takes a look at a wide variety of US drone conversion projects. Archival holdings yielded technical reports on many formerly-manned aircraft drone projects. We will range from Boeing B-17 Flying Fortresses that sampled nuclear clouds, to Grumman F6F Hellcats flown as bombs, to supersonic jet fighters with nobody aboard, to a QB-17 that shot itself down.

What all of the projects in this book have in common is their origination as US manned aircraft and their modification to become unmanned. If it seems unconscionably wasteful to shoot down a B-17 over a desert test range today, it was frugal and a good use of surplus assets in the 1950s. If crewless intercontinental ballistic missiles on one-way trips were the norm for nuclear strategic thinking in the 1960s, only two decades earlier, the US Air Force (USAF) contemplated droning Boeing B-29s for one-way bombing missions into the heartland of Cold War adversaries.

Grainy film footage of drone B-17s being blown out of the sky by missiles became a staple stand-in for any aircraft loss in war movies and television dramas of the early post-war era. Like so many things that touch on popular culture, the history of American drone aircraft is a mélange of the known and unknown.

This book has a simple marching order: it presents the use of formerly manned American aircraft that were converted into drones. The fantastic proliferation and sophistication of purpose-built uncrewed drones in recent years is a different story for a different book. And, of course, other countries developed drones from obsolete piloted aircraft – Britain's employment of Fairey Firefly and Gloster Meteor drones after the Second World War comes to mind – but that falls outside the scope of this volume.

Effort has been made to include verbatim sections of technical reports to preserve the essence and the atmosphere of some pretty remarkable drone flight programmes and projects.

Always, a volume like this could not be completed without the help of many people and organisations along the way. With apologies to anyone inadvertently left out, here are some of the individuals and organisations who helped tell the story of US drone aircraft conversions and deployments over many years of research and compilation, including those now deceased – Air Force Academy Special Collections, Air Force Test Center History Office (and Jeannine Geiger), Air Force Historical Research Agency (and Archie Difante), Gerald Balzer collection, Peter M Bowers, Tony Chong, George Cully, Duncan Curtis, Eglin Air Force Base (AFB) history office, Jim Farmer, Gene Furnish collection, Dr. Richard P Hallion, Dennis Jenkins, Kenneth G Johnsen, Craig Kaston, Donald Keller (and Air Depot), Dave Menard, National Archives and Records Administration, Naval History and Heritage Command, Stan Opatowsky, Planes of Fame Museum (and Ed Maloney), Steve Rainey, Society of Experimental Test Pilots, Frank Tallman and Tallmantz Aviation, Scott Thompson, Don Thomson, Gregg Welling and Gordon S Williams.

Some special notes on sources: Gerald Balzer's extensive photo collection includes images from the Greater St Louis Air and Space Museum (GSLASM), which is cited in this book's photo captions. We are indebted to Gerald Balzer for his generous help, and to the photographers who shared images with him that grew the collection. Likewise, Scott Thompson deserves more than passing mention for his extensive research into the fates of B-17s after the Second World War. His work has informed what we write about QB-17s and DB-17s. Duncan Curtis graciously opened his files on drones, especially QF-86s, to add valuable details to that story. Recollections from QF-16 drone test pilots Steve Rainey and Gregg Welling are their own, and do not represent Boeing, developer of the QF-16, or the USAF.

One other linguistic note that must be mentioned. A celebrated truism, sometimes attributed to author George Bernard Shaw, says, 'England and America are two countries divided by a common language'. That became bountifully evident when proofing my edited manuscript to this volume. One of the marching orders from the publisher was to conform this manuscript to standards of British English and spelling, which can differ widely from American English. So, Dear Reader, please know that I have not abandoned my American writing style. It has just been translated into its British version in the editing process. And grateful I am to have England's Crécy Publishing Ltd, through its Hikoki Publications imprint, giving my drone book its day.

The process of researching, and then writing, a book like *Q-Birds* is an effort that fuelled my passion for American aviation history starting many years ago. I strive to deliver the most accurate effort that I can, but if I have made any errors, alas, I am fallible and I give you my apologies. Editor Tony Holmes also inserted bits of information that go unattributed throughout this book's manuscript. He deserves his own measure of credit and accountability for that.

Legendary aviation historian Peter M Bowers once said he never really finished a book; at some point he simply had to stop and submit his work to the publisher. So, with Pete's words in mind, take this volume as an earnest effort to explore the world of American drone conversion aircraft. There is probably more information to be dug up, but we believe you will find something in these pages that you did not previously know about American drone conversions. Hope you enjoy.

Frederick A Johnsen
November 2023

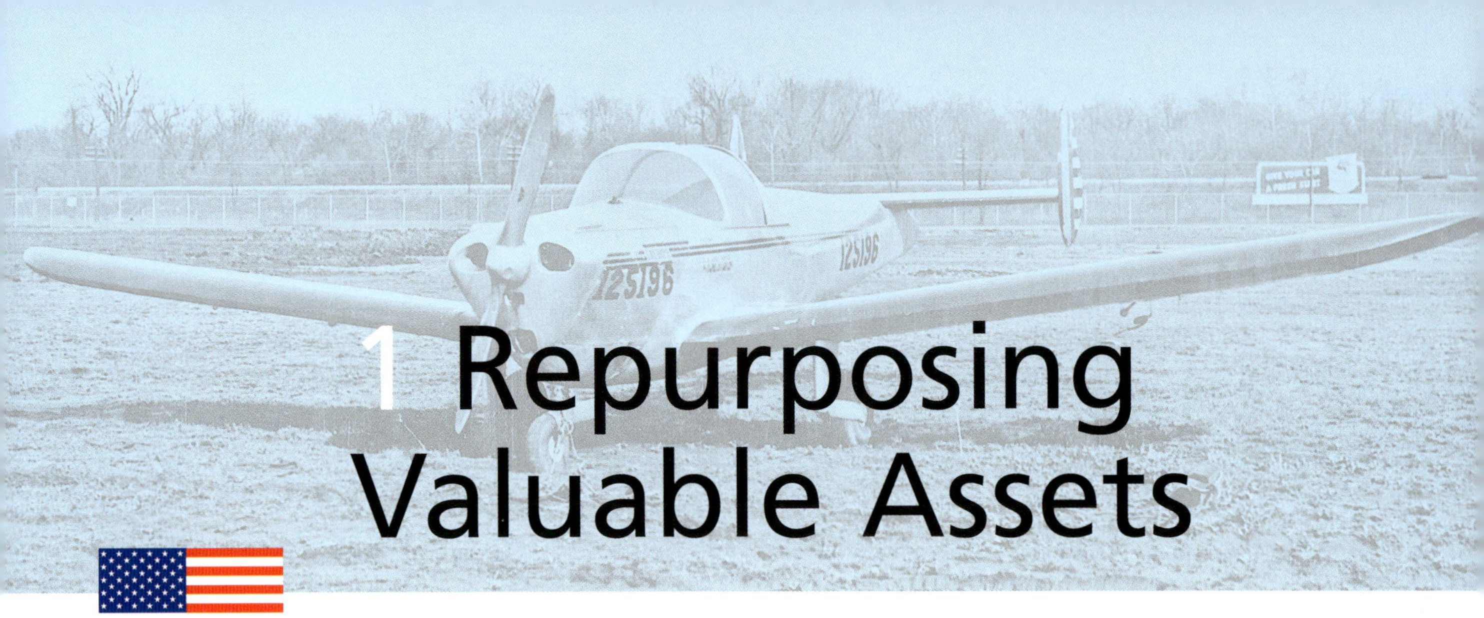

1 Repurposing Valuable Assets

In the midst of the First World War, the US Navy undertook research into aircraft that used gyroscopes and barometers to keep them stable and at intended altitudes. The tests included an unsuccessful purpose-built aircraft that lacked a cockpit, as well as a handful of modified Curtiss N-9 biplanes. The first flight of an aircraft equipped with this type of automatic flying gear came in September 1919. A pilot was still onboard to accomplish take-off and landing, but the concept showed promise.

On 17 October 1918, an unmanned N-9 successfully launched from a catapult designed by John Norden, later of bombsight fame. Although the biplane was programmed for a flight of eight miles over the ocean, at which time it was to descend to the water, the distance measuring and control gear malfunctioned, and the errant N-9 cruised out to sea never to be seen again. Nonetheless, the concept of unmanned aircraft gained headway with the use of this converted N-9. The stage was set. Nearly 100 flights of automatically controlled N-9s were made – most of these had a safety pilot on board. The end of the First World War on 11 November 1918 put the concept of unpiloted aircraft on hold as budgets, and urgency, waned.

In 1920, the US Army Air Service (USAAS) contracted with Lawrence Sperry's new company to outfit three Standard E-1 fighter-trainers as radio-controlled 'flying torpedoes'.[1] The E-1 radio control aircraft were lengthened in the process, and given the serial numbers 64228, 64229 and 64230. Sperry was also the contracted manufacturer of the M-1 Messenger light liaison biplane, eight of which were delivered as radio-controlled 'aerial torpedoes'. These ultimately received the designation MAT for Messenger Aerial Torpedo.[2]

A single Curtiss Robin cabin monoplane bought by the USAAC in 1928 became the XC-10 drone, with its engine remounted. Stabilising dihedral appears to have been added to the wings of the drone. *Gerald Balzer collection*

The Stearman-Hammond Y-1S, designed as an easy-to-fly general aviation aircraft, lent itself to early droning experiments by the US Navy in 1936 as the JH-1. *NACA*

By 1921 the US Navy had embraced the notion of using radios to control an unmanned aircraft instead of relying on mechanical timing devices and simple stabilisers. Test flights in 1923 showed promise, but by 1925 the effort had ended. It would be a decade before the US Navy revived its interest in remotely-piloted aircraft.

In 1928, the US Army Air Corps (USAAC, which had replaced the USAAS two years earlier) bought a Curtiss Robin cabin monoplane which was given the serial number 29-452.[3] It received a modified engine mount, placing the motor higher and closer in line with the wing, blocking much of the forward view available in a standard Robin. The unaesthetic aircraft was flown as a radio-controlled drone and given the nomenclature XC-10. It was said to be the world's first remotely controlled weapon-carrying aircraft. Shoestring interwar defence budgets only allowed the XC-10 to barely survive as a project until 1932.[4]

From 1937, a small number of ageing US Navy Curtiss N2C-2 Fledgling trainers were given a 'makeover', which included the fitting of a tricycle landing gear and removal of the rear cockpit, for use as radio-controlled drone targets. *Wallace via Gerald Balzer collection*

The development of unmanned aircraft in the United States from the First World War into the 1930s was frequently premised on the concept of creating a flying bomb. To achieve this, fundamental remote flight controls and later radio controls needed maturation. Capt Delmar S Fahrney, who would retire as a rear admiral, was charged in 1936 with the task of learning about making remotely controlled targets for ships' gunners. The goal was to give the US Navy a realistic aerial target within three to five years. The starting point was to use existing manned aircraft modified for radio control.

That summer, the US Navy used a pair of Stearman-Hammond low-wing tricycle gear general aviation aircraft, under the designation JH-1, for radio control testing. The JH-1 had started life as the civil aviation Y-1S, designed to be easy to fly. The Stearman-Hammond plant was established in South San Francisco, California, and the company touted that the Y-1S was a safe aeroplane in which non-pilots could quickly become proficient. One story told about the Y-1S stated that a person with no previous piloting experience taxied, took off, flew circuits and returned to land and taxi back to the hangar based solely on verbal instructions made by the instructor pilot seated beside the neophyte.[5]

One of the features of this aircraft was its lack of rudder controls, with turns effected by use of differential ailerons and elevators. This simplified flight control feature, plus the ground handling benefits of tricycle landing gear, possibly influenced the US Navy's choice of the Stearman-Hammond for early radio control studies. Radio control modifications were made at the Naval Aircraft Factory in Philadelphia, Pennsylvania, using specialised radio gear developed at the Naval Research Laboratory.

By 1937, US Navy radio control aircraft work had migrated to Curtiss N2C-2 Fledgling trainers, which ended their days with tricycle landing gear and radio control equipment for use as target drones. Testing was moved to the US Coast Guard station at Cape May, New Jersey. Pioneering the basic set up for drones in the US for decades to come, the Cape May operation used one pilot seated at a cart near the runway, where he manipulated controls similar to the throttle, control column and rudder of the aeroplane. Radio signals translated the ground controller's movements to receivable signals in the biplane, which responded accordingly. The ground controller manipulated the N2C-2 during take-off and up to an altitude of 200ft, when another control pilot in an airborne Great Lakes TG-2 biplane took command of the unmanned N2C-2. Landing was accomplished by a hand-off of the N2C-2 to the ground control pilot.[6]

First flights of the radio-controlled N2C-2 had a safety pilot aboard who could rescue the biplane from a predicament if the remote pilot experienced problems. By November 1937, the testers were ready to launch one of the N2C-2s with no safety pilot aboard. Take-off, hand-off and aerial manoeuvring went well. The approach to landing looked fine, but at touchdown the nosewheel hit too hard and collapsed, followed by the mainwheels folding and the propeller bending. The Curtiss was repairable, and in late December a complete flight with no safety pilot was accomplished without incident. This has been credited as the first time a full-sized aircraft was under radio control without a safety pilot from the start to the finish of the sortie.

The adoption of tricycle landing gear, which made the aircraft easier to manoeuvre than conventional tailwheel style, was a hallmark of the N2C-2 drone. *Wallace via Gerald Balzer collection*

The N2C-2 drone programme gave the US Navy convincing evidence of the feasibility of radio-controlled full-sized aircraft. *Wallace via Gerald Balzer collection*

US Navy ground control pilots quickly realised they would need to make landing inputs that 'felt backward', as they faced the approaching radio-controlled aircraft on landing. For example, a movement of the control column to the left would make the aircraft respond by moving to the right, relative to the ground controller. This issue of orientation remained for years, and was best overcome by experience.

In this era, the US Navy started labelling its radio-controlled aircraft 'drones' as targets for seaborne gunners. In 1939, Capt George Holloman and 1Lt Rudolf Fink of the USAAC were able to observe US Navy target drone operations at firsthand. Their report led the USAAC to request a drone, mother ship and ground control set from the US Navy. From then on, both services would refine drone capabilities to meet their specific needs.[7]

Aside from serving as target drones, radio-controlled N2C-2s were also expended during the course of trials pre-war. In 1938, for example, a solitary N2C-2 was guided into a target ship as a demonstration of a flying bomb. That same year, radio-controlled aircraft targets challenged the gunners embarked in the carrier USS *Ranger* (CV-4). In 1942, an obsolete Great Lakes TG-1 torpedo-bomber was fitted with a large television camera beneath its left wing which was to be used by a remote operator as he guided the biplane to its target, further testing the concept of an attack drone.

By 1940, piloted monoplane combat aircraft were rapidly making earlier generations of warplanes obsolete, and the US Navy converted surplus aircraft like the biplane Boeing F4B/P-12 into unmanned flying targets. Its use had been posited by the USAAC that same year under the designation A-5, intended for converted P-12Es. In 1940–41, it used the prefix letter A to denote a (Power Driven) Aerial Target before its subsequent adoption as A-for-Attack.[8] The USAAC soon migrated away from using full-size aircraft for this purpose, resulting in the A-5 notion being dropped.[9]

The US Navy liked the idea, however, and in 1940 it began converting 23 ex-USAAC P-12Cs, -Ds -Es, and one F-model, to become target drones as the F4B-4A, with newly-assigned Navy Bureau of Aeronautics (BuNo) serial numbers. It is believed the last of the F4B-4As was expended in 1942.[10] A 25 September 1942 official report titled *Location of U.S. Naval Aircraft* lists three F4B-4As on strength with utility squadron VJ-5 at Cape May.[11]

During the Second World War, both the US Army Air Forces (USAAF, as the USAAC was redesignated in June 1941) and the US Navy capitalised on advances in radio control capabilities and television cameras to equip war-weary B-17 Flying Fortresses for the USAAF and Consolidated PB4Y-1 Liberators for the US Navy as explosives-laden expendable drones in Projects *Aphrodite* and *Anvil* (see Chapter 2).

Fleets of wartime aircraft were made obsolete by rapidly advancing aeronautics. These outdated warplanes were available to the American military for droning. Both the USAAF and the US Navy explored the feasibility of using bomb-laden drones for dangerous one-way combat missions, and both services also used surplus fighters and bombers as remote sensing aircraft in nuclear tests. Drones were also handy targets to validate evolving antiaircraft missile systems.

The PQ-13 (an Ercoupe Model 415-C with an O-300 engine) was an abortive experiment at converting a piloted civilian aeroplane for use as a military target drone. This aircraft, given serial number 41-25196, and 41-39099 were evaluated by the USAAC in 1941 but no contract resulted. 41-25196's serial number adorned its fuselage in two locations. *NARA*

The post-Second World War USAF (which became independent of the US Army in September 1947) had among its leaders those who remembered all too well how surplus aircraft from the First World War stifled new aviation developments in the 1920s and gave members of Congress handy, if ill-advised, excuses for not funding new aircraft development and production at a rate the service deemed necessary. Even during the war, some of the motivation for follow-on programmes after *Aphrodite* was the perceived need to divest the USAAF of its older bomber fleet in one-way drone bomb missions, lest these war-weary examples show up on paper looking just as viable as a new aircraft to the unenlightened.

The emergent USAF summarily scrapped older warplanes in places like Kingman, Arizona, and Walnut Ridge, Arkansas. Meanwhile the service husbanded a pocket of brand-new B-17Gs at remote places like Pyote, in the wide open expanses of west Texas in the post-war 1940s. The last B-17Gs delivered by Douglas and Vega under contract, and even the very last Flying Fortress to roll out of the Boeing home factory in Seattle, survived the scrapper. With its nascent wartime experience in droning B-17s, and a belief among some pilots that the big bomber was easy to fly, and therefore should be easy to drone, the post-war USAF went all in on using Flying Fortresses for projects deemed to be too risky for onboard pilots.

As remote pilots gained proficiency and droning equipment improved, the USAF's post-war use of B-17Gs blossomed into an enterprise that flourished for more than a decade. The aircraft went from rustic one-way missiles, to unmanned radiation samplers in atomic tests, to intentional ditching machines, to targets for an ever-more-sophisticated array of anti-aircraft missiles.

Similarly, the US Navy's surfeit of new and low-time Grumman F6F Hellcats, also known for their forgiving flight characteristics with a big wing that made them more gentle than some fighters, gave the service a utility drone that enjoyed more than ten years of service. This narrative, while exploring many fascinating drone programmes in the US, acknowledges the seminal importance of B-17s and F6Fs to the American drone experience.

2 The Beginning

Gen H H 'Hap' Arnold, Chief of the USAAF, expressed interest in expending aged-out heavy bombers on German targets. The experimental iteration that transpired was not a general remote or unmanned bombardment campaign, but a few specific strike attempts at hardened targets that were particularly dangerous to hit, and possibly impervious to a lesser volume of explosives that a normal manned B-17 could carry on a sortie.

The USAAF called the programme Project *Aphrodite*, while US Navy aircraft folded into *Aphrodite* were codenamed *Anvil*. Research into droning timeworn bombers took place both in the US and with the Eighth Air Force in England, and the Flying Fortresses were sometimes identified as 'Weary Willies' (the letters WW were routinely applied to aged aircraft in England to identify them as war-weary).

The ability to control another aircraft in flight had by now been grasped, but the ability to take-off a remotely-piloted bomber was still in the future. Landing such a creation was not desirable with up to 20,000lb of high explosives on board. So the premise for *Aphrodite* was to have a two-man crew take off in the radio-receiver bomber, pass control to an airborne mother ship and then bail out.

On 26 June 1944, Lt Gen James H Doolittle, commander of the Eighth Air Force, directed the 3rd Bombardment Division to undertake Project *Aphrodite* – the use of droned B-17s filled with explosives and flown against hardened German targets. The unit tasked with performing these missions was the 388th Bombardment Group (BG) at Knettishall, in Suffolk. Initially, USAAF *Aphrodite* drones were controlled by Double Azon, an interim device that was used until better control was validated.[12] Single Azon allowed steering in azimuth only, but for *Aphrodite*, a second Azon set was fitted for elevation (pitch) control. This required an operator who could see the drone being directed, or at least see a forward view from the drone provided by early television signals.

Combat sorties, attempted or otherwise, with *Aphrodite* numbered 13 between 4 August 1944 and 1 January 1945. Two *Anvil* aircraft added to the total. In early 1945 *Aphrodite* was discontinued, with the specialised control equipment removed from remaining Flying Fortresses used in the programme.

The emphasis for *Aphrodite* came at a critically frustrating time for Allied planners in the summer of 1944. The invasion of western Europe and the systematic reduction of German war-making capabilities demanded considerable bombardment resources. But the threat posed by V1 and V2 'vengeance weapons' launched from France and the Netherlands and aimed at southern England was very real, and the British government emphasised the need for help in taking out the missile sites. American leaders, sometimes begrudgingly, took bomber assets away from prosecuting other aspects of the war to make destruction of V-weapon sites the priority in Operation *Crossbow*. Results with normal bomb loads proved ineffective against hardened and underground facilities that could be difficult to find. Larger explosives with a dramatically bigger radius of destruction looked attractive for

B-17F 42-30595 *GREMLIN GUS II* was one of the original ten Flying Fortresses converted into BQ-7s for *Aphrodite*. The aircraft was fitted with the Double Azon guidance system during the conversion to pilotless flight. *USAAF*

ending the V-weapon threat in the summer of 1944.

Col Alfred R Maxwell, director of operations for the US Strategic Air Forces (USSTAF) in Europe, was schooled and experienced at developing bombardment equipment and requirements. He opined in a terse message on 20 June 1944 that 'the large rocket sites are practically invulnerable to normal bombing attacks. Strong indications that sites must be neutralized immediately. Believe that success can be attained if large enough loads of explosive can be placed with extreme precision, namely within ten to twenty feet of aiming points. In view of importance of neutralization which you will fully appreciate, every weapon which offers chance of success should be exploited.'[13]

A war-weary droned Flying Fortress or Liberator carrying nine or ten tons of high explosives was only one of several experimental ideas seized upon in those desperate times.

Col Maxwell also considered droning heavy fighters like Republic P-47 Thunderbolts or Lockheed P-38 Lightnings to crash bombs into the targets:

> 'In order to obtain ground penetration of armor piercing or 2000lb George Peter [general purpose] bombs it may be necessary to dive a radio-controlled Peter Four Seven [P-47] or Peter Three Eight [P-38] into site. The control ship should be fast and nimble in order to fly through the heavy Flak at low to medium altitudes. For this purpose we can make available Baker Two Sixes [Martin B-26 Marauders], Able Twenties [Douglas A-20 Havocs], [de Havilland] Mosquitos or Droopsnoot Peter Three Eights. Therefore, control equipment should be selected which can be quickly installed in one of these types.'[14]

Ultimately, the drones developed under *Aphrodite* for *Crossbow* and other attacks in 1944 would be four-engined B-17s and B-24s, led into combat by more B-17s as director aircraft. As early as 23 June, Col Maxwell invoked the name *Aphrodite* for the bomber drone effort in a message requesting television gear to equip the drones for greater accuracy. He also acknowledged initial *Aphrodite* sorties would be controlled by a Double Azon set-up as a makeshift expedient until better radio control gear was forthcoming.[15]

In a 1 July 1944 message to USAAF leadership, Gen 'Hap' Arnold elaborated on his interest in using war-weary bombers:

> 'This suggests an effective method of disposing of our great and growing numbers of war-weary aircraft of all types in all theatres. For example, in Europe crewless aircraft heavily laden with very high explosives might be guided by television principle and could possibly be steered into any remaining objectives in the theatre. In the Far East, such aircraft, operating to maximum range – not radius – could possibly be guided across vast stretches of water and then be steered by heat or magnetic target seeking devices into cities or ships.'[16]

Four days later, plans were approved to convert 500 Flying Fortresses and Liberators into drones, and they were to be guided by 100 control aircraft.

The initial targets for *Aphrodite* were German V-weapon storage and launch sites in the Pas-de-Calais area of northern France. Double Azon-equipped B-17F drones were to be tended by four control aircraft, one Flying Fortress and three Liberators. The control pilots began training in England on 1 July 1944. The drone pilots were given instruction in the proper way to bail out once their aircraft was under control of the mother ship. The second crewmember onboard the drone was a specialist in the use of the C-1 autopilot.

The mission scenario called for two task forces consisting of two control aircraft and one drone apiece. They would fly an assigned route and altitude profile, while checking out control of the drones before the drone crews bailed out. After guiding their first two drones in to their targets, the mother aircraft were to return to pick up another set of drones. A fifth drone assigned to the mission would carry an offensive load of jelled gasoline.[17]

That first *Aphrodite* mission launched on 4 August 1944, its targets being various bunkers associated with

GREMLIN GUS II survived long enough for its Azon gear to be replaced by Castor guidance equipment. It was assigned to a mission that would have seen the German battleship *Tirpitz* in the Alten Fjord in Norway targeted by a large hydrostatic bomb detonated underwater. The weapon was so large that it had to be lowered into the fuselage from above. In order for this to take place, Boeing engineers modified the bomber by removing the fairing behind the cockpit. Once the weapon was in place, the fuselage was faired over again with sheet metal. As can be seen here, the cockpit was left open, leading to 42-30595 being dubbed 'The Roadster'. *Tirpitz* was sunk by RAF Lancasters on 12 November 1944 using 12,000lb Tallboy earthquake bombs, thus sparing 42-30595 from destruction. The bomber was eventually salvaged in June 1946. *USAAF*

B-17G 43-37793 was one of two Flying Fortresses assigned to the 388th BG as Azon mother ships for BQ-7 drones during *Aphrodite*. Unlike the aircraft these B-17s were controlling, neither of the mother ships had seen previous service as bombers – they arrived at Knettishall in June 1944 fresh from United Air Lines' modification centre in Cheyenne, Wyoming. The AN-117-A antennas for the AN/ARW-18 radio transmitter for the Azon system are clearly visible on the underside of the bomber. *USAAF*

V-weapons in the Pas-de-Calais. All four mother ships took off an hour ahead of the drones and climbed to an altitude of 20,000ft over a pre-arranged location. The four drones assigned to the operation took off five minutes apart under piloted control. Navigation aircraft allocated to each task force led the piloted drones to the rendezvous with the control aircraft.

The first drone, assigned to Task Force II and targeting the V1 bunker at Siracourt, flew in a rectangular pattern, with the control aircraft and drone crew finalising transfer of control from the pilot aboard the drone. Its predetermined flightpath led directly over Woodbridge airfield, in Suffolk, where the C-1 autopilot technician bailed out. As soon as he had taken to his parachute disaster struck, as the heavy drone pulled up, stalled, fell off on one wing and dived into the ground, carrying the hapless pilot to his death. An altimeter problem was suspected to have caused the pull-up that started the stall sequence.

Task Force II requested a second drone, which was immediately despatched to it. This time, the set-up procedure, transfer of aircraft control and crew bailout occurred as planned.[18] Since *Aphrodite* relied on visual cues for a successful mission, the appearance of clouds over the second drone's target (the Wizernes bunker) obscured the control pilot's view. The drone was estimated to have hit the ground 500ft from the bunker because of this. It was a grim and inauspicious start for *Aphrodite*, and Task Force II had spent so much additional time collecting a replacement drone that it was recalled home instead of setting up for its intended third target.[19]

Task Force I had an uneventfully successful hook-up with its first flying bomb, with the crew bailing out safely. The drone was led directly over its target, but the control pilot in the B-24 was unable to make the B-17 go down. In a second pass over the target, the drone again failed to dive. By now, the mother ship crew knew they had a drone that flew, but would not dive into the ground, so they circled the B-17 around the target area 'in an effort to get rid of it', according to the after action report. A few minutes later, the drone was hit by Flak and exploded about 15 miles east of its assigned target.

Task Force I picked up another drone and directed it to the second target of the day. The control pilot felt that the B-17 was flying too high and tried to reduce its altitude to the standard attack height of 300ft. However, this manoeuvring caused the drone to impact with the ground some 1500ft short of the target when the pilot initiated its final dive at the wrong time. So ended the first operational sorties of *Aphrodite*.[20]

Two days later, the mother ships went aloft again, followed by two drones. The first drone (a B-17F carrying ten tons of Torpex explosive) was successfully led through the hand-off tasks. While crossing the English Channel, the mother ship lost control of the drone when it encountered a formation of B-24s over the English Channel. The mother ship overshot the drone and then experienced control problems that resulted in the B-17F turning sharply to the left, flipping over onto its back and then crashing into the sea roughly two miles from the coastline of occupied France.

The second drone (a B-17G) was again successfully set-up and control transferred to the mother ship. While set on a course for the Continent, the drone started an uncommanded turn to the right, which the control pilot tried to correct. Failing to respond properly to control inputs, the drone was flown into the Channel by the second mother ship, which was concerned lest the errant drone should wander back over England with its huge load of explosives. The expedient Double Azon control system was suspected of being problematical following these early missions, and its use was discontinued after 6 August.[21] Although the *Aphrodite* crews had now gained experience with the system, their mission success rate was still nil.

US Navy participation in *Aphrodite* involved the creation of just two *Anvil* bombers. One was in the inventory as a PB4Y-1 Liberator and the other was a B-24D made available by the USAAF's 3rd Air Division, an upper command echelon of the Eighth Air Force. The US Navy used two modified Lockheed PV-1 Ventura twin-engined medium bombers as control aircraft. Twenty-seven enlisted sailors and officers were assigned to *Aphrodite*. The US Navy relied on FM remote-control equipment that was considerably more sophisticated than the stop-gap Double Azon.

Once in England, crews experimented with the drone system, studied targets and honed their technique, before declaring 12 August to be the date of the US Navy's first *Aphrodite* mission (which would see the fortress of Mimoyecques targeted yet again).[22] It was a date that would resonate for the wrong reasons. The volunteer pilot of the *Anvil* Liberator was Lt Joseph Kennedy, son of the former US ambassador to Britain, Joseph P Kennedy, and elder brother of the future US president, John F Kennedy.

A forward-looking television camera was mounted in the nose of this B-17F converted into an *Aphrodite* BQ-7 robot bomb. On one drone mission, the camera sent back imagery of the BQ-7's gentle descent and belly landing inside enemy territory without exploding, causing Allied concern about secrets revealed to the Germans. *AFHRA*

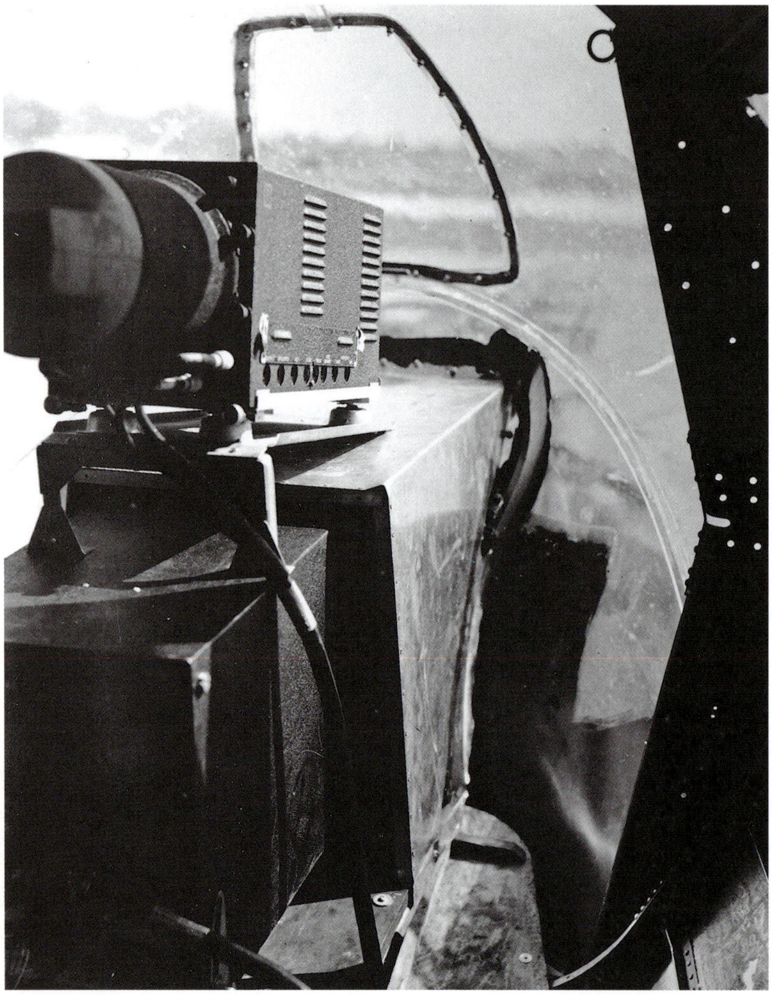

Two PV-1 mother ships trailed the Liberator at an altitude of 2000ft. Control was successfully passed to one of the Ventura crews, and the bomber was manoeuvred by the mother ship. About two minutes later, however, a tremendous blast (the aircraft was carrying ten-and-a-half tons of Torpex) disintegrated the drone south of Halesworth, in Suffolk, before its two crew could bail out. What is sometimes inadvertently overlooked in the discussion of Lt Joseph Kennedy's death is the loss of the second pilot aboard the PB4Y-1 that day, Lt Wilford J Willy.[23]

Further *Aphrodite* missions were delayed until the cause of the detonation could be found. Once it was decided that a faulty safe-and-arming system was the likely cause of the explosion, the arming detonation system was changed to a manual device instead of an electric mechanism. At last, on 3 September, a second US Navy *Anvil* aircraft (formerly a USAAF B-24D) was despatched on an *Aphrodite* mission. The droned Liberator responded to the set-up and hand-off to the control aeroplane pilot. The brace of two PV-1 mother ships escorted the now unmanned B-24 over the North Sea, aiming for U-boat pens at Heligoland, on the German coast. The flight covered more than 350 miles.[24]

Television used in the drones and mother ships was referred to as 'Block', and problems with the latter bedeviled this sortie, as described in a post-mission summary:

> 'The Block operator with a poor picture picked up the breakwater on Dune Island, mistaking it for Heligoland. Eight seconds prior to impact, the Block picture was lost, indicating a hit by Flak on the transmitter. The robot also started into a right turn and the controller dove it into Dune Island. Photos show a large crater near the barracks area and extensive damage to barracks and other buildings.'

In the absence of Block television, the control pilot relied on visual observation of the drone before impact.[25] In the big picture, the results of this mission had been yet another operational failure for the *Aphrodite* drone project, for the concrete U-boat pens remained unscathed. Yet the evidence of extensive damage to outlying structures (both barracks and a fuel dump) at Heligoland was at least a validation of the power of one droned four-engined bomber laden with explosives when guided to a target.

From early September, USAAF *Aphrodite* aircraft used the Castor radio control system that was similar to the US Navy's FM remote-control equipment instead of the problematical Double Azon. By then, drone B-17s and B-24s had been officially designated BQ-7s and BQ-8s, respectively. The first Castor BQ-7 detachment had arrived in England on 2 August 1944, and 12 bombers were converted into drones for the unit at Burtonwood, in Cheshire. Five Flying Fortresses were modified as CQB-17G mother ships at this time, with all modifications to both types being completed by 20 August.

Despite the Castor aircraft now being fitted with improved guidance equipment, the *Aphrodite* missions remained anything but routine, with hazards lurking for the aircrew assigned to them. Indeed, during the first operation for the BQ-7, on 11 September, only one of the two crewmen aboard the drone bailed out successfully following a trouble-free set-up – the other was a fatality, possibly due to an improperly attached static line. Nevertheless, the drone was guided 355 miles to Heligoland. Ten seconds from the target, the BQ-7's right wing burst into flames (Flak was reported in the area) and the drone entered an uncommanded right turn. Other controls remained responsive up to impact, however, and Block television imaging was clear and useful. The aircraft crashed about 300ft to the right of the intended target.[26]

Three days later, Hemmingstedt oil refinery was targeted following a conventional bombing mission by 23 B-17s from the Eighth Air Force on 6 August. Two BQ-7s (and six B-24s of the 458th BG armed with VB-1 Azon 1000lb guided bombs) were sent there. All drone crewmen bailed out safely, and both BQ-7s were escorted without issue for 400 miles. The first drone's control pilot was hampered by unclear imagery, so he guided the aircraft visually to the target. A monitor aircraft on the mission had clearer Block imagery, and reported the BQ-7 crossed over the target at low altitude and overshot by about 200ft as the control pilot misjudged the use of down control.[27]

The second BQ-7 was overrun by its mother ship, forcing the pilot of the latter to execute a 360-degree turn to get behind the drone. Whilst turning, contact was lost with the bomber in the haze, and data received by the control pilot failed to identify the drone's heading and Block coverage only showed water. Lacking sufficient information to point the drone on a heading towards the refinery, or even onward into Germany, the control pilot decided to crash the BQ-7 into the sea rather than risk its flight into friendly territory.[28]

Aphrodite missions did not then resume until 15 October, when two BQ-7s were guided to Heligoland. The first drone, which lost its Block television capability on final approach to the target, was destroyed by Flak at an altitude of 700ft. Control of the second BQ-7 was hindered by low visibility that degraded the Block television coverage. The after action report said this drone 'hit the lower town of Heligoland'.[29]

Sixteen days later, on 31 October, a pair of BQ-7s targeted the Heligoland U-boat pens for a final time. Control issues were reported with both aircraft, and Block television images were poor due in part to restricted visibility. For the first drone, the weather was 'socked in zero–zero' over the target, so the BQ-7 was notionally released on a heading that was wryly said to be 'toward Berlin', although the efficacy of that is dubious. Weather and control issues thwarted the second drone also, and it was released on a heading into the North Sea.[30] Some accounts say it exploded in Sweden.

With its bombardment group identification marking on the tail and nickname on the nose painted out, an unidentified B-17F modified into a BQ-7 drone sits peacefully on an airfield in eastern England in November 1944. The following month the Flying Fortress was consumed in an unsuccessful *Aphrodite* mission. *AFHRA*

This combat-worn B-17F whose gunners had claimed three victories over Luftwaffe fighters became a BQ-7 drone for the *Aphrodite* project. 42-30353, formerly called *TEN KNIGHTS in a BAR ROOM*, had served with the 95th BG prior to being expended along with another BQ-7 on the ill-fated *Aphrodite* mission to the railway marshalling yards at Herford on 5 December 1944. The wind deflector is visible ahead of the open hatch through which the take-off crew would bail out. *USAF*

As late as early December 1944, message traffic on *Aphrodite* lists one 'B-24 Robot' among the spare aircraft available. No indication is given whether this is a war-weary US Navy PB4Y-1 or an ex-USAAF Liberator, and it was not expended.[31]

A change in targeting saw two BQ-7s despatched against railway marshalling yards at Herford, deeper into Germany, on 5 December. The orders were succinct. The primary target was the Herford marshalling yards, the secondary target was the Nienberg marshalling yards and the 'last resort' target was the Celle marshalling yards, 'or any other military objective positively identified as being in Germany'.[32]

By now, drone crews were faring better in bailouts than had some of their early compatriots. Control responses were reported as good this day, although Block television coverage was again 'spotty'. Poor weather made it impossible for the control crew to find the target, so the first drone was despatched in the direction of another city, where the mission team reported it was shot down. The second drone descended through cloud cover and then mushed into the ground without exploding. The *Aphrodite* team figured this was the result of carburettor icing reducing engine power, leading to a power-on approach to the surface. The bomber had probably decelerated too slowly to cause forces sufficiently violent to detonate the explosives.[33]

Ominously, the control pilot reported he could still see a good television image from the nose of the crash-landed BQ-7 after it came to a halt on the ground, confirming the drone and its experimental control equipment were intact for German inspection. Although three escorting North American P-51 Mustangs were told to destroy the grounded BQ-7, and duly acknowledged this order, later message traffic suggested the drone was still intact and had fallen into enemy hands.

Thwarted by poor weather the following morning, it was not until the afternoon of 6 December that two missions were launched to find the downed drone, without success. The search

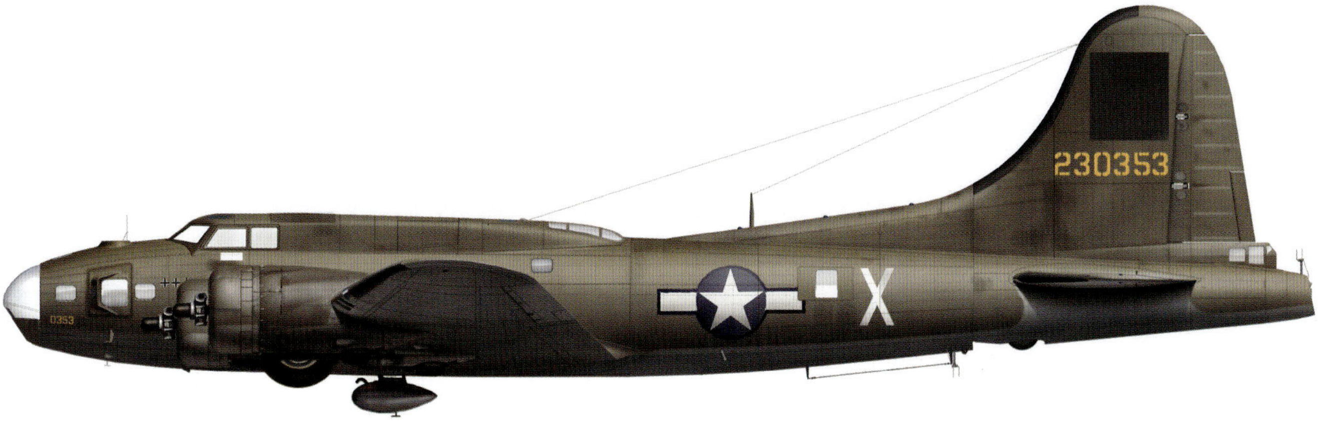

B-17F 42-30353 *TEN KNIGHTS in a BAR ROOM* was converted into a BQ-7 drone for the Project *Aphrodite* series of combat sorties over Occupied Europe. The aircraft was expended on an unsuccessful mission against railway marshalling yards at Herford, in northwestern Germany, on 5 December 1944.

was not helped by the various conflicting reports on the exact whereabouts of the BQ-7. The control pilot gave one location, a photo-reconnaissance aircraft stated another spot and a third area was indicated by fighters that had accompanied the mission. Maj Gen Carl Spaatz, commander of USSTAF, sent the following message to Lt Gen Doolittle on 19 December:

> 'Everything possible should be done to locate and determine the status of the *Aphrodite* baby which landed intact in Germany. If located, it should be destroyed regardless of possibility that compromise may by now be complete. In view of explosive content, suggest napalm may be practical.'[34]

On 20 December, following more weather delays, searches were again launched despite the Eighth Air Force believing there was little chance the drone would be found. Although contemporary *Aphrodite* messages preserved in the Air Force Historical Research Center file on the topic did not resolve the fate of the intact BQ-7 in German hands, a 1952 summary of drone history made a cryptic reference to its apparent end. 'Later intelligence reports indicated a sudden demise of enemy personnel who were making a check of the TNT-loaded drone.'[35]

1 January 1945 was a day of near-continual action for both the Allies and the Luftwaffe, with the latter employing an estimated 700–800 aircraft in a dawn attack on Allied airfields on the Continent in Operation *Bodenplatte*. New Year's Day also saw the Eighth Air Force sortie more than 700 heavy bombers against ten or more German cities, concentrating on rail centres and Oil Plan targets.

One more mission that day would wrap up the *Aphrodite* project. Two BQ-7s flew to Oldenburg, in North West Germany, to target the city's power station. Control was good en route, but the visual smoke trail generators fitted to the drones were not working. The first drone did not have Block video equipment installed, and the second drone's Block system was inoperative. The first BQ-7 hit the ground about two miles beyond the power station even though the control pilot applied down control at the right time for expected target intersection. The second drone hit the ground about five miles from the target as it made a turn for a second run-in. Altimeter failure was suspected.[36]

A bleak explosion in a snow-covered farm field somewhere in the vicinity of Oldenberg, in North West Germany, on 1 January 1945 was an epitaph for the end of *Aphrodite* as a drone BQ-7 Flying Fortress failed to hit its meaningful target (the city's power station) that day. *USAF*

There is no charitable way to cast *Aphrodite* as an operational success. However, in the development of droning technologies, the efforts made with the project paved the way for ever more precise drone techniques and equipment, and before year's end, the USAAF would be remotely launching BQ-7s in stateside tests. Meanwhile, in January 1945, *Aphrodite* was stood down even as its proponents lobbied for a modified second round of sorties against Germany.

The decision to halt *Aphrodite* and potential offshoots was motivated, at least in part, by objections downgraded to reluctance expressed by Prime Minister Winston Churchill in 1945. Lt Gen Barney M Giles, deputy commander of the USAAF, wrote to Maj Gen Carl Spaatz on 27 April 1945:

> 'For your personal information, there has been received, shortly after President Roosevelt's death, a lengthy message from the Prime Minister [Winston Churchill] to the President which removed official objection to our war-weary program in terms of the greatest reluctance. He expressed willingness to endure added misery and hardship, but acknowledged the probable correctness of the American military plans. Due to the tone of the message and the circumstances on the Western Front, the President has directed that the project concerning war-weary explosive laden aircraft will not be pressed further in Europe at this time.'

Lt Gen Giles added, 'Accordingly, we will not reinstitute such operations', although he reserved the option of revisiting it on German targets 'if the situation seems to warrant it at a later date'.[37] Unknowable to the generals at that time was how quickly Germany would surrender on 8 May 1945.

The nature of the war-weary unmanned aircraft effort that had been contemplated for 1945 looked at the possibility of hitting large industrial target areas in Germany, possibly on a bigger scale than the 1944 *Aphrodite* efforts against hardened targets. British reluctance, echoed by some US planners, centred around the belief that 'the employment of these bombers will expose London, which is a unique target and already under attack by long-range rockets, to similar attacks by German war-weary bombers', explained Maj Gen John E Hull, Assistant Chief of Staff of the US Army's Operations Division.[38]

Nevertheless, Maj Gen Spaatz expressed enthusiasm for continuing the development of droned bombers. 'I am convinced that further development and experimentation in the Zone of the Interior [continental USA] should produce an effective weapon of tremendous power for use against Japan', he wrote to Lt Gen Ira Eaker, deputy commander of the USAAF, on 3 May 1945.[39] Ultimately, tests with a droned BQ-8, which had Pacific War overtones, did not lead to combat use of bomber drones against Japan.

Gen 'Hap' Arnold, a proponent of using unmanned war-weary bombers against German targets, asked Brig Gen Grandison Gardner, commander of the Air Proving Ground at Eglin Field, in Florida, to write to Maj Gen Spaatz with details that favoured the use of the 'Weary Willies'. What Gardner told Spaatz in February 1945 survives as a remarkable encapsulation of USAAF droning accomplishments and ambitions. His letter reveals what some planners were contemplating for the future of unmanned warplanes, and sets the tone for post-war visions of drones as missiles.

Gardner looked ahead to the day when four-engined drones would take off remotely. If the date of that first remote four-engined takeoff is lost to us for now, it is likely that it happened in post-war 1945, and was incorporated with landing strategies in time for Operation *Crossroads* (two nuclear weapons tests conducted at Bikini Atoll, in the Marshall Islands) in July 1946. Like a prehistoric insect preserved in amber for future inspection, Gardner's letter is reproduced here in full because of its significance to the USAAF drone story:

> 'Gen Arnold asked me to write you a personal letter and tell you what we have learned regarding the operation of pilotless war-weary aircraft, believing that you may not have obtained all the pertinent information through official cables.
>
> 'We have flown enough of these craft now to be quite confident that we can operate them successfully under a wide variety of conditions, and that we should be able to employ them usefully in many situations. I am aware of the fact that you have had considerable experience with them in the theatre, and that you undoubtedly know more about them than we do. We may, however, have learned some things that will supplement your experiences.
>
> 'We ran a series of tests on airplanes descending from medium high altitudes (8000ft to 14,000ft) on part throttle under automatic pilot control so as to get estimates of what the probabilities might be of their hitting within a pre-designated area if flown into the ground without change of automatic pilot settings during descent. We checked our estimates of this method by actually crashing a B-24 descending from 13,000ft with an initial rate of descent of 500ft per minute set into the automatic pilot. After the pilots bailed out, the airplane remained in flight for 55 miles with only a slight change in direction.
>
> 'Due to the fact that power increases with increased atmospheric density on descent, the path angle gradually flattens out and distances may vary 35 to 40 miles in descending from 10,000ft. We thought that the morale effect of this uncertainty might be one of the most important attained from

these weapons. If set with rate of descent sufficient to land within an hour, the chance of their returning would be negligible.

'We have had considerable experience flying pilotless airplanes by air-to-air remote control. Our experience shows that the missile airplane (sometimes referred to as the Baby airplane) can be flown into a small area target. This air-to-air control has been accomplished with and without the aid of a radar navigational link between the control or Mother airplane and the Baby. With the radar navigational link, we have been able to fly the missile as far as 35 miles ahead of the Mother and bring it into an area target with accuracy sufficient to hit a large factory. The radar navigational link involves the use of a new piece of equipment (AN/APN-21), which I believe is now available for theater use.

'This air-to-air controlled bombing is accomplished by bringing the missile down to an altitude of about 300ft on its final approach to the target. Experience shows that the problem of the airplane's trajectory when diving from 300ft becomes relatively minor, and that the missile can be accurately controlled into a specified area.

'We have conducted extensive tests in remotely controlling pilotless aircraft (Orphans) from a ground control station. We are convinced that from 5000ft we can hit an area three to four miles on a side (nine to sixteen square miles), and that from 10,000ft we can hit an area six to eight miles on a side (thirty-six to sixty-four square miles). We have expended two heavy bombers by this system of control. In one case the airplane landed 1.2 miles from the expected point of impact. In the other case, the airplane landed 0.7 miles from the expected point of impact.

'Accurate control has been obtained to ranges of 85 miles with the airplane at line-of-sight altitudes. We have actually dropped bombs by such remote control 23 miles from the control station, with errors averaging not greater than 840ft, and believe that as experience increases we may be able to do better bombing by this method than with standard airborne radar bombing equipment. While we can accurately place the airplane in space, we are still deficient in controlling it through the final dive into a target, and believe that we can drop bombs and bring the airplane home perhaps to better advantage than we can crash the entire load. We have not yet tried to take off or land four-engined airplanes without the pilot, however.

'Thinking more of the needs of the Pacific Theater, we have tried long-range missions, flying the Baby airplane from a Mother airplane in not too close proximity, and think that we can probably run long-range operations successfully, although we are not quite so ready to guarantee the success of missions beyond a few hundred miles. The missions controlled from the ground station may have to be limited to 50 or 75 miles until equipment has evolved further and our experience has been increased.

'In our various tests we have tried out a variety of fusings and feel sure that we can specify a fuse that will be positive, provided it is armed before the pilot leaves the airplane; and we believe that the arming can be just as safe as in conventional aircraft bomb loads. We are doubtful about the advisability of using higher-powered and more sensitive explosives than TNT because of the extra hazard and occasional loss of an airplane and crew, which would far outweigh the advantages of the not very high percentage of additional explosive power.

'We have an officer in your theatre at the present time who has most likely called upon you before now, and who is able to give you the best information we have on fusings and loadings. His name is Maj Robert R. Milner, of the Ordnance Department. If we can be of help to you by sending other officers who have now had some experience and training in this job, from both the radar and the ordnance point of view, we will be very glad to let you have them on a temporary basis whenever you request them.

'We feel that the most useful employment of pilotless aircraft in your theatre would be in weather unsuitable for other operations, and by remote control from the ground. We feel that they could be quite successfully operated over distances such as those separating our present most forward positions and the German Ruhr and Rhine Valleys. The ground control system requires an SCR-584 radar set, modified for 100 miles range, a variable PRF [pulse recurrence frequency] for control, and the 100-mile automatic plotting board. The airplane equipment consists of the modified AN/APN-7 beacon now designated as AN/APN-21, the C212/UP selector unit, and the C1 Remote Trim Board.

'The pilotless airplanes could start most anywhere, and as soon as they come within the range of the SCR-584 station, and the pilot and the SCR-584 operator have made their control checks, the pilots may bail out.

'As to the objection of having to have pilots bail out on each of these missions, we have so far had ten volunteers, and it appears that we could continue to get volunteers indefinitely. I feel that the next step, however, should be perfection of equipment and procedure for take-off without the pilot, and a later step should certainly be the development of equipment and procedure to make landings without the pilot so that the same airplane could carry bombs over on repeated trips.'[40]

The shelving of pilotless bomber sorties from England in the interest of protecting London from German missions of the same nature led at least some in the USAAF planning chain to consider reviving some form of 'Weary Willie' effort from air bases outside Britain. The rapid denouement of the European War overtook any efforts to invigorate some form of *Aphrodite* follow-on, however.

Project *Willie Orphan* unfulfilled

In January 1945, USAAF proponents of pilotless bombardment aircraft continued modification of seven war-weary bombers for use as drones in the European Theatre of Operations. Two of the seven aeroplanes would be fitted with the Black Maria beacon and considered part of Project *Aphrodite*, but the remaining five bombers would carry different gear, and were differentiated by being called the 'initial test of *Willie Orphan*'.[41] The two *Aphrodite* bombers in this set were to be controlled by an airborne mother ship, while the five *Willie Orphan* drones were to be controlled from a ground station.[42]

As 1945 dawned cold in England, a rationale for *Willie Orphan* was enumerated by USSTAF. Among points made in a memorandum generated by the organisation was the plan for using 'war-weary radio-controlled aircraft as robot bombs'. The intended purpose and objectives of *Willie Orphan* were telling – 'To destroy or damage area targets in support of tactical and, in a limited sense, strategical operations'. No longer present was the concept of pinpoint target selection, as had been tried unsuccessfully with *Aphrodite* the previous year. And the objectives left no doubt about what *Willie Orphan* proponents were touting. They viewed this proposed drone programme as a method 'to immediately counter the psychological effect of the German V1 and V2 program with a controlled robot bomb of far greater destructive effect and, consequently, of higher psychological value'.[43]

Willie Orphan's planners envisioned using both war-weary B-17s and B-24s to create these robot bombs, and they created lists of components for droning kits specific to each type of aircraft. While some of the *Orphans* might be controlled from another aeroplane, others were intended to be controlled by a ground station via SCR-584 radar 'near the frontlines opposite the selected target'. That addressed range limitations inherent in the ground radar stations of the period, and had the additional effect of getting the whole US robot bomb-launching operation out of Britain. The *Orphans* would be capable of carrying 'up to 20,000lb of TNT or Torpex'.[44]

Willie Orphan mission methodology with a ground radar station was described as follows:

> 'Volunteer pilots and co-pilots fly the aircraft from an advanced and relatively isolated landing field, navigating to a pre-arranged point where contact is established by VHF radio with the SCR-584 ground radar station. The pilot sets up the C-1 auto-pilot and radio control, and the operation of the aircraft is turned over to a controller at the SCR-584 ground station. After remaining with the aircraft an adequate time to insure [sic] that the radio controls are functioning properly, the pilot and co-pilot bail out upon instructions from the ground station. The robot is then directed to the target area by a controller using radio controls and referring to the position of the aircraft which is shown accurately on the SCR-584 plotting board.
>
> 'As the robot approaches the target area, the controller reduces engine power and causes the robot to assume a trajectory that will result in it falling within the target area. It is estimated conservatively that at operational limits of control a target area of four miles square can be hit with reasonable certainty. Targets which are located at shorter range and which require less altitude for line-of-sight control could be attacked with somewhat better accuracy.'[45]

War-weary aircraft were to be stripped and radio control equipment installed at the Burtonwood depot. Although testing of the drones – the majority of the technical work – was to be accomplished in England, the final checkout and launch would take place from a Ninth Air Force airfield on the Continent according to the ultimately unfulfilled *Willie Orphan* plan.[46]

The Ninth Air Force looked at the locations of SCR-584 radar sites on the Continent in January 1945 and used a formula that said a *Willie Orphan* robot flying at an altitude of at least 5000ft could have a range of 50 miles. With typical radar sets placed only ten miles from the frontlines, that distance put many German cities under the shadow of *Willie Orphan*, including the western Ruhr area – Mönchengladbach, Dusseldorf, Cologne, Düren, Bonn, Euskirchen, Koblenz, Trier, Saarbrücken, Wiesbaden, Frankfurt, Baden-Baden, Freiburg, Stuttgart, Mannheim and other industrialised areas. With the all-seeing radar plotting board for SCR-584 sets, it was posited by the Ninth Air Force that inclement weather and night conditions would favour robot operations when enemy defences would be hampered.[47]

Airfields A-58 (Coulommiers) or A-70 (Laon-Couvron) were considered by the Ninth Air Force to be good candidates for the Continental take-off site for *Willie Orphan*.[48]

The emphasis of *Willie Orphan* was simply stated. It was a high-explosive answer to German V-weapon attacks, and lacked the intended precision of the older *Aphrodite* programme. The rapid conclusion of the war in Europe denied the Ninth Air Force the chance to use *Willie Orphan* in combat, but its build-up was a significant commitment to droning technologies.

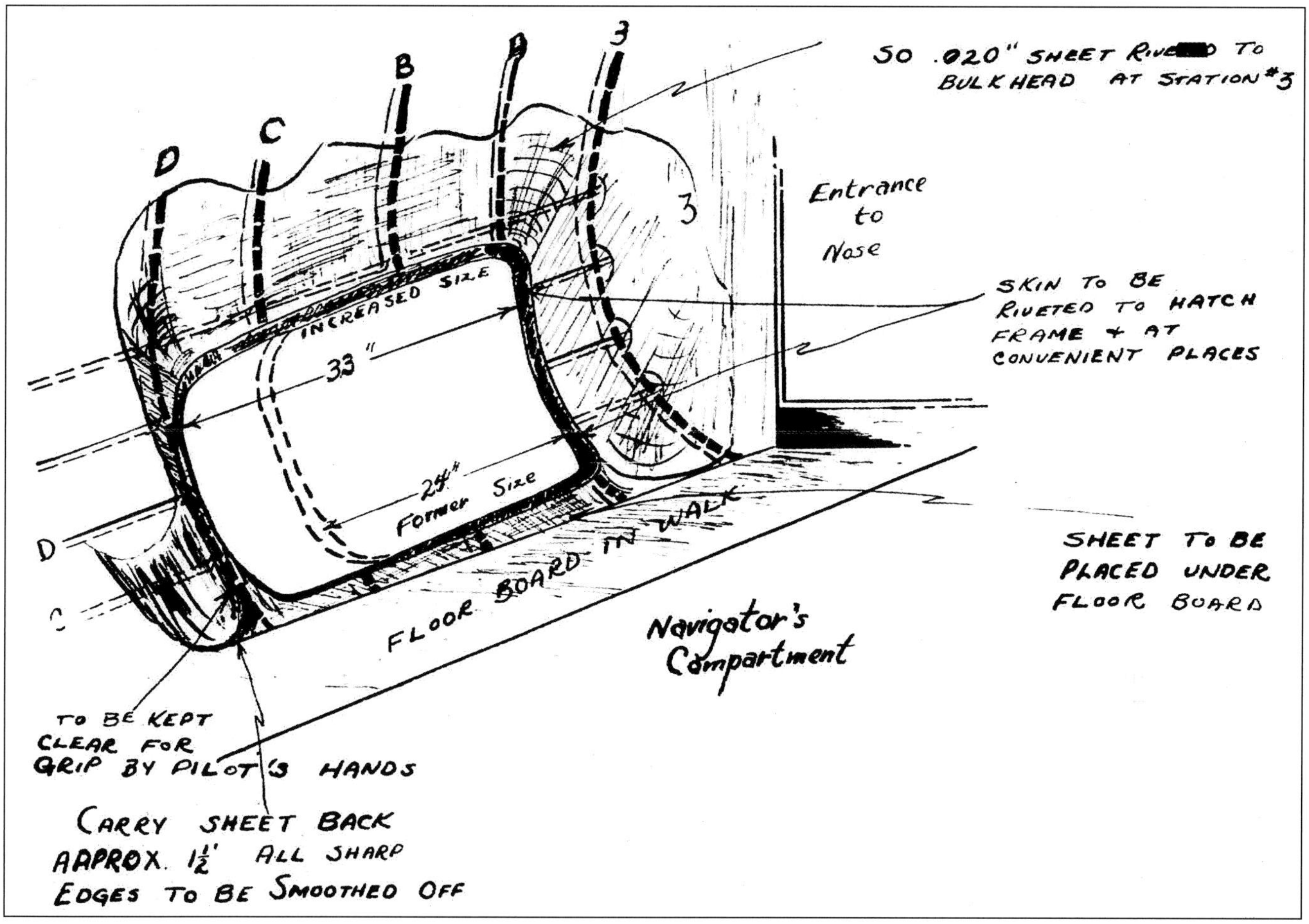

A working sketch instructed Eighth Air Force mechanics how to improve airborne egress for the pilots of *Aphrodite* B-17s by making some sheet metal fairings and enlarging the hatch opening. The hatch door was removed and the hatch was widened by nine inches to a width of thirty-three inches. *AFHRA*

Making an *Aphrodite* BQ-7

When *Aphrodite* was on the table for 1944 delivery, the USAAF developed specific instructions to guide the team who stripped and prepared war-weary B-17s to create BQ-7 drones. Among the salient points was the painting of uppersurfaces of the wings and the vertical tail chrome yellow – the same bright colour as propeller tips – for enhanced visibility. This was a logical variation on dark olive camouflage that was intended to diminish the appearance of a regular B-17 when looking down upon it from another aircraft. The yellow had some visual benefit until winter sorties, when snow on the ground made the wings more difficult to spot than if they had been a dark colour.[49]

A significant change to the factory B-17 fuselage was the widening of the forward escape hatch from 24in to 33in, extending the opening rearward, now left open without a hatch. The one-way flight of these BQ-7s made this bigger aperture sufficient for the short life of the droned Flying Fortress bomb. The enlarged opening made it easier for the crew to clear the aircraft. The inside of the fuselage was skinned over around the hatch opening to remove projections that might get in the way of a quick exit. But one portion in the lower left corner was unskinned, providing a place for the crewman to grip. Outside of the hatch on the forward fuselage, a bent sheet metal wind deflector further facilitated departure of the drone crew after setting the fuse on their explosive-laden BQ-7.[50]

The war-weary B-17s were to have all equipment that was not necessary for safe flight removed. This included armament, gun mounts, bombsight and related hardware. The Plexiglas astrodome was to be replaced with flat sheet metal. The drive to purge weight from the drones included removing the B-17s' bomb-bay door motors and worm gear mechanism, with the doors bolted shut to the central catwalk structure. All wheels and tyres were to be replaced with new ones, and brakes were to be in perfect working order. Since the one-way missions of the BQ-7s in *Aphrodite* could be accomplished with less than a full fuel load, the outboard wing Tokyo tanks were to be drained, disconnected and plugged.

Consideration was given to making more room in the cockpit for the pilots who would need to get out of the cockpit with parachutes to leave the drone over England. The plans for modifying the BQ-7s included a drawing and text describing replacing the co-pilot's seat with a smaller navigator's stool. The modification

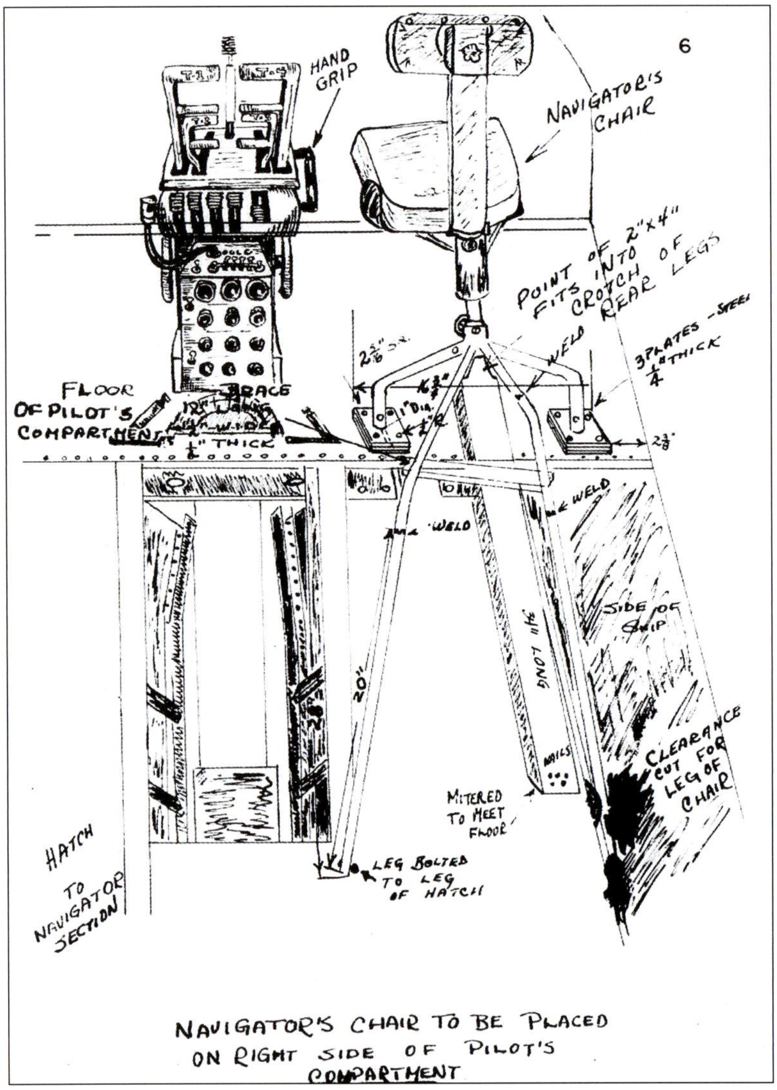

A notebook sketch for *Aphrodite* showed how to instal a navigator's chair on the right side of the drone cockpit for use on the short take-off flight before the crew of two bailed out. *AFHRA*

A modified 75-gallon drop tank became the smoke tank of choice for *Aphrodite* missions, providing up to an hour of uninterrupted smoke trail for the director pilot to track the BQ-7 drone. The duration of smoke could be extended by turning the flow on and off as required during a mission. *USAF*

required the welding of two 20in-long lengths of 1in pipe to the rear legs of the navigator's seat to accommodate the B-17's cockpit floor levels.[51] It is not known how universal this modification was, for film of a later stateside drone BQ-7 cockpit in 1945 shows both original pilots' seats intact just before the aircraft was sent on a mission to destruction.

The smoke tank, the contents of which helped the control pilot with guiding the drone once it was under his sole command, was to be mounted to the centreline keel at the bomb-bay – a location that proved injurious to one pilot as he bailed out and struck the tank, hurting himself and possibly causing the tank to malfunction. An M-10 smoke tank was tried, but it had insufficient capacity. The answer was found in modifying a standard 75-gallon drop tank with electrically-operated solenoid valves, giving the control pilot access to about one hour of continuous operation that could be extended in duration by starting and stopping the smoke trail at will.[52]

A full load of Torpex high explosives in a Flying Fortress fuselage had a net weight of 18,425lb, which meant a gross weight of 21,105lb including boxes and shoring. Torpex was cast in boxes that measured 6in x 12in x 17.5in. It was important to locate the Torpex boxes near enough to the BQ-7's centre of gravity to avoid a dangerous out-of-balance situation. Accordingly, 13,230lb (gross weight) of Torpex was placed in the bolted-shut bomb-bay. This represented 210 boxes of the explosive, each with a gross weight of 63lb. Another 100 boxes of Torpex, weighing more than three tons, packed the radio room, while twenty-five boxes were nestled in the pilot's compartment aft of the seats.[53]

To facilitate bailout by airmen not primarily trained in parachute operations, the Irving Airchute Company made modifications to its T-5 parachute for use by *Aphrodite* drone crews, devising appropriate static line and freefall parachutes for the job. Observations on *Aphrodite* included in the final report documentation included:

> 'It has proved advisable to have a professional parachute instructor, preferably a paratrooper, spend a week with these men showing them how to leave the aircraft, how to guide their chute on the way down, and the proper method of striking the ground and recovering.'[54]

The Castor phase of *Aphrodite* used mostly off-the-shelf radio equipment, except for two customised items – a time-delay relay and relay board, which were *Aphrodite*-specific. In addition to basic aircraft manoeuvring, the radio equipment enabled the control pilot to turn smoke on or off, turn the television in the drone on or off and adjust throttle settings in the BQ-7. The gear was also designed to show the control pilot the current heading of the drone even if it was out of sight of the control pilot. Mechanical devices to turn knobs on the C-1 autopilot of the robot drone to effect the pitch axis

Unlike later drone programmes that became increasingly sophisticated, *Aphrodite* needed onboard pilots for take-off, after which they bailed out when a director aircraft took control. *Aphrodite* two-man take-off crews were given a concentrated course in parachuting techniques. *AFHRA*

and roll axis were commanded by radio signals from the control aeroplane. A compass in the drone was monitored by television to tell the control pilot what heading the BQ-7 was on.[55]

The two pilots aboard *Aphrodite* drones for take-off needed some specific systems training, as described in project documentation:

> 'The principal part of their training time is occupied with instruction in the setting up and operation of the C-1 Automatic Pilot. A minimum of four hours ground instruction and ten hours flight instruction is considered necessary in their C-1 training.'[56]

Aphrodite planners made a change in how the Rebecca/Eureka radar navigation system worked by placing the typically ground-based Eureka transponder in the drone, while Rebecca was carried by the control aircraft. As described in contemporary USAAF *Aphrodite* papers, 'Rebecca in the control plane can interrogate the Eureka and determine the direction and distance of the missile in case it becomes lost to the controller'. Rebecca had a directional antenna that could help locate where the Eureka device was, and Rebecca used the time it took to receive return signals to establish distance between it and Eureka.[57]

A robotic mechanical arm was clamped to the conveniently designed B-17 throttles, enabling all four engines of an *Aphrodite* Flying Fortress to be adjusted simultaneously in drone flight. *AFHRA*

Other radio and visual finding aids were built into *Aphrodite*, but sometimes none of these systems helped crews find lost drones during actual combat sorties.

Eglin-tested BQ-8 drone

The growth in development and production of heavy bombers for the USAAF during the Second World War led to an inevitable surplus of early models even while the conflict raged on. In addition to the BQ-7 Flying Fortresses tried during *Aphrodite*, at least one ageing B-24D was droned and controlled by a special Liberator and, evidently, a B-29 in tests at Eglin Field. As previously noted, the radio-controlled Liberator carried the nomenclature BQ-8.[58]

Eglin's test E-44-60 – titled Testing a Stripped War-Weary B-24D Aircraft – was undertaken to determine whether a radio-controlled Liberator could be flown more than 1500 miles at 15,000ft at a cruising speed of 200mph, with climbs made at 190mph. The B-24 was to be taken aloft by a crew of two and orbited at 5000ft while a B-29 mother ship assumed control of the drone Liberator. Then, in the fashion of *Aphrodite* B-17s, the pilots were to bail out of the drone.[59]

During the Eglin tests, the Liberator pilots remained on board, but did not handle any controls once the mother ship took over at 5000ft. Testers determined the BQ-8 could perform the mission with throttles set at 2250rpm and 36in of manifold pressure. About 2400 gallons of aviation gasoline were consumed by the BQ-8.[60] This mission profile was envisioned for potential combat use in the Pacific.

Bell P-59 Airacomet reluctant robot drone

The Bell P-59 Airacomet occupies a rare place in American aviation history as the United States' first jet aircraft. If the Airacomet's performance was modest, it nonetheless validated some concepts of jet-propelled aircraft. Sixty-six P-59s, from XP-59A through P-59B, were built before the later Lockheed P-80 Shooting Star proved its merit as a superior jet fighter.

P-59B 44-22633 was modified as a radio-controlled drone intended for spin testing that would not risk the safety of an onboard pilot. This precaution was made after Bell pilot Jack Woolams experienced a serious spin event over Muroc Army Air Base (later renamed Edwards AFB), California, in an Airacomet in 1944. By 1946, the once-secret P-59 programme was nearing an end, and the drone P-59, nicknamed 'Reluctant Robot', operated from the Muroc main base area instead of the isolated North Base complex where the XP-59A had made its first flight on 1 October 1942.[61] Its purpose as a spin tester may have waned with the ageing of the P-59 programme, but its utility as a drone technology demonstrator remained viable.

The 'Reluctant Robot' was equipped to use a transmitting television camera capable of relaying flight information and special stress and strain gauge data back to researchers on the ground. Painted bright orange, the drone Airacomet was sometimes seen in the company of another P-59 mother ship painted black. The drone could also be controlled from a truck-based ground station.[62]

The 'Reluctant Robot' was also flown from Wright Field, Ohio. Its demonstration flights had a safety pilot on board, but the promise of such a high-performance aircraft drone was not lost on Bell, already immersed in development of the XS-1 that would challenge supersonic flight. Bell and USAAF Air Technical Service Command researchers posited that a pilotless radio-controlled high-performance aircraft might probe the speed of sound without endangering the life of an onboard pilot. Bell and the USAAF also demonstrated the ability to transmit flight test data from the 'Reluctant Robot' to a ground station by means of telemetry as well as the onboard TV camera.[63]

Although some engineers envisioned the ability to test new high-performance aircraft to destruction, while receiving flight test data up to the moment the unoccupied machine disassembled in flight, ultimately test pilots would rule the day in experimental flight research, including the first supersonic flight. Decades later, a sub-scale remotely-operated model of an F-15 Eagle would be used for dangerous tests over Edwards AFB. The 'Reluctant Robot' outlasted most P-59 Airacomets to become a static display at Edwards AFB for decades, repainted in various schemes over the years until it was decided to keep the aircraft in a standard silver colouration as a P-59B.

3 Stand-off for Safety

The wartime efforts of *Aphrodite*, hobbled by the need to have humans on board to take off in the drone B-17 before bailing out, showed the need for improved drone technologies and abilities. Intentional destruction of a BQ-7 circa November 1945 that was captured on film reveals an improvement in capabilities: this drone takes off unmanned.

With peace, the development of droned aircraft stayed alive as both the USAAF and the US Navy embraced emerging remote-control aircraft technologies. Controlled uncrewed aerial vehicles were embraced as ways to deliver unmanned missiles to distant targets, as well as a way to probe and measure hazardous nuclear blast clouds with unmanned aeroplanes and, lastly, a realistic way to replicate hostile aircraft for anti-aircraft gunnery (and later missile) testing and training.

Operation *Crossroads*

The first big show for post-war droned aircraft was Operation *Crossroads* in July 1946, which included two atmospheric atomic bomb blasts for which US forces wanted detailed measurements. The USAAF modified a number of B-17Gs into drones and mother ships, while the US Navy used drone F6F Hellcats to fly closer to the radioactive plume than was considered safe for aircraft flown by humans. Plans called for four radio-controlled B-17 drones and five mother ship control Flying Fortresses on *Able Day* – the airburst portion of the test.

For a special probe of the mushroom cloud generated by the first *Crossroads Able* blast, four F6F drones guided by pilots in Hellcat mother ships were part of a large contingent of Grumman fighters made available for the operation. For the *Able Day* 1 July airburst weapon, three of the F6F drones passed

The *Crossroads Able Day* nuclear blast on 1 July 1946 provided opportunities for drone B-17s and F6Fs to probe the mushroom cloud and environs, collecting atmospheric samples. *USAAF*

through the column of radioactive gases intact while a fourth Hellcat drone went out of control and crashed before the drop had taken place. The surviving drones were demonstrably radioactive after their exposure to the blast column.[64]

In the reams of documentation printed following Operation *Crossroads*, the purpose of the Hellcat drones on *Able Day* was noted as:

> 'To collect air samples for the Manhattan Project by means of specially designed filters; in addition, the drones were to provide data on the effects on aircraft of forces released by the explosion by means of automatic recorders and to obtain close-up photography of the blast through the use of gun cameras in all drones and a remote-controlled standard motion picture camera in one drone.'[65]

One of the F6F drones had an unexpected wild ride in the rising column from the *Able Day* blast. As the effects of the explosion created powerful updrafts, the unmanned Hellcat was quickly lifted more than a mile upward, exiting the plume far higher than its drone director F6F pilot had anticipated for the return flight to safety. The fighter director on board the aircraft carrier USS *Shangri-La* (CV-38) located the wayward fighter drone and vectored the mother ship to a rendezvous. Fifty-five miles from the mushroom cloud, mother and drone were reunited for a successful flight to the island of Roi, where the three remaining drones and their mother ships recovered.[66]

A US Navy after action report supplied more details on the errant F6F drone:

> 'One Navy drone was swept upward, in passing through the cloud, from 20,000 to 26,000ft. This was the greatest change in altitude recorded of any drone sent through or above the cloud, and it may have been caused partially by a tilt of the aircraft when released by the mother. The drone was recovered with some difficulty but was safely landed.'

The report noted that aircraft like the F6F drones that passed through the cloud from the *Able Day* blast 'remained lethal [from radioactivity] for several days'. The US Navy bluntly said, 'Indications are that the highly radioactive materials, even within the hot column of gases and the mushroom cloud, have no permanent effects on operating aircraft, power plants or electronic equipment, although it is questionable as to whether a pilot would survive'. That encapsulated the succinct argument for the use of drones in nuclear testing.[67]

Quantification of the effects and evolution of a nuclear blast was a huge priority for the United States so that it could comprehend the ramifications of the weapon the country had produced in secrecy during the war. The US Navy and the USAAF

Although US Navy F6F-3K Hellcat drones were serviced ashore during *Crossroads*, they launched from an aircraft carrier to probe the nuclear blasts. *US Navy/NARA*

This Operation *Crossroads* F6F-3K Hellcat with a yellow tail would be guided to the hazardous nuclear blast area at Bikini Atoll by a manned F6F-5. Thirty F6F-3K drones and thirty F6F-5 mother ships were involved in the Bikini Atoll tests.

provided fleets of photographic and sampling aircraft, both piloted and droned, for use in *Crossroads*. Two charts in a USAAF-centric book published immediately after *Crossroads*, and intended for use by planners, show stacks of aircraft by altitude during the *Able Day* aerial and *Baker Day* underwater detonations, including F6F Hellcat drones and mother ships loitering at several levels.

For the *Able Day* aerial bomb dropped by a B-29, five Hellcats were stationed at 10,000ft – two F6Fs, 'Yellow 1' and '2' S-Drone Control, one F6F 'Yellow Dog' Drone and F6Fs 'Yellow 3' and '4' S-Drone Control. At 14,000ft, one F6F was listed as 'Skylight Photo', while just above at 15,000ft, two F6Fs were shown as 'Blue 1' and '2' P-Drone Control, one F6F was 'Blue Dog' Drone and two F6Fs were 'Blue 3' and '4' S-Drone Control. With their pilots sucking oxygen at 20,000ft, two F6Fs carried the tags 'White 1' and '2' Drone Control, one F6F was 'White Dog' Drone and two F6Fs were 'White 3' and '4' S-Drone Control. The Hellcats of *Able Day* topped out at 28,000ft, with two F6Fs as 'Red 1' and '2' P-Drone Control, one as 'Red Dog' Drone and two more F6Fs as 'Red 3' and '4' S-Drone Control.[68]

The *Baker Day* device detonated on 25 July was anchored in the water 90ft below the surface in an area where the ocean depth was 180ft. For *Baker Day*, two photographic Hellcats, identified as 'Skylight' and named 'Sugar' and 'Roger' (first mission), were shown at an altitude of less than 1000ft above the surface of the ocean. At 5000ft, F6Fs 'Blue 1' and '2' were P-Drone Control aircraft for one F6F 'Blue Dog' Drone, while two more F6Fs at that altitude were 'Blue 3' and '4' S-Drone Control aircraft. Loitering at 9000ft, F6Fs 'White 1' and '2' provided P-Drone Control for one F6F 'White Dog' Drone, while F6Fs 'White 3' and '4' were S-Drone Control. At 10,000ft, four F6F 'Skylight Photo' aircraft are shown. Hellcat participation for *Baker Day* capped out at 14,000ft with F6Fs 'Red 1' and '2' P-Drone Control, F6F 'Red Dog' Drone and F6Fs 'Red 3' and '4' as S-Drone Control. F6F 'Skylight Photo' aircraft 'Roger' (second mission) was also tallied at that altitude.[69]

Shangri-La hosted all Hellcat drones and mother ships for *Crossroads*. A US Navy after action report on aviation components of the operation described the effort needed to equip sufficient Hellcat drones and mother ships for the 1946 atomic tests:

> 'The preparation and furnishing of drones, control planes and related technical equipment required a major development and manufacturing program, largely handled by the Naval Air Material Center [NAMC] at Philadelphia and the Pilotless Aircraft [Navy] Experimental Utility Squadron [XVJ] 25, later designated as the VX-2 Detachment, and assigned as Task Unit 1.6.14 in the JTF-1 Operation Plan.[70]
>
> 'This program involved the accelerated production at the Naval Aircraft Modification Unit [NAMU], Johnsville, Pennsylvania, of a total of thirty F6F-3K drones and thirty F6F-5 control airplanes. Additional equipment required consisted of radio control equipment, design and installation of radioactivity filters, installation of Geiger counters and indicators and installation of VGTA recorders in a number of the drone aircraft.'[71]

It is remarkable to consider the first notification of formal participation by the US Navy's Bureau of Aeronautics (BuAer) in Operation *Crossroads* came in the second half of January 1946. Less than six months later, the massive drone operation would be in place and functional. At a 17 January meeting with representatives from the Los Alamos National Laboratory (creators of American nuclear weapons), members of BuAer described the capabilities of the US Navy's drone programme to place unmanned aircraft in areas of potential radiation danger.

A NULLO F6F-3K drone launches from an aircraft carrier in May 1947. *Thomas E Doll via Gerald Balzer collection*

At that time, the USAAF suggested using drone B-17s for sample gathering during *Crossroads*. However, according to a US Navy historical account, in January 1946 the USAAF was less certain it could safely recover the drone B-17s without crash-landing them. The US Navy offered F6F Hellcat drones that it said could be launched from an aircraft carrier and recovered safely on a nearby island runway.[72] Ultimately, the USAAF perfected drone B-17 recovery operations, and both Flying Fortresses and Hellcats served as useful, and reusable, drones for *Crossroads*.

XVJ-25 at Atlantic City, New Jersey, was assigned the task of Hellcat drone operations for *Crossroads* on 21 January 1946. This unit – which became Drone Controller/Guided Missile Development Squadron (VX) 2 in mid-March – was located not far from the NAMU at Johnsville. Fortuitously, the latter was already undertaking an F6F drone conversion programme.

Early in the planning for *Crossroads*, the Hellcat drones and their mother ships were to be based aboard the escort carrier USS *Saidor* (CVE-117), which was also tasked with providing photographic

Brightly coloured F6F-3K Hellcat drones were prepared for US Navy participation in *Crossroads* and photographed at NAS Atlantic City, New Jersey, on 13 March 1946. Tail colours identify different radio frequencies used by the aircraft. *US Navy/GSLASM via Gerald Balzer collection*

This Operation *Crossroads* F6F-3K Hellcat had a pink tail that identified its radio frequencies for drone missions in the two nuclear weapons tests conducted at Bikini Atoll, in the Marshall Islands, in July 1946.

support for the operation by launching piloted camera-equipped F6F-5Ps. The number of Hellcats needed for photo duties and drone purposes grew in the planning phase to the point where the entire drone operation was relocated to the larger fleet carrier *Shangri-La* to deconflict this tasking from the F6F-5P operations on board *Saidor*.

As preparations for *Crossroads* unfolded, on 22 January the US Navy requested that NAMU hasten completion of twenty F6F-3K drones and twenty F6F-5 mother ships for the nuclear tests. On 1 March this number was increased to twenty-six drones and thirty mother ships, and, still later, four more drones were readied, making a total of thirty F6F drones and thirty F6F mother ships. US Navy planners initially embraced, and then rejected, the use of multi-place scout or torpedo-bomber aircraft as mother ships for *Crossroads* since some of the drone flights would be at altitudes where fighter performance was required. It had been wisely decided the mother ships needed to match the drones in performance.[73]

At the NAMC in Philadelphia, tests verified that the drone control equipment to be carried by the Hellcats could withstand the rigours of catapult launching. Radioactivity filters were devised for the Hellcat drones, and plans were made for the installation of Geiger counters and the availability of protective goggles for the already-trained F6F-5 drone director radio control pilots from other US Navy sites who were now gathering at Naval Air Station (NAS) Atlantic City, New Jersey, in advance of *Crossroads*. Monitoring the Geiger counter had, at first, been deemed the province of a radiation crewmember when the mother ships were envisioned to be multi-seat aircraft. Now, it was up to a single pilot to fly his F6F-5, direct the F6F-3K drone and listen to a Geiger counter for radiation warnings.

Crossroads F6F-3K 'Drone 11' photographed at NAS Atlantic City in March 1946. *US Navy photo via Steve Ginter/ GSLASM/Gerald Balzer collection*

A US Navy officer shows how to remove a contaminated air sampling device from a Hellcat in preparation for *Crossroads* in 1946. *NARA/Gerald Balzer collection*

As previously noted, the four Hellcat drones earmarked for flying through the *Able Day* nuclear plume were fitted with a VGTA recorder which created a record of velocity, acceleration, time and altitude. They were also equipped with film cameras, three F6F-3Ks carrying 16mm gun cameras and the fourth fitted with a 35mm Mitchell motion picture camera on a wing bomb rack. Because radio channels were limited in number, the signal to start the cameras was ingeniously tied to the channel used for the drones' brakes, which would not be employed until landing.[74]

USS *Shangri-La* (CV-38) transited the Panama Canal with a flightdeck full of F6F Hellcat drones and directors in 1946 en route to the Pacific for *Crossroads*. The drones, brightly painted, are clearly visible in this aerial view of the aircraft carrier. A total of thirty F6F drones and thirty F6F mother ships were assigned to *Crossroads*. *NHHC*

Paper filters to collect data on radioactivity were to be housed in a device jointly developed by the USAAF and the US Navy. The device had a requirement for quick retrieval of the paper filter from a stand-off distance of six to ten feet. Tests of a Geiger counter aboard an F6F-5 proved it could sustain a catapult launching, but the audible signal from the Geiger counter could not be distinguished by the pilot over the engine noise in the cockpit. Efforts to amplify the sound failed. The answer came in the form of a micro-ammeter mounted to the Hellcat's instrument panel, giving the pilot a visual-only cue for radioactivity levels.[75]

The drone unit joined *Shangri-La* at Naval Operating Base Norfolk, in Virginia, where it departed for the west coast on 18 March. Arriving at NAS North Island, in San Diego, California, the F6F crews trained aboard *Shangri-La* and at Naval Air Auxiliary Field (NAAF) Chula Vista, otherwise known as Brown Field.[76] By then, the unit had become VX-2, with the drone operation being undertaken by a detachment from the parent squadron. In April,

Hellcat drone practice operations at Brown Field, near San Diego, in April 1946 preceded their use in *Crossroads*. A ground control pilot, at ease in a wooden classroom chair, manipulates the control box to land the Hellcat. *NARA/Richard Porcelli/Gerald Balzer collection*

the unit fitted micro-ammeters for the Geiger counters into the cockpits of its Hellcats. It also upgraded the drones' paper filter device. Training sorties were made with Hellcat mother ships over the desert site near Alamogordo, New Mexico, where radioactivity levels remaining from the world's first atomic explosion could be registered by the airborne Geiger counters.[77]

In the months leading up to the *Crossroads* deployment, F6F crews repeatedly practiced launching Hellcat drones from *Shangri-La* and then recovering them on an airfield runway just as would be the case during the real operation, when they would take off from the carrier and land on the island of Roi. The US Navy's brain trust of drone operators did not include many Naval Aviators with high-performance fighter experience or recent aircraft carrier service, so an intensive flying training programme was initiated to bring the drone pilots up to speed with the powerful Hellcat. This included high-altitude indoctrination and carrier landings. From 26 January to 14 March, refresher training in F6F aircraft, drone and drone control operations took place from NAS Atlantic City. From 18–31 March, refresher training in carrier take-offs and landings was the order of the day aboard *Shangri-La* as the vessel headed to San Diego.[78]

Once the VX-2 detachment reached NAS North Island, complete tactical operations were performed on a daily basis from nearby Brown Field when weather ceilings permitted. Typical training and mission scenarios are detailed in the following *Crossroads* report:

> '[A drone mission] included early morning checkouts by mechanics and electronics personnel before the primary and secondary control aircraft were airborne. The Field Control Unit took over next and checked out drones for each airborne control group. When a satisfactory check to all stations was completed, a safety pilot made a normal take-off in each drone. The primary control group then took over at a safe altitude and proceeded with the drone to the practice area. The drones were climbed to their assigned altitudes, leveled off, and their speeds stabilized. On the "bombs away" signal, they were released on course for the target, and the primary control groups fell astern. The secondary groups then flew a precise zig-zag course calculated to intercept the drone after it passed over and was a safe distance from the target. Recovery was by the Field Recovery Unit at Brown Field. The afternoon training program included radio control work, test and familiarization flights, auto-pilot run-ins on drones, and practice control landings.'[79]

The drone controller seated at his station on the flightdeck in the left foreground sends an F6F drone on its way. Launches like this during *Crossroads* put remote Hellcats in harm's way without endangering pilots. *GSLASM/Gerald Balzer collection*

Some early drone launches from *Shangri-La* were made with a pilot onboard. When full-up dress rehearsals of the intended *Able Day* flights of Hellcat drones and drone directors were made off the California coast, Santa Rosa Island stood in for Bikini Atoll and Brown Field represented the airstrip at Roi that would recover the drones during *Crossroads*. On 3 May the *Crossroads* Hellcat team conducted the first NOLO (No Live Operator) of an F6F from a carrier deck as part of a dress rehearsal. A pilot sitting in a chair on the carrier's flightdeck controlled the NOLO Hellcat.[80]

Protective goggles to guard against flash injury were initially intended to be issued to the F6F-5 drone director pilots, but these reduced visibility to the point where the pilot had virtually no vision capability. The F6F-5 lacked an autopilot, making the use of goggles impossible. A partial fix, similar to something used for instrument training, was to line the F6F canopy with amber Plexiglas and provide the pilot with blue goggle lenses. The combination of blue and orange substantially reduced visibility outside the cockpit. Spotlights installed in the cockpit and trained on the instrument panel increased the visibility for the pilot to enable flight inputs based on instrument readings.[81]

With the arrival of all components of *Crossroads* in the Pacific, 24 June was designated *Queen Day* during which all of the aircraft and other participants flew their assigned missions just as they would on 1 July for *Able Day*.

USAAF B-17 *Crossroads* drones

As with other participants in the hurried preparations for *Crossroads*, the USAAF perfected techniques for launching and landing four-engined Flying Fortress drones, and handing their control off to airborne mother ship B-17s, in a remarkably short time span. A *Crossroads* historical report said:

> 'Training at the Clovis [New Mexico] Army Air Base was carried on by the Air Instrumentation and Test Requirements Unit (TU 1.5.3) in the operation of four-engine drones and drone control aircraft. Directed by technicians from Wright Field, experienced B-17 air crews were trained in taking-off and landing drones by remote control from the ground and from the air. They were also given refresher courses in ground and flying training.'[82]

As the USAAF technicians and aircrews raced to make their B-17 drones optimally useful in time for *Crossroads*, the skies around Clovis, New Mexico, glittered with bright silver and yellow modified Flying Fortresses. A *Crossroads* after-action historical report said:

> 'At Clovis Army Air Base the objectives of the Group were to train ground and air crews to operate four B-17 Drone Aircraft, four B-17 Drone Control Aircraft, and one B-17 Master Drone Control Aircraft. The four drones were

Early in 1946, at Roswell, New Mexico, the USAAF demonstrated its capabilities by flying a drone B-17 next to a drone director B-17. Here, the drone's ground control pilots are operating their equipment from a Jeep. The effort was part of the build-up for *Crossroads* later that year. From the photograph it appears cold desert winds made it necessary to wear coats with upturned collars – perhaps this undated image coincides with early drone operations in February 1946. *USAAF/NARA*

This Flying Fortress drone at Roswell in early 1946 was an aged camouflaged B-17G with an early-style Plexiglas nose, rather than one of the brand new low-time G-models that would be used as an operational drone during *Crossroads* later that year. *USAAF/NARA*

specially equipped with air filters and air-collector bags to gather air samples of the cloud and cloud columns resulting from the atomic bomb burst. Cameras were also installed in the drones to photograph the cloud at close range.'[83]

Experienced USAAF drone operators from Wright Field travelled to Clovis to help train the *Crossroads* crews. The first training flights took place on 11 February 1946, followed four days later by full-up training using both the airborne and ground control equipment for the droned Flying Fortresses. A contemporary report noted:

Below: Crossroads B-17 drones were fitted with air bags (top right) in the bomb-bay for atmospheric sample gathering during the atomic tests. *AFHRA*

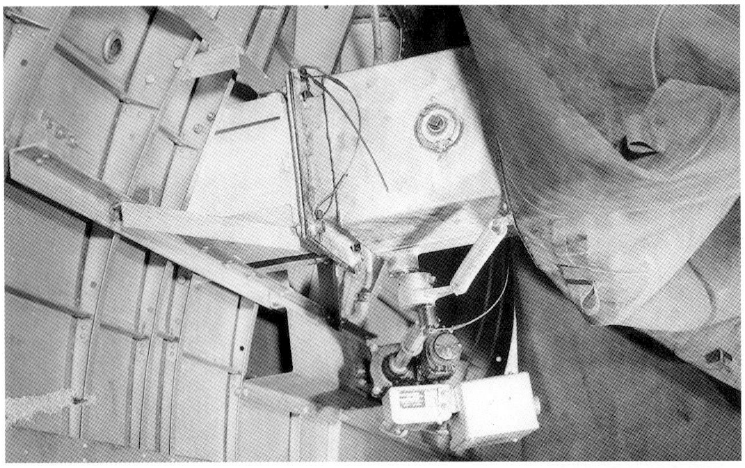

The *Crossroads* air bag support structure installed into the bomb-bay of a B-17 drone. *AFHRA*

This *Crossroads* B-17 drone in bright yellow and black markings flies under remote control. The rectangular section faintly visible in the top turret location is where the atmospheric sample collector would be installed for operational missions. *AFHRA*

The air bag intake scoop mounted on the outside of one of the B-17's bomb-bay doors for *Crossroads* sampling. *AFHRA*

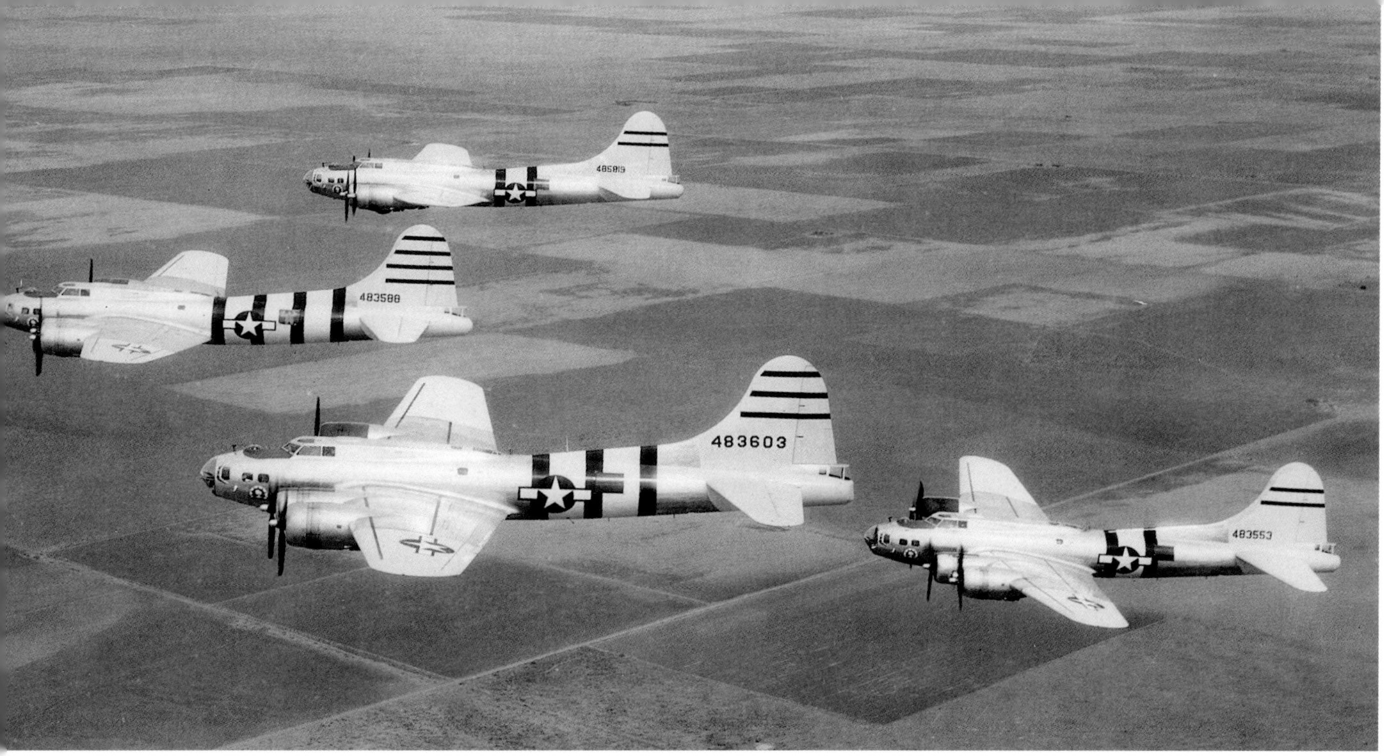

C Flight's shiny new *Crossroads* drones undertake a piloted cross-country jaunt to Roswell for staging before heading to the Pacific for the 1946 nuclear shots. *AFHRA*

'Flight training stressed long-range navigation and cruise-control missions, radio-controlled landings and take-offs, and both high- and low-altitude missions to achieve coordination between mother and drone aircraft. Also much time was devoted to ground approach and the development of standard operating procedures for all phases of drone operations and control.

'Training was initiated for sixteen crews, and 138 flying hours of radio control, and 90 hours of metal stick [control column] training were flown prior to the termination of training at Clovis Army Air Base. The average individual flying training completed was as follows: pilots, co-pilots and radio control pilots – 19:30 hours; navigators – 37:30 hours; radio operators – 17:30 hours; RCM observers – 4:00 hours.'[84]

The *Crossroads* B-17 drones had television transmission capability in the aft fuselage to provide onboard views to the remote pilot in the director aircraft. The television antenna was fitted atop the tail gun emplacement. *AFHRA*

A gaggle of seven drone and director B-17s fills the ramp, probably at Roswell in April 1946 in preparation for *Crossroads*. *USAAF/Gene Furnish collection*

During training and testing, USAAF crews proved they could operate a drone B-17 as high as necessary – sometimes above 25,000ft. This validated the high-altitude functionality of drone control equipment and television and telemetering units. Above 28,000ft, the television gear experienced problems with motor brushes arcing. New high-altitude brushes were installed, but results were not entirely satisfactory, and the evaluation of this continued as the unit made ready to deploy to the Pacific.

The USAAF B-17 drones needed a robust and nuanced capability to land safely – something that was less critical for earlier iterations of droned Flying Fortresses intended for one-way trips as flying bombs. The first set up for wheel brakes on the B-17 drones for *Crossroads* used valve action that imparted equal braking to both mainwheels. This was too simplistic an answer, and, as described in a *Crossroads* report, 'was definitely hazardous, particularly in crosswind landings. Thus a device was incorporated into the braking system whereby differential braking was possible. This device operates so that an application of right or left rudder produces a similar application of the right or left brake, and has resulted in considerably more positive control during the landing roll'.[85]

Ten yellow-tailed B-17 drones are lined up on the crushed coral ramp at Eniwetok, along with six Flying Fortress mother ship director aircraft and a pair of lifeboat-carrying SB-17s for search and rescue. *Gene Furnish collection*

A USAAF public information officer strikes a pose with one of the B-17 drones at Eniwetok during the *Crossroads* effort. *USAAF/Gene Furnish collection*

The brilliant yellow paint of a *Crossroads* B-17 drone provides the backdrop for three public information officers dressed in mixed flying gear on Eniwetok in 1946. *USAAF/Gene Furnish collection*

The USAAF B-17 drones and mother ships took up residence on Eniwetok Atoll, 185 nautical miles to the west of Bikini Atoll. From there, drone and director crews engaged in frequent training sorties in the time leading up to *Able Day*.

The drone B-17s, with their camera installations and sampling gear, were rare machines with high value for the impending *Able* and *Baker* missions. As such, training flights, even when ground operators made the take-off and landing, were conducted with a safety pilot aboard the drone B-17 in case his hands-on inputs were needed to save the aircraft. On 27 May, eight seconds after take-off, the B-17 drone identified as 'Fox' was taken over by its onboard safety pilot when the bomber swerved and would have crashed without intervention. Safety pilots intervened in B-17 drone training missions on several occasions. During training on Eniwetok (later also spelled Enewetak), B-17 ground control pilots made 124 take-offs and 140 landings with the droned Flying Fortresses, implying onboard pilots made 16 take-offs.

Able Day called for four B-17 drones and five B-17 mother ships to be aloft, and the unit trained for this several times in advance. *Able Day* was to be the first *Crossroads* B-17 mission flown with no safety pilots aboard the drone Flying Fortresses.[86]

The *Able Day* operation on 1 July was the first of two 'big shows' for *Crossroads*, and it would furnish proof of the efficacy of the drone aircraft. The four USAAF B-17 drones and four B-17 mother ships took off, performed their mission as briefed and returned to base. Two of the drones were badly buffeted, but came through and were landed successfully. One drone was damaged on landing when the B-17's brakes failed to hold and it ran off the end of the runway.[87]

Judging by the men standing casually in its proximity, this *Crossroads* sampling B-17 drone must not have been measurably radioactive when the photograph was taken. The Cletrac with a long tow rope could be used to position radioactive drones in a remote location after a mission, with groundcrew access limited to brief sessions while wearing dosimeters to track radioactivity. *USAAF/Gene Furnish collection*

B-17G drones, newly out of a surplus park, stand ready for duty at Eniwetok as part of the *Crossroads* test shots in the summer of 1946. The droned B-17s collected radioactive airborne samples and performed other tasks too dangerous for human crews. *USAAF/Gene Furnish collection*

Drone director *ABLE Mable* – possibly the complete name is *ABLE Mabel No 5*, serial 44-85818 – forms the backdrop for aircrew assigned to *Crossroads* in mid-1946. *USAAF/Gene Furnish collection*

Between 1 and 25 July, some rearranging of camera gear took place aboard the B-17 drones. The 25 July *Baker Day* underwater blast would have different characteristics above the surface of the ocean than were seen on *Able Day*'s air burst. B-17 drones again penetrated the blast plume on *Baker Day*, gathering atmospheric samples and making photographic recordings of the scene.

The operators experienced some difficulties with variations in the flight characteristics of the several B-17 drones used in *Crossroads*. Inherent variances between servo and motor mechanisms in the different droned Flying Fortresses of the day were especially problematic when landing the radio-controlled aircraft. Control inputs could produce differing levels of response from different B-17s – the final inputs to a landing made such variations sporty at best. The continued operation of drones by the USAF over the years was met with ever-evolving ingenuity in ways to improve the reliability, repeatability and overall utility of drones.

B-17 drone use in Operation *Sandstone*

In April–May 1948, the next series of atomic testing at Eniwetok used three nuclear devices mounted on 200ft towers. Twelve QB-17G drones as sampler aircraft and an identical number of DB-17G controllers were assigned to *Sandstone*. A report following the testing summarised the drone activity:

> 'TASK UNIT 7.4.2 (DRONE UNIT). This unit was made up of 460 men from the 1st Experimental Guided Missiles Group [EGMG] at Eglin Field, Florida. Men from this task unit operated 24 B-17s, 12 of which were drone control aircraft and 12 were unmanned cloud sampling aircraft. Contaminated drones were landed at Enewetak, where the radioactive cloud sample filters were removed by LASL [Los Alamos Scientific Laboratory] personnel. The drones were decontaminated at Enewetak and then returned to Kwajalein [in the Marshall Islands] where the unit was stationed.'[88]

Wright Field civilian photographer Gene Furnish posed with *Crossroads* B-17 44-83588 on Eniwetok. Beneath the front of the circular 58th Wing emblem, a small wind deflector is visible at the leading edge of a ventral camera port installed in the drone. *USAAF/Gene Furnish collection*

With the ventral panel opened, the downward and forward-looking camera on this B-17 drone is being fitted with a red filter at Eniwetok for *Crossroads*. *USAAF/Gene Furnish collection*

In the summer of 1947, the USAAF pondered, and rejected, the possibility of using B-29 Superfortresses as drones for *Sandstone*. A lead time estimated at two years would be needed to bring B-29 drone engineering, modifications and operations up to the same level of proficiency already available with B-17s, making this out of reach for *Sandstone*. As the drone unit prepared for *Sandstone* duties, it was observed that not every pilot could become a successful radio control drone pilot. The number of pilots entering training increased to accommodate the higher than expected attrition rate of unsuitable candidates.

The timing of the blast for *Sandstone* required the B-17 drones to be airborne before daylight, so on 20 October 1947 the drone unit made its first night radio-controlled take-off. Additional exterior lighting on the B-17 drones aided remote pilots in visualising the attitude of the drone at night.

The drone QB-17s collected samples of particles from the radioactive shot clouds. Eight participated in the first two shots of *Sandstone* and seven were used in the third, and final, shot. The samples were collected on filter papers located in sheet metal boxes mounted where the chin and top turrets of the B-17 had originally been.

Three flights were made through the radioactive blast cloud by each of several QB-17s, after which they landed at Eniwetok. Once the aircraft had stopped rolling, their tails were checked for radioactivity and a tow bar attached to each drone's tail. The QB-17s were then towed into an area at the eastern end of the runway on the lagoon side of the island. The area was isolated by rows of debris including junked heavy construction equipment, trucks and steel landing mats. This heavy debris barrier acted as a barricade in the event a drone failed to stop on landing. It also served to attenuate radiation issuing from contaminated drone QB-17s.[89]

Manned *Crossroads* B-17 drone 44-83519 with large black and yellow bands undertakes a test sortie with an unidentifiable unpainted director B-17 during testing and training over New Mexico, circa April 1946. *USAAF/Gene Furnish collection*

Retrieval of the filter papers from the drones involved *Sandstone* workers running to the drone bombers to extricate the filter canisters with as little exposure time as possible. Protective clothing and subsequent showering were used to minimise the possibility of lingering radioactive exposure. The drones were left isolated in this parking area for several days to allow radioactivity levels to diminish with natural decay processes. Then the QB-17s required servicing to prepare them for the next shot in the *Sandstone* series.

One groundcrewman would taxi the QB-17 from its initial parking spot to a wash area, probably downwind, where water runoff and airborne spray would be less likely to cause contamination to workers. A filmed account shows the groundcrewman who taxied the QB-17 dropping from the hatch and sprinting away from the aircraft to avoid prolonged exposure.

To decontaminate the QB-17s, they were monitored for radioactivity levels, washed, rinsed and monitored again. The wash solution could include kerosene and distilled water. The engine areas were contamination hotspots because the presence of oil and grease in tight passages accommodated the unwanted retention of radioactive particles. Following decontamination, the QB-17s still retained some radioactivity, but levels of radiation had decayed or otherwise been lessened to allow some maintenance to be carried out. Maintainers were limited to a maximum of 90 minutes in proximity to the QB-17 at that time. Anyone working around the drones post-mission was monitored for radiation exposure according to reports.[90]

Four of the QB-17 sampling aircraft were additionally fitted with strain gauges, pressure gauges and accelerometers to record initial blast effects and turbulence encountered in the mushroom cloud. The timing of the *Sandstone* blasts was a compromise that acknowledged the need of B-17 director crews to have sufficient daylight to guide the QB-17s properly. A gamma ray measurement needed darkness to record visible light emission. Pre-dawn practice flights determined the earliest opportunity to launch QB-17s while still having sufficient darkness for the gamma study. For the 15 April *X-Ray* blast, eight QB-17s were positioned and launched from Eniwetok.

QB-17 44-83664, with the call sign 'Drone 14', became uncontrollable and crashed into the sea in spectacular fashion minutes before the *X-Ray* detonation. The pairing of Mother and 'Drone 14' started off haltingly when the latter nosed up on take-off as its airspeed bled off to 120mph. The nose of the Flying Fortress was forced down by a constant input of the down-elevator signal. The drone then appeared to be under control, and was subsequently guided toward its intended location for the blast.

44-83664 was on a correct heading at 14,000ft, with the blast detonation about two minutes away, when it commenced a rogue vertical climb as the remote pilot watched helplessly. At the time of this climb, the mother ship was not transmitting any

Military and civilian members of The Adventurers Club pose with a banner proclaiming their organisation in front of a *Crossroads* B-17 drone on Eniwetok. The corps of photographers and other technicians recruited for *Crossroads* included Hollywood motion picture talent to ensure outstanding film coverage. *USAAF*

Low and to the right, a B-17 drone returns to Eniwetok under the control of a B-17 mother ship nearer to the camera. Crews practiced hand offs between ground control drone fliers and airborne remote pilots in the director B-17s. *USAAF/Gene Furnish collection*

Crossroads remote pilots had this televised view of instrument readings from the B-17 drones they were controlling. *AFHRA*

LAMP INDICATES ONE OR MORE OF THREE SALVO SWITCHES ARE ON
WARNING
MARKER BEACON
VACUUM
LEFT ENGINES
RIGHT ENGINES
FUEL PRESSURE
DOWN
CYL. TEMP °C HEAD
LOCK
CLOSED
THROTTLE
CLOSED
LOCKED LOW PITCH
HIGH R.P.M.
FORMATION STICKS
AUTOPILOT
C-1 AUTOPILOT
CENTERING
SENSITIVITY
LOCK

The windswept palms of Eniwetok wave behind this *Crossroads* B-17 director taking off. *AFHRA*

signals to the drone. 'Mother Ship 14' immediately transmitted a full-down elevator signal which produced no response in the QB-17. 'Drone 14' stalled on the left wing, dropping into a vertical dive that instrumentation showed to reach 250mph, accompanied by gyrations. After briefly levelling out, the drone dived again, this time attaining an incredible 380mph before the errant QB-17 executed two complete inside loops – something unheard of for such a bomber. More movements described as gyrations ensued before 'Drone 14' entered a 260mph dive that culminated in a spectacular explosion as the wayward bomber hit the ocean. With no recoverable wreckage to inspect, informed speculation about the cause of 'Drone 14's' spectacular departure ranged from an unknown source of spurious up-elevator radio commands to a short in the C-1 autopilot system.[91]

Other *Sandstone* adventures included a QB-17 that did not have full braking available. Differential braking was adroitly employed by the remote pilot just short of ground-looping the big bomber, and a series of nylon ropes across the runway at the far end saved the day. The first three ropes broke as the bomber contacted them, rolling at about 45–50mph. The fourth, fifth and sixth ropes held, and the QB-17 was saved.[92]

The second *Sandstone* shot, code-named *Yoke*, detonated just before sunrise on 1 May (variously reported as 30 April). At that moment, a QB-17 passed overhead at 20,000ft to photograph the detonation. The drone encountered severe buffeting and did not perform subsequent sampling passes since the additional radioactive exposure might have damaged the film in its cameras. The third shot of *Sandstone*, *Zebra*, on 15 May (or 14 May, depending on the source) yielded QB-17s that were measurably hotter than after the previous two shots. Three of the men removing the sampling paper filters received radioactive burns to their hands that ultimately required skin grafting.

During *Sandstone*, the QB-17s recovered on Eniwetok after blast missions while the mother ships landed at Kwajalein Atoll. Following *Sandstone*, the QB-17s were cleared to return to Eglin Field once their radiation levels were recorded as below 0.016 R/hr (roentgen/hr).[93]

With time for practice and proficiency, a *Crossroads* drone on the ramp brackets another yellow-and-black striped drone coming in to land while a director B-17 is off to the left in the background. *AFHRA*

Opposite: B-17 drones assigned to *Crossroads* were fitted with mechanical arms adapted to the unique Flying Fortress throttle quadrant, grasping all four throttles with a metal bracket for uniform settings on all engines. *AFHRA*

An elevated platform on the flat surface of Eniwetok provided a suitable vantage point for ground control pilots of B-17 drones during *Crossroads* in the summer of 1946. *AFHRA*

While the QB-17s on Eniwetok cooled from their radiation exposure, they were washed down with a mixture of kerosene and Gunk (a commercial product used for cleaning aircraft exterior surfaces), followed by a tri-sodium phosphate bath. The last step in this process was a water rinse. Following a cool-down period, the QB-17s were monitored for radioactivity, and the duration for which personnel could be around the aircraft varied in the number of allowable hours based on radiological readings. One of the QB-17s was washed with only water, and this proved ineffective. The chemical washes were then performed to get this drone decontaminated.

Radiation observations showed the engine oil in the QB-17s was radioactive from flying through the atomic cloud, but levels were not considered high enough to warrant oil changes until after the final drone sampling flight of the series. The nature of the work of decontaminating the QB-17s during *Sandstone* is captured in the instruction to the men spraying the aircraft to avoid having the hoses contact their clothing because they 'had become contaminated in the radioactive puddles beneath the planes'.[94] Effective radiation monitoring of workers was necessary in an effort to assure their well-being.

Crossroads B-17 drone modifications included the fitting of an air sampling device where the top turret had formerly been located. *AFHRA*

This view looking forward also shows the B-17 drone's dorsal air sampling device. *AFHRA*

The B-17 drone air sampling device mounted in the top turret location. *AFHRA*

Far left: The B-17 drone's dorsal air sampling device had a quick-release mechanism to facilitate the removal of radiated sample paper following a mission. *AFHRA*

Left: In this photograph, the B-17 drone's dorsal air sampler is shown with its sample removal panel open. *AFHRA*

The B-17 drone's control equipment mounted on the navigator's table during the *Crossroads* era. *AFHRA*

Above: Groundcrew hurry to remove radioactive sampler equipment from a QB-17 modified with a special chin sampler position after the *Zebra* shot during Operation *Sandstone*. *NARA*

Top left: A remotely-operated crane arm plucks a sample gathering device from a QB-17 during Operation *Sandstone*. *NARA*

A *Sandstone* QB-17 in the process of post-mission decontamination. *NARA*

As mother ships were shepherding drones back from the blast during *Sandstone*, the radiologist occasionally recommended greater separation between mother and drone due to radiation levels in the QB-17s.[95]

While acknowledging its obsolescence in the post-war world, one *Sandstone* after action report was effusive in its praise of the venerable B-17 Flying Fortress as a drone aircraft:

> 'B-17 remote control aircraft are ideally suited for this type of work despite the obsolescent control equipment installed in them. It is extremely doubtful that any other aircraft could have been as completely satisfactory at the present time. It's (sic) proven stability, flexibility, and uncritical flying characteristics have made themselves felt during almost all of the flights due to the somewhat unscientific methods of remotely flying them.'[96]

A pilot who has just finished moving a 'hot' QB-17 to the decontamination station receives a radioactivity check on Eniwetok during *Sandstone*. *NARA*

An armed MP keeps unauthorised personnel away from a washed *Sandstone* drone. Depending on circumstances, access to QB-17s immediately after nuclear sampling missions could be limited in duration, and more relaxed after a cooling period had elapsed. *NARA*

Frequent and thorough washing of clothing and personnel, monitored by radioactivity checks, was intended to keep *Sandstone* crews safe. *NARA*

After working on a *Sandstone* QB-17 post-mission, this groundcrewman is scrubbing himself down with soap and water to remove any radioactive contamination. *NARA*

QB-17s and QT-33s of Operation *Greenhouse*

The use of Second World War B-17s as drones for nuclear blast sampling worked well in the 1940s on tests like *Crossroads*. However, as the capabilities of bombers, and bombs, increased it became apparent the QB-17s could not attain sufficient altitude for some sampling needs. Lockheed QT-33As, developed from the T-33A Shooting Star (a lengthened two-seat trainer based on the F-80 Shooting Star fighter), eventually began to come on line to supplement the venerable QB-17s during nuclear tests.

Five QT-33A drones and an identical number of DT-33A drone director aircraft made their service debut during the four detonations codenamed Operation *Greenhouse* in April–May 1951. They worked alongside 18 QB-17s and 15 DB-17s for three of the blasts. The QB-17G identified by the last three digits of its serial number as 666 was lost on the *Item* shot on 24 May, QT-33A 928 was destroyed on the *Dog* shot on 7 April and QT-33As 929 and 940 crashed on the *Easy* shot on 20 April.[97]

The ten QB-17 drones were heavily contaminated from flying through the radioactive cloud soon after the *Dog* explosion. Four days of decontamination effort were required before aircraft maintenance could be safely conducted. For *Easy*, the drones began sampling runs right after the detonation. Two QT-33s, measuring blast and heat effects, were lost. One came down in the sea and the other jet crash-landed on Bokoluo, part of the Marshall Islands. The QB-17 drones had all landed at Eniwetok by 0925 hrs.

For the *George* shot on 8 May, H-hour was postponed until 0930 hrs – a delay of 3 hrs 11 min from the original schedule – to allow more daylight for drone aircraft operations to compensate for anticipated cloud cover. During the *George* explosion, some control of a QT-33 at 29,000ft was lost. Its drone mission was aborted, and the aircraft made a safe recovery. Shot *Item*, the final *Greenhouse* blast on 24 May, used fewer drones than other tests, and a QB-17 was lost at sea.[98]

QB-17 and DB-17 operations for *Greenhouse* were described in the following report:

> 'Each drone was controlled by personnel aboard a B-17 controller aircraft. One or more of the drones and their controllers were supervised by personnel aboard another B-17, the master-controller. For this experiment each drone was to make one pass through the shot cloud. Each drone entered the cloud at a different altitude. The manned B-17s – the controllers and master controllers – did not enter the cloud.'

Radioactivity was tabulated for the QB-17s:

> 'Readings of gamma intensity in drones penetrating the cloud were over 1,000 R/hr. In drones penetrating the cloud stem, gamma readings exceeded 100 R/hr.'

Tradescantia flowering plants were carried aboard three QB-17s that each made two passes through the shot cloud from the *Dog* explosion at 16,000ft, 18,000ft and 20,000ft. These plants were tested for their ability to be organic indicators of radiation exposure, or biological dosimeters. Plants and mice were placed in drones for the *Easy* and *George* blast

Two days after the *Greenhouse Easy* shot on 20 April 1951, a contaminated QB-17 is washed down on Eniwetok. A radiation hazard sign adorns the lower forward fuselage ahead of the entry/escape hatch. *NARA*

cloud surveys. Eight QB-17s were airborne for each shot except *Item*, passing through the shot cloud at 16,000ft, 18,000ft, 20,000ft, 22,000ft, 24,000ft, 26,000ft, 28,000ft and 30,000ft.[99]

The Naval Radiological Defense Laboratory (NRDL) and Army Chemical Center (ACC) collaborated on contamination and decontamination studies during *Greenhouse*. Mindful that they were intentionally trapping radioactive materials from the atmosphere, the team studying contamination and decontamination worked out a plan. They devised 40 panels coated with various materials that were taped to the wings and horizontal stabilisers of several QB-17s and then carried through the shot clouds. For *Dog* and *Easy*, all eight drones carried panels. For *George*, four drones carried panels, but one of the QB-17s had to return to base before it went through the cloud. During the *Item* shot seven drones carried test panels. A few hours after the shots, panels were removed from the drones. A test report said:

An operator reaches out the back of a shielded motorised device intended for the safe removal of radioactive samples from a container beneath the nose of a QB-17 during *Greenhouse*. *NARA*

> 'To remove the panels, a man carrying a hooked pole walked to the drone from a truck positioned about 100ft upwind. He used the hook to engage a loop hanging from each panel and pulled the panel off of the plane. Other panels are taped to the underside of the wing just behind the leading edge. Holding the panel at the end of the pole, he returned to the truck, where a second man grasped the panel with tongs and put it in a box. After a number of panels were collected, they were taken by truck to another location, where a crew of four men with tongs and poles tipped with scalpels stripped off the remaining tape. They then re-boxed the panels. Some panels were flown to NRDL and ACC about ten hours after the shots; others were kept in the proving ground for initial study and flown to the laboratories two days after the shot.'[100]

Two QT-33s and two QB-17s were flown a specified distance from several of the *Greenhouse* detonations to measure blast effects on airframes. For the *Dog* shot, QT-33 No 1 was lost. It drifted to the left and bounced several times on take-off, ultimately crashing in the lagoon. QT-33 No. 2 dragged its right wingtip tank on take-off, and subsequent inspection after the mission showed scratches on the tank but not a lot of damage.

The QT-33's horizontal displacement from the *Dog* blast was 8580ft, with the shockwave striking the QT-33 from the rear and below. The drone jet flew at a high enough altitude so that its slant range distance from the detonation was 11,600ft. The post-mission inspection did not reveal evidence of any shock damage to the structure, although black lettering paint was blistered and panels that were painted yellow had a brown scorch tint. Probes indicated the QT-33 experienced a rapid temperature rise of 70°F above ambient.[101]

Greenhouse's use of drones in 1951 marks a turning point in aircraft development, with modern jet-powered QT-33s flying alongside essentially pre-war piston-engined QB-17s. The QT-33 shockwave experiments revealed scorched paint, but not apparent airframe damage. When QB-17 'Drone M' (44-83537), a product of an earlier design era, took a shock hit from the *Dog* blast, the results were different. The DB-17 director aircraft released the drone on a specified heading at an airspeed of 138 knots. When the shockwave hit, the unmanned Flying Fortress 'bounded about 300–400ft with a nose-high attitude, dropping IAS [indicated airspeed] to 89 knots and changing direction 30 degrees', a report said of the incident. Loss of down elevator control was noted. The blast effects hit the underside of the QB-17's fabric-covered elevators, and radiant heat caused the fabric on the lower side of the elevators to depart, possibly after charring from the blast.[102]

Despite this damage causing instability that left the aircraft susceptible to stalling, the drone director managed to complete a safe, if somewhat dramatic, landing. A post-flight inspection of the QB-17 revealed more damage than testers had initially realised. The ailerons had also been damaged, while the fabric-covered control surfaces lost much of their lower skin in the blast. It was said at the time that if the extent of compromise to the QB-17 had been known, it is possible the team would have elected not to try to land the drone on the Eniwetok runway. A report on the incident noted:

As soon as QB-17s landed following *Greenhouse* activity, they were towed to the decontamination area by a tug with an extra long tow bar that placed the tug operator at a greater distance from the radioactive drone. This photograph was taken on 8 May 1951 – the day of the *George* shot. *NARA*

'Other minor evidences of heat, such as blistering of paint on the black letters and the black surfaces and on the black compass-antenna housing and charring of a wooden plug, were found by careful examination of the airplane.'

No major structural damage was reported. The damage was done while the QB-17 was at a slant range from the blast at 18,380ft nearly three-and-a-half miles distant.[103]

For the *Easy* shot (thirteen days after *Dog*), a test report stated:

'It was considered imperative that the fabric surfaces of the QB-17 drone airplanes be protected. The materials on hand at Eniwetok were examined and considered for use as protective coats. Several materials, such as white paint, aluminum paint, wrapping paper and two kinds of wrapping foil were selected as most promising. Alternatives such as fabricating metal surfaces and covering the fabric surfaces with thin sheets of soft aluminum were considered and then discarded because they were too time-consuming or because they required unavailable material.'[104]

Interestingly, Strategic Air Command (SAC) nuclear bombers including Convair B-36s and Boeing B-47s and B-52s later adopted glossy white undersurface paint as a reflective blast heat protectant.

For the *Greenhouse Easy* shot, after on-site quick tests of various protective materials were made in an oven at 1000°F, a concocted foil application was deemed helpful, as described by a report on the effort:

'The foil selected consisted of laminated materials as follows: one layer of gauze impregnated with glue, one layer of brown wrapping paper, one layer of foil [apparently aluminium], and one layer of plastic [rather tough, but very slightly heat resistant]. The fabric horizontal surfaces [elevators and ailerons] of three B-17 drones ["M", "N" and "O"] were covered with this foil. The foil was doped to the fabric, and the edges of each sheet were sealed with a metal-foil-backed adhesive tape borrowed from Project 6.1. The surfaces were flight-tested before shot day to make sure that the protection was not likely to come off in flight.'[105]

The *Easy* shot of *Greenhouse* provided more proof of the need for unmanned aircraft in such a hostile test environment when a QT-33 (Drone 3, in the 'Alice Position') spiralled out of control shortly after the blast, its radio control systems likely ruined by heat damage from the blast wave. The drone jet was at a slant range of 6160ft from the shot.

Shortly thereafter, QT-33 Drone 2, in the 'Betty Position', failed to come under full control of the mother ship after the jet's run at a pre-arranged distance from the blast. The drone had been controlled by radar for the pass, after which controllers found that recording equipment could not be switched off. The QT-33 could not be landed by the radar director, and neither the mother ship director nor the ground director could attain enough control of the drone to effect a safe landing. As reported after the test:

Long poles and quick movement by the groundcrew indicate the level of radioactivity in the presence of this QB-17 after a sortie during *Greenhouse* in 1951. *NARA*

> 'The decision was made to crash-land the drone, according to a previously arranged plan, on Bogallua Island. The airborne director attempted directional and altitude control while the radar director reduced power. The airplane crashed and burned. It was estimated that the airspeed at impact was approximately 225 knots.'[106]

Because of residual radioactivity on Bogallua Island, the QT-33 wreckage could not be accessed for a day. The destruction of the QT-33 in the crash landing and subsequent fire prevented the determination of the level of damage that might have been contributed by the blast effects.

QB-17 'Drone M' performed its pass successfully. Once the DB-17 mother ship returned to the proximity of the drone, control was satisfactory, but the mother ship could see the partially exposed right main tyre was on fire. Otherwise, the aircraft appeared undamaged. The director crew lowered the landing gear on the drone to extend the flaming tyre as far from the airframe as possible. Eventually the fire was extinguished. The QB-17 with the damaged main tyre was kept aloft while the other drones were landed, just in case the stricken aircraft suffered a landing mishap that could have blocked the runway. The damaged drone landed safely, rolling to the right near the end of its run.

A subsequent inspection of the QB-17 revealed little other damage. Some of the experimental foil covering the fabric control surfaces was burned, but the surfaces themselves appeared undamaged. Pressure damage associated with the detonation was listed as the cause for access panels that were found popped open, damage to the bomb-bay doors and rear entry door and other similar items. Slant range to the blast was just over 11,000ft.[107]

QB-17 'Drone N', in the 'Doris Position' for the *Easy* shot, was flying at 17,510ft slant range from the blast. The shock wave hit the drone from the front and below. Because of the location assigned for this position, it was not feasible to manoeuvre the drone to miss the cloud plume. This QB-17 entered the turbulent area of the cloud about 54 seconds after time zero. Because it passed through the cloud, 'Drone N' could not be examined until it was decontaminated. Wing/fuselage fairing strips were bent and partly detached, leading testers to conclude the wings had flexed upward substantially. While no unusual wrinkles or permanent deformation of the wing could be ascertained, it was noted that paint had flaked from some rivet heads. Although the testers could not confirm it conclusively, they said there was some evidence to suggest the wings of this QB-17 took a permanent set, or bend, from the loads encountered that day.

The *George* shot on 9 May saw an array of drone and support aircraft sent aloft again. Amongst them was QB-17 'Drone N', which flew line abreast with its mother ship and the master director B-17, with spacing of 1000ft between them. The drone experienced the shock wave 32 seconds after detonation, the mother ship two seconds later and the master mother aircraft a second after that. The only crewmen of the two manned B-17s to experience some heat from the blast were those seated beside windows. The three Flying Fortresses experienced a tail-up pitch from the rear and below as a result of the blast shock while flying some 42,600ft in slant range from the detonation. Even at this distance, the camera hatch doors on the drone were blown open by the shock wave.[108]

QB-17 'Drone P' was the last aeroplane assigned to the *George* test shot to take off, since it was slated to be at the lowest altitude – 14,000ft – and did not require extra time to climb. Its slant range distance of more than 60,000ft from the blast meant 'Drone P' was likely to return with little or no damage from the shock wave and blast effects, which hit the QB-17 from the front and slightly below.

The results of *Greenhouse* led to a proposal to the USAF to configure additional aircraft types, specifically Republic F-84 Thunderjets, B-29s and B-47s, as drones to use in the parameters of future tests, presumably because more modern types were needed to quantify blast effects on operational frontline aircraft. Later, when QB-47s were created, it was for a different purpose – replicating likely hostile bombers.

AD Skyraider drones of Operation *Upshot–Knothole*

The ability of tactical aircraft like the Douglas AD Skyraider to deliver a nuclear weapon to a target and safely egress the area without succumbing to blast effects was studied in Operation *Upshot–Knothole* in Nevada in March–June 1953. For the tests (which numbered eleven shots in total), Skyraiders were flown in conjunction with a series of nuclear explosions, the aircraft being positioned where ADs could expect to be when they were overtaken by blast effects from air bursts.

AD-2K BuNo 122363 and early-build XBT2D-1 BuNo 09103 were converted into drone aircraft and instrumented for the measurement of atomic weapon effects. The Skyraider was to be in level flight attitude, with its tail toward the blast in a vertical plane containing the burst point simulating an escape position of an AD-type aircraft following delivery of an atomic weapon. The results were expected to also provide useful data for other aircraft types that might be in the vicinity of a nuclear blast.[109]

The Skyraiders were fitted with Naval Air Experimental Station Type I Remote Control Equipment. Each of the droned Skyraiders flew as manned aircraft in lower-risk missions for *Upshot–Knothole* before their drone sorties in order to gain data for testers. For NOLO operations, a test report explained:

> 'The drone take-off was under the control of a pilot at a ground station located beside the runway. Once airborne, the drone was

turned over to a pilot flying a Navy Model F8F "mother" control plane. Upon arrival at the test site, control was turned over to a pilot at the radar plotting board. Using data from the radar plot and from telemetering direct reading meters, the pilot guided the drone to its predetermined position relative to the burst at time zero. Following the test, the "mother" aircraft again took control and the drone was returned to the base, where the pilot at the runway station controlled the drone landing.'[110]

The drone and mother ship contingent for the *Annie* shot (on 17 March) included one AD-2 drone codenamed 'Duck Bill Dog', two Grumman F8F Bearcat mother ships codenamed 'Duck Bill 1' and '2' and two AD-4 Skyraider armed escorts codenamed 'Duck Bills 6' and '7'. These code names would be repeated in other shots of this test series (sometimes including a third escort, 'Duck Bill 8'). When equipment difficulties precluded using the AD-2 as a drone, it was piloted at 17,000ft Mean Sea Level (MSL) and 9000ft beyond ground zero at detonation, providing data useful for the intended drone positionings closer to the blast.[111]

The *Nancy* shot, on 24 March, was the first time a NOLO drone sortie had flown in an atomic test in the US Zone of the Interior. An array of manned sampler aircraft on this shot included F-84Gs, with pilots and their Thunderjets being monitored for radiation exposure – indicative of the reason why drones were used for high-risk exposure during the test shots.

Data for thermal and blast effects was obtained for all of the shots except Shot 7, codenamed *Simon*, on 25 April when the Skyraider drone was destroyed at shock arrival, along with all data. Shot 1 was accompanied by a manned Skyraider flight, with the aircraft 16,800ft from the blast when the shock reached it. Shot 2 (*Nancy*) was accompanied by a drone AD-2 positioned closer to the blast, the aircraft being 10,900ft away when the shock arrived. Temperature sensors recorded rises in heat on aluminium surfaces of varying thickness and colour, the latter ranging from blue to heat-resistant white and aluminised lacquer.[112]

The fateful *Simon* shot saw the immutable laws of physics deliver a 'one–two punch' to the drone Skyraider, downing the aircraft on the Nevada desert in the T-1 Yucca area. The unavoidable denouement followed a nuclear blast that had an actual yield more than 30 per cent larger than what was forecast. The AD-2 drone was positioned in flight based on calculations for the smaller yield bomb. The actual thermal radiation severely damaged or weakened all the blue-painted skin on the underside of the Skyraider's wing. The aircraft was 5900ft higher than the atomic blast and just 6700ft in slant range from it. Testers estimated a temperature rise of 500°F on blue-painted skin that was 0.064in thick, and an astounding 1200°F rise on thin 0.016in skin. The testers reported:

> 'The top side of the wing gave no indication of thermal damage other than softening of standard blue paint on 0.016 skin on the aileron, where the underside skin was completely destroyed. The above information was obtained from the wing outboard panels and sections of the elevator

For Operation *Upshot–Knothole*, two droned US Navy Skyraiders and their F8F Bearcat directors probed the sobering limits of airframe survivability while escaping the effects of a nuclear blast. *NARA*

Droned AD-2K Skyraider BuNo 122363 was helping the US Navy quantify nuclear blast damage effects on flying aircraft during Operation *Upshot–Knothole* tests in Nevada when it came apart in flight over the T-1 Yucca area on 25 April 1953. Thermal radiation damage and the aftershock from the *Simon* shot inflicted mortal damage on the Skyraider's wings.

> and horizontal stabilizer which were torn off at shock arrival and received only minor additional damage due to the fall. Evidence indicates that the wing failure resulted when the thermally weakened skin was further damaged by shock effects, thereby reducing the overall strength of the wing. The sections of the empennage were torn off when struck by the wing panels.'[113]

Shot 8 (*Harry*, on 19 May) used the XBT2D-1 as a drone. For this flight, the skin on the belly and wings of the dark blue drone was stripped back to bare aluminium, except for panels on the ailerons and elevators. No thermal damage was visible on any unpainted surface on the drone. Blue-painted portions showed damage from heat. The aircraft used in this test had exposed wheel wells for the main gear, whose tyres were painted with a white heat resistant paint. In spite of being directly exposed to thermal effects, the painted tyres showed no signs of heat damage.[114] Testers noted the value of white-painted surfaces:

> 'The extreme importance of aircraft skin surface finish is readily seen in the results from Shot 7. Heat resistant white painted panels remained intact where similar panels with standard blue paint, subjected to identical thermal radiation, were completely destroyed. Bare aluminum held up almost as well as heat resistant white, but in all cases experienced higher temperatures. It is to be noted here that heat resistant white and standard white paint afford roughly the same protection as long as the finish is not charred. At thermal levels high enough to seriously affect the standard white surface, it proves to be no better than aluminized lacquer.
>
> 'Field analysis of the structural failures which caused the loss of the drone in Shot 7 were conducted by project personnel and representatives of the Structures Department, Douglas Aircraft Company. Indications are that the aircraft might have survived had the under skin been bare aluminum or painted heat resistant white instead of standard blue. The coating of other thermally vulnerable items, such as fabric seals and rubber tires, with heat resistant white paint permitted them to withstand approximately four times the thermal radiation that they could in their natural state.'[115]

A big takeaway from the test report underscored the significance of light skin finishes:

> 'Heat resistant white paint provides aircraft skin with a greater degree of protection from thermal radiation than any other surface finish tested. Next to heat resistant white, bare aluminum appears to offer the best protection against thermal damage. Aircraft skin painted standard blue is extremely vulnerable to thermal damage, being able to stand less than one-third of the thermal radiation withstood by skin painted with heat resistant white. Use of white or light colored paint on tires, aerodynamic seals and other dark colored materials provides similar protection against thermal radiation.'[116]

The XBT2D-1 drone (known as 'Duck Bill Dog 2') caused tense moments for the director crew in an F8F Bearcat during the set up for Shot 8 when the drone took a heading toward populous Los Angeles and refused commands to change course for 15–20

Groundcrew calibrate the radio control equipment fitted in the nose of a QF-80 drone at Indian Springs AFB on 6 April 1953 prior to the jet's participation in the *Dixie* shot during *Upshot–Knothole*. *National Nuclear Security Administration*

minutes before H-hour. A technical summary blamed the errant Skyraider on 'some outside frequency interference'. Neither the F8F nor the ground station could interact with 'Duck Bill Dog 2' for several minutes. Then, the frequency interference stopped and the Skyraider responded, allowing the director pilot to line the aeroplane up and insert it in its intended position in time for the detonation at H-hour. The flight ended with a successful drone landing at Indian Springs AFB, Nevada, to the relief of all.[117]

Upshot–Knothole's *Dixie* shot, on 6 April, marked the first use of jet drones in the US Zone of the Interior for a nuclear test. Two USAF QF-80 Shooting Stars, codenamed 'Brow Beat 2' and '3', participated that day. Four DT-33s served as director aircraft, codenamed 'Brow Beat 1', '4', '6' and '9'.[118] A redacted test report described this initial jet drone operation as follows:

> 'The Project 4.1 drone phase encountered a little difficulty in that the first drone did not penetrate the cloud but went under it. Drone No. 2 penetrated the very bottom of the cloud and recorded a reading of 4000 r peak intensity at the wing tips. The drone landings and take-offs were very successful.'[119]

On 7 May two QF-80 drones and four DT-33 directors were involved in the *Encore* 'Effects' shot, with the drones penetrating the blast cloud after initially missing it. By manoeuvring in flight the drones made a 180° turn and collected valuable blast cloud samples.[120] Eighteen days later, the QF-80 and DT-33 entourage that was scheduled to participate in the *Grable* shot under the call sign 'Brow Beat' cancelled because of ground winds at Indian Springs AFB. A QB-17 located at the same site also cancelled.[121]

Tail numbers for the QF-80s are listed in test documents as '58698' and '58644'. The QF-80 drones were equipped to carry research animals and gamma radiation measuring devices.[122]

One report from *Upshot–Knothole* was not overly charitable about the usefulness of the drones. This document suggested:

> 'In the event of future studies of external gamma radiation dose rate and integrated dose in clouds from weapons up to 30 KT [kiloton] yield, it is recommended that consideration be given to the utilization of high-speed manned aircraft. The use of manned aircraft would provide more accurate data on area and altitude of penetration and transit time through the cloud. Such studies may also include evaluation of the shielding

QF-80B 45-8599 was one of two drone Shooting Stars involved in the *Dixie* shot. Only one of the QF-80s successfully penetrated the nuclear blast cloud caused by the detonation, and both aircraft returned safely to Indian Springs. Wingtip pods trapped radioactive particles for evaluation. *National Nuclear Security Administration*

characteristics of the aircraft in the various crew positions. Especially attractive advantages of employing manned aircraft are the increased control, maneuverability and resulting ease of hitting the cloud, elimination of ground control radar facilities, and decreased probability of aircraft loss. It would permit utilization of a type of aircraft suited to extensive instrumentation and capable of flying well above 30,000ft, a combination not available in present drone aircraft.'[123]

The author of the report was subsequently vindicated, for there appears to have been a greater reliance on fast piloted jets in later years for atomic sampling missions. Nevertheless, the drones did their job of collecting samples and without having to risk pilots' lives in the early years of nuclear weapons development in the Cold War. Eventually, their baseline groundwork did not need to be re-accomplished with each new blast test. The contribution made by the drones was valuable. From burning landing gear rubber on a QB-17 to the scorched crash of a Skyraider overtaken by too much blast, the drones performed an essential research service without risking a human crew onboard.

QF-80B 45-8599 and its DT-33 drone director prepare to depart Indian Springs on 6 April as part of *Upshot–Knothole*'s *Dixie* shot. This mission marked the jet drone's nuclear test debut in the US Zone of the Interior, with two QF-80s and four DT-33s participating in the flight. *National Nuclear Security Administration*

4 Hellcats for Targets and Training

The F6F Hellcat was an inspired Second World War fighter design. Boasting the right mixture of power and flying qualities, it was the mount of choice for a generation of fighter pilots, more than 300 of whom became aces in the war against Japan. With VJ Day bringing the global conflict to an end, and the rapid advancement of the jet age immediately post-war, Hellcats quickly lost their status as frontline fighters in the US Navy. However, their availability made them prime candidates for droning, while other manned F6Fs served as drone director aircraft.

The US Navy's aircraft nomenclature at the time attached the letter K to the alphanumeric designation of piloted aircraft that were converted to drone use. This resulted in F6F-3K and F6F-5K drone variants. As detailed in Chapter 3, Hellcat drones were extensively used in Operation *Crossroads* in 1946.

An F6F-5K drone carrying a single 1000lb bomb is positioned at *Boxer*'s port bow catapult on 2 September 1952 for a combat sortie experiment that will be its final flight to destruction. *NARA/Tommy Thompson/GSLASM/Gerald Balzer collection*

F6F-5K BuNo 77633 was part of a small force of Hellcat drones used in combat strikes during the Korean War. The Hellcat drones, each armed with a single finless 1000lb or 2000lb bomb, were launched from USS *Boxer* (CV-21) whilst it sailed off the coast of North Korea in August–September 1952. The television camera pod under the right wing transmitted imagery back to the AD-2Q Skyraider mother ship controlling the Hellcat.

Hellcat drones in combat

In August–September 1952, as the Korean peninsula was fought over by communist and United Nations' forces, the US Navy launched six F6F-5K drones from the carrier USS *Boxer* (CV-21). A mother ship took control of the droned Hellcats at carrier take-off. With each F6F-5K carrying a 1000lb or 2000lb bomb mounted on the centreline station, the Hellcats were employed against particularly well defended ground targets to avoid piloted aircraft falling to communist anti-aircraft fire.[124]

The F6F-5Ks used a television guidance system. This caused some unique issues aboard the crowded *Boxer*, as noted in the carrier's after action report for the period:

> 'The starboard wing of the F6F-5(K) could not be folded when the television camera pod was installed. Due to space limitations on the hanger (sic) deck, this often interfered with scheduled work and with spotting for flight operations.'[125]

The F6F-5K drones launched from *Boxer* in August–September 1952 were awkward to handle once the television pods were installed beneath the starboard wing, necessitating that the latter be kept extended. With the catapult bridle being installed by the flightdeck crew for launch, this F6F-5K shows its bomb load and television pod.
NARA/Tommy Thompson/GSLASM/Gerald Balzer collection

An F6F-5K drone is readied for a catapult launch from *Boxer* as its ground handling pilot steps out of the cockpit. An AD Skyraider, likely operating independently of the drone mission, roars down the right catapult. Other Skyraiders guided the Hellcats to their targets. *GSLASM/Gerald Balzer collection*

The equipment in the aircraft involved in the drone operations required 30 minutes to warm up and check after the Hellcats were brought up to the flightdeck. The after action report suggested removing additional regular aircraft to create sufficient space on the hangar deck for the preparations. 'This would make possible an immediate launch when the planes were brought up, and would not interfere with other scheduled operations'. It was necessary for *Boxer* to keep a steady course while the F6F-5K drone gyro stabilisation was checked, and until the drone was launched.[126]

Drone launches were controlled from the air by AD-2Q Skyraiders from VC-35, with two of these aircraft being brought aboard *Boxer* along with a pair of drones. The drone operations took place while the carrier was otherwise engaged in maximum effort conventional air strikes with a full complement of 80 aircraft on board. The after action report noted:

> 'In order to bring the two drones and two AD-2Q control planes aboard, it was necessary to keep two of the ship's ADs on

Flightdeck crew aboard *Boxer* prepare to launch an F6F-5K bomb-laden drone on 2 September 1952. The results of several sorties were disappointing. *NARA/Tommy Thompson/GSLASM/Gerald Balzer collection*

'Overshadowed' by an F9F Panther, an F6F-5K drone carrying a 1000lb bomb on the centreline station is readied for combat on 2 September 1952 aboard *Boxer*. As previously noted, when the television camera gear was attached to the right wing, the latter had to remain extended, cramping operations on a crowded carrier.
NARA/Tommy Thompson/GSLASM/Gerald Balzer collection

the beach. Replacement drones were brought aboard as others were expended.'

F6F-5Ks were launched from 28 August, when one example left *Boxer* 'under control of two AD control planes'. Another Hellcat was launched the following day, and two more on 1 September – the final two Hellcat drones of the operation launched twenty-four hours later.[127]

The F6F-5Ks used in combat were assigned to Guided Missile Unit (GMU) 90. *Boxer*'s Photo Intelligence Section provided target imagery for the squadron.[128] The results of using the Hellcat bomb-laden drones were tallied as one hit, four misses and one operational abort.[129] The expenditure of droned Hellcats against Korean targets appeared less rewarding than research into purpose-built missiles.

Hellcats at Chincoteague

F6F-5Ks were outfitted for use as drone targets in a series of flights undertaken by VX-2 at Naval Aviation Test Station (NATS) Chincoteague, in Virginia's Eastern Shore region, from June 1949 through to March 1950. Used to evaluate the effect of small arms incendiary rounds on aircraft in flight at high altitude, the unmanned Hellcats carried fuel in the cavities where wing-mounted machine guns and ammunition were normally housed. Initially, approximately 25 gallons of fuel, stowed in one- and five-gallon cans, was deposited in the starboard wing bay of the Hellcat drones for live fire tests conducted by other manned F6Fs.[130]

The first four test flights in what was unofficially dubbed 'Project Hotwing' saw the manned F6Fs fire on the Hellcat drone from above and behind at about 200 yards. The piloted Hellcats fired strings of ammunition ranging from five to fifteen rounds in a burst. The attacking aircraft carried two Browning M2 0.50-calibre machine guns in the outboard stations.

The rest of the test flights were made with F6F-5K drones carrying a gun in the cockpit, mounted and aimed to fire into the same aircraft's left wing. Weapons installed were either 0.50-calibre or experimental 0.60-calibre machine guns or 20mm cannon. These tests were considered more reliable than the free-firing flights. For the gun in the cockpit flights, a 15.5-gallon fuel tank was made of galvanised steel sheet metal and installed in the left wing gun bay. The weapons fired bursts of three to six rounds by remote control. The testers noted that the multi-round bursts made it impossible to determine if only one shot would be sufficient to propagate sustained ignition in the fuel tank.[131]

The study included the use of 0.50-calibre M23 incendiary (T48), 20mm M97 high explosive incendiary (HEI) (T23), 20mm M96 incendiary, 0.60-calibre incendiary (T36) and 0.60-calibre armor-piercing incendiary (T39) ammunition. The availability of unmanned fighter aircraft was a boon to the testing of these weapons and their effect on various fuels. The testers variously used 115/145 octane aviation gasoline and JP-1 and JP-3 jet fuels in the target fuel tanks.

It was concluded that 'fires can be initiated by incendiary ammunition at altitudes of 29,400 to 34,000 feet at indicated air speeds of 110 to 150 knots,

This red F6F-5K drone met a watery end. While drone controllers worked to keep their aircraft operable for multiple missions, the nature of a drone's service was hazardous, and ultimately destruction was likely. *GSLASM/Gerald Balzer collection*

and once initiated, they can be sustained to a damaging degree'. The 115/145 octane aviation gasoline was found susceptible to fire from all of the rounds except the 20mm M97 HEI. 'JP-1 fuel was the most resistant to ignition of sustained fires. The results obtained with JP-3 fuel show that it will ignite, and that sustained burning can be obtained with all rounds tested except the 20mm M97'. The testers observed that JP-3 fires resulted in greater damage than fires fed by the other fuels, suggesting higher heat generated from the JP-3.[132] 'The maximum true altitude at which positive results were obtained was 34,000 feet, this being the approximate operating ceiling of the control photographic aircraft', the report noted.

A table of test flight results created following the NATS Chincoteague Hellcat drone trials is a casual litany of the demise of unmanned F6F-5Ks in the sea and marshes off the Virginia coast. The first firing flight, on 5 July, which saw a second Hellcat firing on the drone, produced no hits. The following day, hits were observed on the Hellcat drone, with evidence of ignition prior to the drone crashing into the sea. With the weapon mounted in the drone, the third flight prompted ignition of aviation gasoline and loss of the F6F-5K in a marsh. On the sixth flight of this series, another drone crashed into the sea. Several other F6F-5Ks sustained damage on landing, including one wheels-up event. At least seven drones were reported as crashed during the tests, which is not surprising considering that the goal of the tests was to fire weapons into the aircraft in flight.[133]

The NATS Chincoteague Hellcat drone trials were emblematic of the times. The US Navy had hundreds of near-new F6F-5s that were surplus to the needs of the fleet, and naval aviation was in the midst of transitioning from high-octane gasoline to jet fuel, as were other major world powers. Knowledge of the volatility of various fuels and ammunition used against aircraft in flight was urgently needed.

On one wintry flying day, the airborne control pilot and his ground-based counterpart both lost sight of their F6F-5K drone as they were attempting a hand-off of responsibility as the aircraft was returning to Chincoteague in deteriorating weather. The Hellcat staggered across the airfield at low altitude and low power, crashing in oyster beds beyond the base.[134]

The USAF conducted its own high-altitude tests of a QB-17 Flying Fortress with a 0.50-calibre machine gun mounted to fire into the drone's outboard wing gasoline tank, and these flights are detailed in Chapter 12. The USAF also tested some 'gun-and-fuel situations' using a manned B-29 with a bomb-bay trapeze to lower the fuel tank target away from the main airframe. The test report that summarised the US Navy's Chincoteague Hellcat drone trials also noted, 'The B-17 and F6F drone firing tests seem far more realistic than the trapeze tests and represent true combat conditions to a far greater degree'.[135]

On 8 August 1957 over the Mojave Desert at China Lake, an AIM-9B AAM found its mark, causing the F6F-5K target to shed parts amid a ball of fire. *US Navy*

Photographed in April 1961, weathered F6F-5K drone BuNo 77722, with a pilot aboard, has been fitted with wingtip camera scoring pods. *Clay Jansson/GSLASM/Gerald Balzer collection*

Sidewinder versus Hellcats

When the first Sidewinder air-to-air missile (AAM) was flight launched over the Mojave Desert on 14 May 1952, the target was a droned F6F. The Hellcat did not produce a heat signature sufficient to attract an infrared seeking Sidewinder, so groupings of T-131 tracking flares ranging from six to sixteen in number were affixed to the old prop-driven fighters to make them more suitable targets.[136] Three years later, in 1956, the US Navy developed the Naval Ordnance Test Station Model 702A flare for the F6F-5K and the Ryan Q-2A Firebee target drone. Magnesium, Teflon and a special wax fuelled the 702A flare, which had a burn rate of 60 seconds on the ground and up to 80 seconds at 65,000ft. The 702A flare also found a home on Grumman F9F-6K Cougar jet drones.[137]

US Navy research leapfrogged high-output flares for target drone enhancement purposes, as well as for missile tracking and as decoy flares for operational aircraft. The USAF also pursued decoy flares as protection for its bombers.

On 16 August 1956, during a missile test flight from NAS Point Mugu, on the coast of California, a nightmare for drone operators happened when an F6F-5K went wandering over southern California, unresponsive to radio signals. Posing a threat to the greater Los Angeles area, the drone Hellcat was attacked by a pair of Northrop F-89 Scorpions, carrying a total of more than 200 Mk 4 2.75in unguided rockets, scrambled from Oxnard AFB. The jet fighter crews failed to down the stray F6F, which eventually ran out of fuel and crashed in the desert east of the town of Palmdale. Virtually all of the collateral damage caused by this incident emanated from the Mk 4 rockets, which started a number of brushfires that took 500 firefighters two days to bring under control, damaged buildings in the town of Palmdale and destroyed a pick-up truck. Fortunately, no one was injured.[138]

As previously noted, thousands of Hellcats were in the US Navy inventory when the Second World War ended in mid-August 1945. In fact, the last F6F-5 rolled out of the plant in November of that year. As effective as the Grumman fighter was in wartime, it was quickly outmoded by F8F Bearcats and later models of the Vought F4U Corsair, with the latter type remaining in production until 1954. Jets were also on the way. It is little wonder that so many F6Fs were available and expendable for use as drones. If Hellcats are rare gems today, their large numbers after the war meant 238 F6F-5K drones were still counted on inventory by the US Navy on 31 July 1957. A table of allowances bearing that date showed the following placement of F6F-5Ks:

31 July 1957 US Navy allowance and location of aircraft:

40 F6F-5K at [NAS] Point Mugu, A9 status [A9 = Research and Development, Ageing in Tour]

1 F6F-5K at NAS Pensacola R&D [Research and Development], A9 Status

1 F6F-5 at NACA Moffett/Ames, U Status [U = Loan by the US Navy]

22 F6F-5K at [NOTS] China Lake R&D, A9 Status

45 F6F-5K at NAS Norfolk O&R [Overhaul and Repair Department] BuAer FA, MZ Status [MZ = Storage]

15 F6F-5K at [NAS] Pensacola O&R BuAer FA, B Status

7 F6F-5K at [NAS] Pensacola O&R BuAer FA, C Status

6 F6F-5K at [NAS] Pensacola O&R BuAer FA, DD Status

2 F6F-5K at [NAS] Pensacola O&R BuAer FA, E4 Status

1 F6F-5K at NAS Johnsville, A9 Status

20 F6F-5K at San Diego O&R BuAer FA, NY Status (NY = Storage)

1 F6F-5K at Pool BuAer FA Litchfield Park, Y Status

1 F6F-5K at Litchfield Park Storage Facility, D4 Status

1 F6F-5K at Operational Development Sqn VX-2 [NATS] Chincoteague, A9 Status

7 F6F-5K at FASRON 8 [NAS] Alameda, C9 Status

2 F6F-5K at VU-3 R&D [Naval Auxiliary Air Station] Ream Field [Imperial Beach], A9 Status

1 F6F-5K at Fleet Utility and Drone Control Sqdn VU-3 Brown Field [NAAF Chula Vista], AQ Status

24 F6F-5K at Fleet Utility and Drone Control Sqdn VU-3 Brown Field [NAAF Chula Vista], A8 Status

9 F6F-5K at Fleet Utility and Drone Control Sqdn VU-3 Det A Naha, A8 Status

10 F6F-5K at Fleet Utility and Drone Control Sqdn VU-3 Det B [NAS] Barbers Point, A8 Status

1 F6F-5K at Fleet Utility and Drone Control Sqdn VU-4 [NATS] Chincoteague, AQ Status

9 F6F-5K at Fleet Utility and Drone Control Sqdn VU-4 [NATS] Chincoteague, A8 Status

9 F6F-5K at Fleet Utility and Drone Control Sqdn VU-10 [Naval Station] Gtmo [Guantanamo] Bay, A8 Status

2 F6F-5K at NAF [Naval Air Facility] Advance Base Oppama, B Status

1 F6F-5K at NAF Advance Base Oppama, EJ Status

238 F6F-5K aircraft in total

There was still room for the occasional F6F-5K Hellcat drone in the world of F9F Cougar drones at Point Mugu when this photograph was taken in April 1961. *GSLASM/Gerald Balzer collection*

If some F6F drones ended their days in a spectacular fireball, others skidded in on one final landing and then served up parts to keep remaining Hellcats airworthy. This F6F-5K reposed in a boneyard at China Lake in January 1962.
Clay Jansson/GSLASM/Gerald Balzer collection

Last Hellcat Drone from Pensacola

The January 1958 issue of *Naval Aviation News* noted the end of the line for US Navy F6F-5K Hellcat drone conversions after eight years of production at NAS Pensacola's Overhaul and Repair Department. After earlier Hellcat drones for programmes like Operation *Crossroads* were completed by the US Navy's facility at the NAMU in Johnsville, production of F6F-5K drones was switched to Pensacola, Florida, in 1949. With fleets of surplus Hellcats to choose from, the Department overhauled each aircraft before installing the drone gear, thus providing the US Navy with proven and reliable drones for many years.[139]

Long after F6F-5K Hellcat drones had passed from the scene, wreckage, typically identifiable by the characteristic F6F vertical fin, dotted the desert at Naval Ordnance Test Station (NOTS) China Lake. The waters surrounding San Nicolas Island (sometimes spelled San Nicholas in older military documents), off the coast of southern California, hide the remains of many other Hellcat drones.

This crashed F6F-5K drone on the range at China Lake left its vertical fin as a tombstone in the desert, and it was still visible when photographed in January 1978. *Frederick A Johnsen*

5 P4Y-2K/QP-4B Privateer Drones

The Convair PB4Y-2 Privateer naval patrol bomber was a direct progression from the B-24 Liberator, the aircraft using the same essential fuselage contours with a seven-foot extension ahead of the wing accommodating its sophisticated electronics suite used for surface search operations. Salient Privateer design features included the departure from the B-24's twin tails to a towering single fin and rudder, augmented by horizontal stabilisers with some dihedral to enhance handling characteristics.

The production run of PB4Y-2s totalled 739 and three prototypes, with the latter being converted and stretched from earlier PB4Y-1 Liberators. Even after attrition, the US Navy had hundreds of Privateers in desert storage at Litchfield Park, Arizona, following VJ Day, plus more still in squadron service pending the arrival of sufficient numbers of Lockheed P2V Neptunes. As with the USAAF and its access to factory-fresh B-17Gs for droning in the immediate post-war years, the US Navy had Privateers to spare.

As previously noted, during the Second World War the US Navy created comparatively rustic drones using PB4Y-1 Liberators. Laden with explosives for crash-delivery into a high-stakes target, these Liberators were taken off by a pilot and co-pilot who then turned control over to a director aircraft before the drone crew bailed out. The wartime PB4Y-1 drones' systems were not developed sufficiently to permit remote take-offs or landings. All that changed in 1952 when the Naval Air Development Center (NADC) at Johnsville (a location it shared with the NAMU) undertook state-of-the-art droning of three PB4Y-2s. Thereafter, they were designated P4Y-2K, with the 'B' deleted in US Navy nomenclature generally and the 'K' signifying a drone.[140]

Red P4Y-2K Privateer drone BuNo 59872 flew from Point Mugu and San Nicolas Island. Man-rated, Privateers sometimes ferried workers to and from San Nicolas. *Jim Morrow collection*

The Privateer drones, larger than the QB-17s employed by the USAF, were configured by striking a balance between drone capabilities and economy. It was a tightrope act performed by the US Navy. On the one hand, the Privateer drones were expensive enough that their preservation for multiple missions was desired. On the other hand, the very reason they were being droned was because they were at very real risk of being downed by a missile fired at them, from the ground (or at sea from a ship) or from an aircraft. The radio control capabilities installed in the three Privateer drones at Johnsville included differential wheel braking. With differential braking selected by the external drone pilot, deflection of the rudder would apply increased braking to the mainwheel on that side of the Privateer. This enabled a more precise line-up for take-offs and landings.[141]

Specifications for the Privateer drones called for them to be able to operate from runways 200ft wide and 5000ft in length, clearing a 50ft obstacle at the end of the runway under control of a remote pilot. Crosswinds as high as 20 knots had to be accommodated by the drones, as per the operational specification stipulated by the US Navy for Johnsville's engineers and technicians.

Although crewed Privateer operations required at least a pilot, co-pilot and flight engineer, the drone control functions were created to allow a single pilot to make a remote take-off in the modified Privateer. Airborne drone mother ship pilots in special Grumman F7F Tigercats or F8F Bearcats could operate the P4Y-2K drone in the cruise phase of its sortie while also flying their director aircraft. The P4Y-2K could be controlled visually or out of sight at a distance as far as 30 miles, using radar to establish position and altitude.[142]

Manoeuvres expected of the P4Y-2K were not excessive, and a remote pilot could set altitude hold and the droned Privateer would then execute standard rate turns. With adjustment to the P-1K autopilot carried by the Privateer drone, it could climb as steeply as 30 degrees, dive at 45 degrees and enter a 45-degree bank. Streamlined cylindrical camera pods were mounted to each wingtip of the P4Y-2K to provide comprehensive camera coverage of approaching missile shots.[143] In later years, the contours of Privateer wingtip camera pods would evolve.

The US Navy's earlier experience with droning previously manned aircraft centred on single-engined aeroplanes like the Hellcat. The four-engined Privateer, remotely-piloted from take-off to landing, needed to be able to have its Pratt and Whitney R-1830 engines controlled to the degree necessary to complete the drone mission. When some synchronisation ideas failed to work properly, the Johnsville team set all four propeller control units to 2400rpm for the lowest limits of their range. That was a high setting compared to normal crewed operation of a Privateer, and not conducive to long engine life. However, according to a NADC officer at Johnsville, 'this is not a factor with a target drone where any flight may be its last'.

Fuel mixture controls were left in Auto Rich for all operations. In the event of an inflight engine failure, an automatic rudder trim tab feature would keep the P4Y-2K on course. Limitations in the radio control system for the Privateer meant propellers could not be remotely feathered on failed engines.[144] From the rustic limitations on engine controls in drone mode, one can infer the US Navy had sufficient quantities of appropriate R-1830s to support P4Y-2K operations as replacements for expired engines.

While the USAF liked to drone its surplus tailwheeled B-17s, the US Navy showed that the tricycle gear P4Y-2 (later QP-4B) Privateer four-engined patrol bomber was a suitable candidate for remote pilot operation. This view of BuNo 59872 was also taken at Point Mugu. ***Jim Morrow collection***

The modified Privateer drones were expected to be able to absorb substantial damage and still be controllable for a safe return to base. The Johnsville modification team used an interlock between wing flaps and landing gear to ensure a stray signal would not retract flaps until the landing gear was cycled. This would prevent the aircraft mushing on take-off if the flaps were inadvertently retracted early in flight, and also in the landing phase. Should the first landing approach be waved off, the Privateer drone had enough power to complete go-arounds with flaps and gear extended.

Building on what they knew, the Johnsville team used essentially the same radio receivers in the P4Y-2Ks as in F6F-5K drones. The Privateer drones carried sufficient gasoline for ten hours in the air. This was enough to enable them to take off, climb to altitude, proceed to the hot missile range area, make at least ten passes of fifteen miles each and return to base. The ability of a ground pilot to operate the Privateer drone when it was many miles out of sight meant that his airborne equivalent in the mother ship could hand off control to a ground pilot and allow only the P4Y-2K to enter potentially dangerous skies where missiles would be launched.[145]

The first of the Privateer drones was delivered in December 1952 to what was then called the Pacific Missile Test Center (PMTC) at Point Mugu. After the first three Johnsville-modified P4Y-2Ks proved their worth, future conversions of Privateers to drones were to be accomplished at the US Navy's large Overhaul and Repair Department workshop in San Diego.[146]

Privateers quickly proved their merit at Point Mugu, and over the years more were converted. Still in service in 1962 when aircraft nomenclature changed to a unified system for all US military branches, the P4Y-2K became the QP-4B, with the Privateer's final basic designation as P-4 falling between the new Lockheed P-3 Orion maritime patrol aircraft and the Martin P-5 Marlin flying boat. Spanning two decades of US Navy service, the last QP-4B Privateer drone was downed on 18 December 1964, according to an account in the Point Mugu *Missile* newspaper.[147]

By then, the Privateer drone fleet available at Point Mugu comprised just two aircraft – 'Opposite 31' and 'Opposite 35'. Occasionally, one of the QP-4Bs served as a piloted shuttle aircraft, taking workers out to the US Navy's drone airstrip facility on San Nicolas Island. 'Opposite 31', nicknamed 'Lucky Pierre', had its luck run out on 18 December. Flying from the US Navy's facility on San Nicolas Island, it was destroyed by a missile fired from a Douglas A-4 Skyhawk assigned to test squadron VX-4.

There was never a dull moment for ground control pilots. Here, a photographer has caught a Privateer drone at an alarming angle while landing on San Nicolas Island.
Craig Kaston collection

Finished in Insignia Red and marked with eight mission symbols beneath the cockpit, QP-4B drone BuNo 59872 was one of a small fleet of Privateers that served US Navy target needs at Point Mugu/San Nicolas Island. The last QP-4B was downed in December 1964.

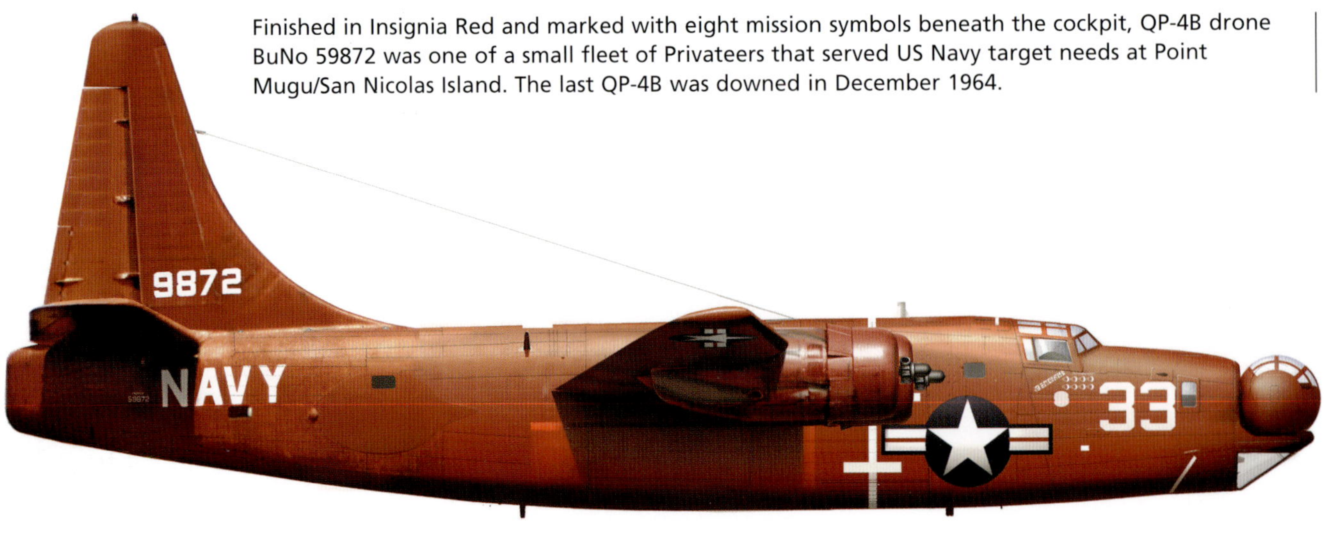

The Privateer's NOLO mission profile had the aircraft manoeuvring at altitudes ranging from 500 to 1000ft. US Navy personnel at San Nicolas Island watched the drama unfold as a missile hit 'Opposite 31' in the right bomb-bay area, but failed to bring the drone down. On the last planned fighter interception of the test, a missile punched into 'Opposite 31's' right wing, ripping it from the red Privateer's airframe and rolling the QP-4B into its final plunge to the sea.[148]

Capt (then Cdr) Bert Creighton was the Executive Officer of VX-4 when he conceived the test that would down the last Privateer drone. A version of the AGM-12 Bullpup air-to-ground missile (AGM), fitted with a 250lb warhead, might also be guided in flight at an airborne helicopter or other slow-moving aircraft by the pilot launching it. As the war in South East Asia increased in intensity in the mid-1960s, concerns had been expressed about the possible threat posed by enemy helicopters. In response to this threat, Creighton wanted to test his ability to guide a Bullpup AGM as an air-to-air munition. The AGM-12 relied on contact fuses for detonation, but for Creighton's anti-aircraft test, the weapon featured a proximity fuse like other air-to-air armaments used at this time.[149]

In flight after launch, a Bullpup missile emitted two flare flames that helped the pilot visually guide the weapon to its target by means of a joystick. Creighton figured the heavy Bullpup, usually fired on a descending path, might have a hard time climbing to the Privateer's height if he released the missile at an altitude lower than the QP-4B. So he released the AGM-12 at the same height as the drone, about a mile distant over the Pacific Ocean. Critics who thought this test would fail were surprised when Creighton's Bullpup passed directly over the Privateer before its proximity fuse detonated the missile, shedding propellers from the stricken Privateer. The QP-4B rolled over on its back and spun toward the sea below.[150]

Despite Creighton's unexpected success, the Bullpup was never operationally fielded as an AAM as its employment would leave the launch aircraft highly vulnerable because the weapon's visual guidance system relied on the launch pilot remaining behind the missile to observe the track of its two flares. Competing with fire-and-forget purpose-built AAMs, Bullpups did not enter the air-to-air arena despite the weapon downing the last airworthy Privateer at Point Mugu.

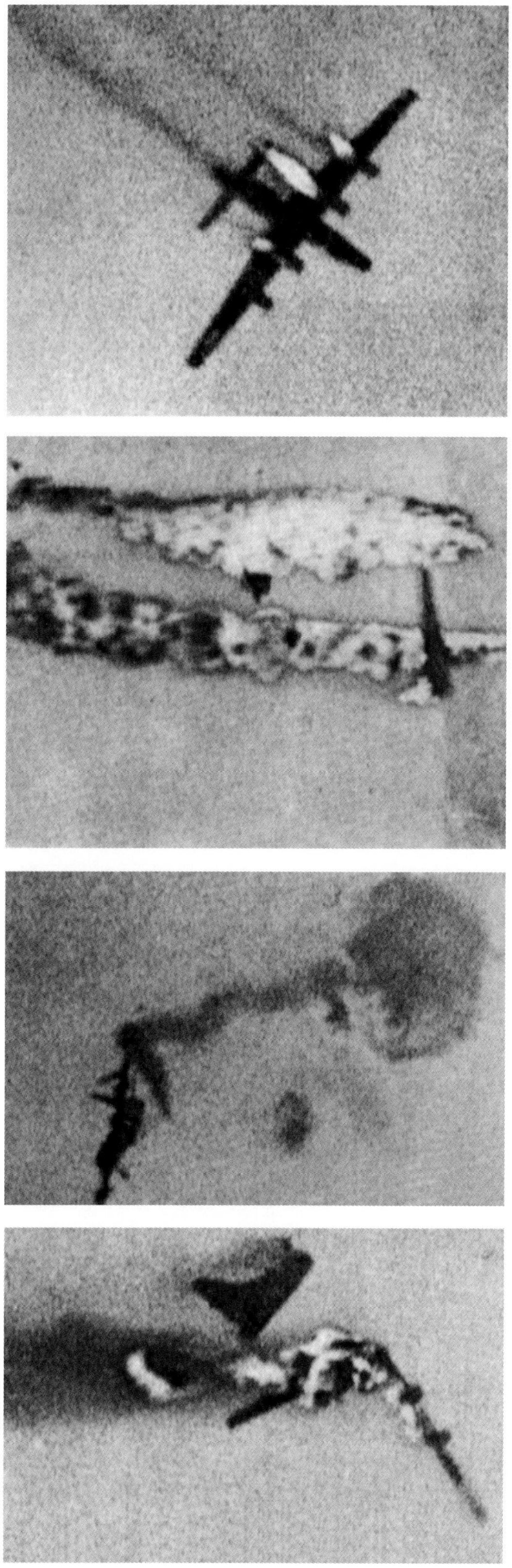

A P4Y-2K meets a fiery end after being struck by a SAM-N-7 Terrier during a test flight off the California coast in 1956. Terriers also launched against a number of QB-17s during the weapon's development trials. *US Navy*

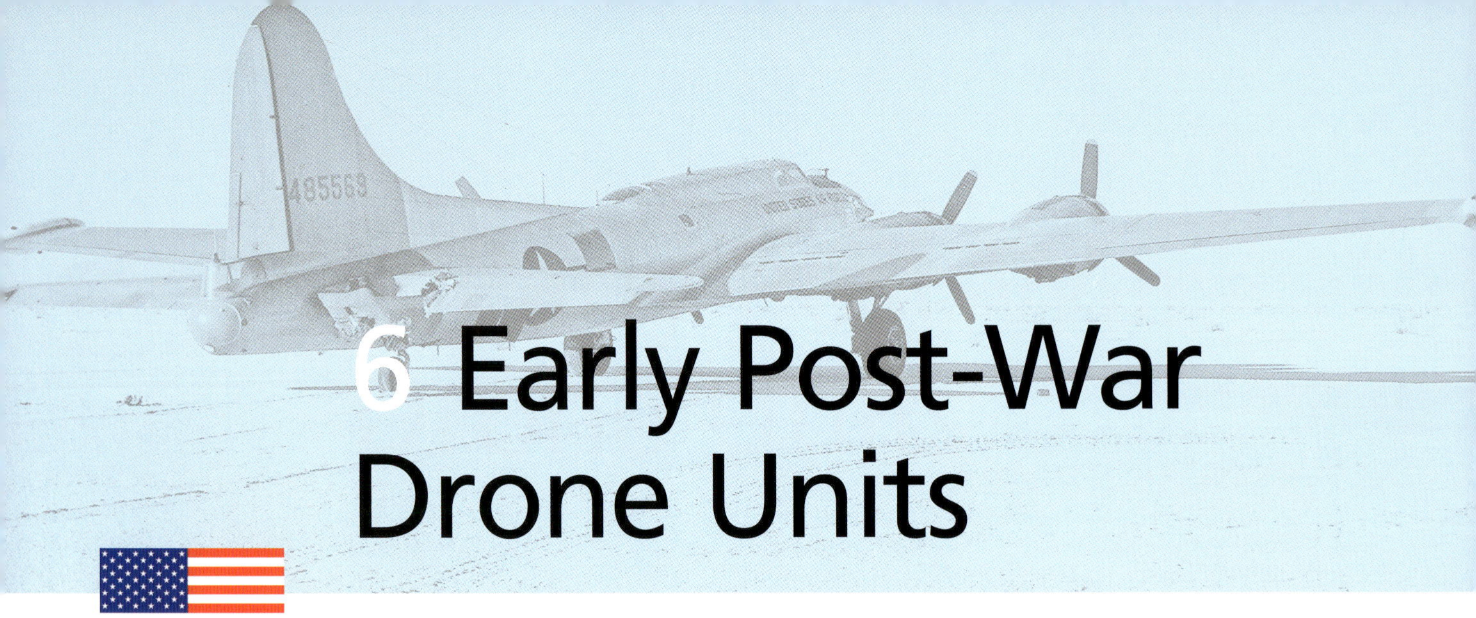

6 Early Post-War Drone Units

Evolution of USAAF/USAF droning of manned aircraft can be viewed through the window of unit histories of some of the organisations involved. The drone-keepers were faced with personnel turnover and loss in the final months of 1945 following VJ Day, as well as new demands for improved drone capabilities in the nascent Cold War.

Drone nomenclature evolved both during and after the Second World War. When first fielded, special droned B-17s were called BQ-7s. BQ, which stood for Bomb, Controllable, was the nomenclature in use from 1942–45. Early post-war B-17 drones were occasionally referenced as MB-17s, with MB standing for Missile Bomber. Adding to this, some of the drone Flying Fortresses had previously been designated TB-17Gs when used as trainers. Paperwork from this era sometimes lists drones as MTB-17Gs and directors as DTB-17Gs. The designation of the letter Q to denote an aerial target came into use in 1948, and droned Flying Fortresses have frequently been called QB-17s since then.

The cold weather refrigerated test hangar at Eglin hosted this drone B-17 in 1948 to learn the effects of low temperatures on the electronics fitted in the aircraft. *AFHRA*

Project *Remote*

Project *Remote* was one of the early post-war programmes to make use of B-17 drones, and it was initiated to demonstrate how such an aircraft could be used as a long-range guided missile. With *Crossroads* Not Under Live Local Operator (NULLO) flights having only lasted about five-and-a-half hours, a longer flight lasting about 15 hours was set for the return of Flying Fortress drones and mothers from the Pacific after the completion of the nuclear tests.

Two drones and two mothers duly left Hilo, Hawaii, on 5 August 1946 and landed at Muroc fifteen-and-a-half hours later, along with one master mother Fortress. Two Douglas C-54 Skymasters flew the ground control equipment from Hilo, overtaking the drone flight en route to Muroc. Their cargo was set up in time for the B-17 drone arrivals.[151] Just two years after *Aphrodite*, the ability to control and navigate B-17 drones had improved significantly as the USAAF/USAF contemplated how to develop unmanned missiles to deliver warheads.

Multiple records of multiple events

Interesting details on the deployment of drones in the first fifteen years after World War II come from a variety of sources. Units associated with specific nuclear and missile tests documented their use of drones, and USAF drone units, home-based at Eglin AFB but ranging over other US and overseas locations, kept their own accounts. This volume explores both narrative trails, with occasional overlaps.

As briefly noted in Chapter 1, when the USAF needed additional B-17s for conversion to drones and directors in 1950, remote Pyote AFB had the goods. It had become known for its rattlesnake population during the Second World War when Flying Fortress crews trained there, and after the conflict had ended, the same dry conditions that accommodated the reptiles made the flat terrain of Pyote a prime location for parking surplus bombers.

Pilots from the 550th Guided Missiles Wing at Eglin evaluated B-17Gs parked in rows in the desert at Pyote and selected the examples they wanted converted to drones and directors under Project MX-1113. Six B-17s were brought out of storage and made ready for flight in February 1950.

In preparation for Project *Greenhouse* nuclear duties in 1951, eighteen four-engined pilots were selected for training to become 'air-beepers' – a nickname assigned to pilots of drones of the era. While Eglin's Auxiliary Field No 6 hosted training for the B-17 drone and director crews, modified *Greenhouse* Flying Fortresses began arriving at the Florida base from June 1950.

USAF B-17 drone operations of this period built on lessons learned from tests like Operation *Crossroads* in 1946. As described for Operation *Sandstone*, a nuclear test that preceded *Greenhouse*, take-offs and landings of QB-17s were accomplished by ground station pilots, since drone pilots in airborne director aircraft had difficulty judging altitudes near the ground from their elevated perch. A radio control Jeep parked at the end of the runway controlled the QB-17's movements in azimuth by remotely manipulating the bomber's rudder and brakes. Another radio control Jeep at the side of the runway actuated elevators and throttle settings. As soon as the QB-17 was airborne, the ground azimuth pilot relinquished control to the director aircraft by voice as it flew above and behind the drone.

To land the QB-17, the airborne director brought it within about three miles of the runway. The drone was held at an altitude of 800ft and an airspeed of 135mph. Under direction of the ground azimuth pilot, control of the drone reverted to the ground pilots, who accomplished the landing. The elevator ground pilot and the airborne control pilot each had the ability to observe selected instruments aboard the drone via television.

The limited television signal range of 20–30 miles in this era placed an effective limit on how far the QB-17s could fly from their control pilot. Radio signals were sometimes good out to 60 miles, and an extreme of 100 miles had been achieved. Ten VHF radio channels were available to accomplish drone operations. Elevator, rudder, flaps, throttle, engine RPMs, landing gear and brakes were systems accessed during a typical QB-17 mission.[152]

In preparation for *Greenhouse*, drone director B-17 crews used two nearby south Alabama towns as a simulated initial point and target so that they could hone the skills needed to place a QB-17 properly at the right time in the nuclear blast sequence. A navigator aboard the director used both search radar and dead-reckoning to get the drone accurately placed. The training helped navigators and drone 'air-beeper' pilots gain the level of close coordination they would need to make *Greenhouse* B-17 sorties successful.

The training flights over Alabama were made at a low enough altitude to dispense with the need for oxygen. The actual *Greenhouse* flights would be higher, necessitating the donning of oxygen masks.

Eglin group leads the way

The 1st EGMG lived for droning at Eglin in the post-war era. On 13 January 1947, the unit participated in the flight of a QB-17 from its home to Washington, D.C. to publicise drone capabilities. The Flying Fortress orbited the Washington, D.C. area for about an hour, having also originally been scheduled to demonstrate dropping bombs at sea. Inclement weather between the Capital and Eglin prevented the drone's return to the Florida panhandle, so it was landed at Bolling Field, in the District of Columbia.[153]

The first B-17G drone ditched in the Eglin tests was 44-83528, a veteran of *Crossroads*. During the war, B-17s earned a reputation for staying intact and afloat after ditchings. *NARA*

As well as undertaking this long-distance flight, the 1st EGMG was also in the process of preparing for Service Test 9-47-2 – the ditching of droned B-17s to better understand the forces at play when an aircraft hits the water. One outcome of the tests was to compare full-scale ditching results with the results obtained by using models.[154]

Testers made it clear they were not interested in quantifying the B-17's ditching characteristics, which were at least anecdotally known to be quite good from a number of splashdowns of Flying Fortresses during the Second World War. With B-17s having a reputation for staying intact and floating, this specific aircraft offered testers a high likelihood that the instrumentation and recording equipment needed for the ditching tests would be reasonably protected. They also opined that a sub-scale model B-17 was likely to remain more intact following the ditching than a real example since the model would be inherently above scale strength in its structure. Furthermore, in the late 1940s, surplus B-17s were readily available, and had already proven themselves adaptable to radio-controlled flight.[155]

The test plan called for ditching two of five allocated B-17s nose-high, near stall speed, for the least forward motion possible, and then stalling two others at a higher-speed in a power-off no-flaps glide to get the lowest sinking speed attainable. The fifth B-17 drone was earmarked to re-test whichever method of ditching promised the best results.[156] Ultimately, seven QB-17s were dunked in Florida waters, with two ditchings made before the five-aircraft test.

On the morning of 6 June 1947 the first of the B-17s scheduled for drone ditching ploughed into the waters near Eglin. The sortie was judged effective. Four passes were necessary before ditching could occur, as the water control station (the equivalent of a normal ground control station, except water-borne) experienced difficulties in controlling throttle settings on the first pass and was unable to cut the engines. Elevator deflection control was ineffective on passes two and three, but on the fourth pass all systems worked and the drone water control pilots ditched the B-17 at the desired three-point attitude with a seven degree incline which was deemed perfect for the best test results.[157]

Damage to the ditched B-17 was less than anticipated. Wartime experience had shown low-wing Flying Fortresses to be easier to ditch and remain largely intact than were high-wing bombers like the B-24. The first ditch test B-17 drone received a six-foot by three-foot hole in the fuselage just aft of the ball turret location. Not surprisingly, the Plexiglas nose cap was cracked. Flaps showed the effects of water impact, and the inboard propellers, which would have contacted the water slightly sooner than

Left: A motion picture camera sturdily mounted in the rear fuselage of a B-17 drone would record the action as the bomber hit the water during an Eglin ditching test. *NARA*

Below: The first B-17G drone ditched in the Eglin tests was 44-83528, a veteran of *Operation Crossroads. NARA*

the dihedral-raised outboard props, were bent, while the outboard propeller blades did not show evidence of impact. The landing gear extended at some point during the ditching, and testers believed the undercarriage relay was activated upon impact. No damage to the gear was noted.[158]

The essential incompressibility of water influences the dynamics of an aircraft ditching. Water can be displaced by a body entering it, but the contact of an airframe with the water can lead to structural deformation or breakage because there is no compression factor in the water. The huge white plume of spray erupting from the surface of the water as the B-17 ditched was the most dramatic manifestation of displacement of the water. There was a rapid deceleration as the drone entered the water, and this transferred energy to the components of the drone.

Testers noted the floodlights mounted in the B-17 to illuminate test instruments for film recording were wrenched from their mounts upon impact, rendering any subsequent documentation useless. A sturdier lighting system was immediately devised for future ditching tests. As it turned out, no instrumentation of the ditching was obtained because the time-limited camera system in the cockpit had been activated during the third abortive pass, and its three-minute time span had been used up well before the fourth and actual ditching pass occurred. Testers were nonetheless happy with the physical post-ditching evidence they found when evaluating the Flying Fortress.[159]

Heading over the Gulf of Mexico, a pair of veteran *Crossroads* B-17s set up for the final flight of the drone, in the lead, with the mother ship following close behind. The B-17G drone was expended in ditching tests conducted to quantify airframe stresses from water landings. *NARA*

The second B-17 to be ditched entered the water at the 4-Mile Point Ditching Site just after 0800hrs on 22 October 1947. Only one pass was needed to get the bomber in the water, touching down at 88mph with a three-degree nose-high incline to the surface. The aircraft planed on the

B-17 drone ditching tests continued into 1949 from Eglin. The aircraft's positive survivability in ditching scenarios made it a useful drone to instrument, allowing researchers to quantify forces and accelerations acting on a large airframe as it contacted the surface of the water. *USAF/J Baer-Riedhart*

Salvage operations are underway for an intact ditched B-17 drone near Eglin. *USAF/J Baer-Riedhart*

surface for about 300ft before settling in the water, remaining afloat. Once again, the landing gear extended in the water, possibly due to a water-caused electrical short in a micro switch. Testers observed that small skin punctures could allow water to ram in and tear the skin. Internal pressure shattered the right waist window Plexiglas outward. Some belly and bomb-bay doors wrinkling and damage was noted, and the right wing flap was ripped loose from its hinges.[160]

It must have been a heady time for drone operators at Eglin. Low-time late-model B-17s were being extracted from desert storage and made ready for risky new remotely-piloted missions that almost certainly led to a spectacle of destruction akin to the staged public steam locomotive collisions of the early 20th century.

The 1st EGMG initially leveraged the ditching sorties as a way to provide training for drone crews in advance of the impending *Sandstone* deployment to Kwajalein and Eniwetok for nuclear cloud sampling. However, after the second ditching, the programme was put on hold to concentrate on training for *Sandstone* and another USAF priority effort.[161]

In 1947, the 1st EGMG trained new drone and director Flying Fortress pilots, starting with control column work using the equipment installed in the B-17, and moving on to various cruising control set-ups with trainees in director B-17s or manning ground stations.

Surface craft, including a barge with a salvage crane, surround a ditched B-17 drone near Eglin in 1947. *USAF/AFHRA*

Retrieved from the water and still draining, this ditched B-17 drone will reveal the science of water impacts to researchers. *USAF/J Baer-Riedhart*

A candidate for scrap now, this B-17 drone was sacrificed to learn the physiology of large aircraft ditching off Eglin in 1949. *USAF/J Baer-Riedhart*

Twelve O'Clock High

When the Twentieth Century-Fox Film Corporation needed a sky filled with Flying Fortresses to dramatise its motion picture *Twelve O'Clock High* (which focused on Eighth Air Force bomber operations in England in the Second World War), the availability of QB-17 drones and their directors was leveraged for the film. Hollywood duly came to Eglin in April–May 1949 to film some of the movie's iconic scenes.[162] The G-model bombers were outfitted and camouflaged to represent B-17Fs for the movie.

It was a major project for the 1st EGMG, commencing on 1 April. Twelve of its B-17s supported Twentieth Century-Fox Film Corporation's production efforts in various areas of the Eglin complex, as well as at Ozark Army Air Field in Alabama, which masqueraded as wartime England. The Flying Fortresses were painted in early April, shortly after which turrets were added. That month, USAF crews rehearsed formation flying, and filming began in May. Hollywood's legendary movie pilot Paul Mantz used a modified North American TB-25 Mitchell camera aeroplane for the flying scenes. The 1st EGMG history described the B-17 used in a famous belly landing scene as follows:

> 'A drone aircraft, which had been returned to storage previously from this unit, was made operational again and used in the filming until it was deliberately bellied in by Mantz for a crash sequence in the film.'

This landing, as well as other airfield operational scenes, took place at the Alabama airfield site that later became part of the US Army's Fort Rucker complex. Some serial number references suggest the bellied-in Flying Fortress was 44-83592, an ex-DB-17 director and not a drone.[163] B-17 researcher Scott Thompson states that the bellied-in Flying Fortress was listed by the USAF as 'reclaimed' on its official chronological record card.

DB-17G 44-83592 is crash-landed at Ozark Field, in southern Alabama, by Hollywood pilot Paul Mantz during the filming of *Twelve O' Clock High* in 1949. Instructed to simulate a typical forced landing of a combat-damaged B-17, Mantz, as the sole pilot aboard the aircraft, slid the bomber on its belly through a row of tents in one of the most famous scenes ever shot for an aviation film. *James H Farmer collection*

Airmen wash the 'Hollywood paint' from an Eglin B-17G in the first half of 1949 after the filming of the motion picture *Twelve O' Clock High* had finished in the region. A number of drone and director aircraft were used to recreate a wartime B-17 bomb group. *USAF*

Lt Col Albert L Haley, commander of the 1st Experimental Air Service Squadron, acted as liaison officer between the USAF and the Twentieth Century-Fox Film Corporation crew. Some squadron members also had bit parts in the film. Shooting wrapped up at Eglin during the first week of June. After that, groundcrews could be seen scrubbing the 'Hollywood paint' from the B-17s.[164] The resulting film, released in 1950, has earned praise from aviation enthusiasts as well as organisations studying leadership practices.

3200th Drone Group

To fulfil the USAF's obligation to support SAM-A-25 (later MIM-14 Nike surface-to-air missile (SAM)) and AAM-A-2 (later GAR-1/AIM-4) Falcon AAM development at the White Sands Proving Ground in New Mexico's spectacular and isolated desert, the 3200th Drone Group stood up Detachment 1 at nearby Holloman AFB, with an intended one-year duration, on 17 July 1951. The Holloman detachment had seven Flying Fortresses in different mission configurations by the autumn of that year. These accrued flight time in training for the impending drone target missions.[165]

By this time, the 3200th Drone Group had better tools and greater experience to enable more sophisticated drone operations, as described in the unit history:

> 'The primary function of the Group was remote control flying of pilotless aircraft, either day or night, through all practical maneuvers including takeoffs and landings. This necessitated a continuous mandatory training program in all components of remote control operation by the units.'[166]

In December 1951, the 3200th was redesignated the 3205th Drone Group.

Rise of Nike and the QB-17

Cold War (and pre-Cold War) urgency led to the remarkable expenditure of B-17s to perfect the groundbreaking Nike SAM. The same escalating technologies that had made the Flying Fortress obsolete by 1945 also argued for the creation of new and more capable means of defending against enemy bomber attacks.

In January 1945, with the war in Europe still raging, the US Army was already formulating its need for an anti-aircraft missile system with capabilities that would outstrip conventional anti-aircraft artillery. While the US defence establishment was leaning forward with new long-range bomber designs, in the last half of the 1940s there was a presumption that potential adversaries like the Soviet Union were doing the same. This rationale meant North America was no longer impenetrable to enemy aircraft.

This thinking set the USAAF to work devising jet interceptors to meet any incoming bomber threat, while the US Army envisioned a ring of SAM sites in the US that would be a last-ditch defence for any hostile bombers that managed to evade the USAAF screen. The problem required accurate and timely placement of an explosive warhead in proximity to inbound bombers of ever-greater capabilities in altitude and speed.

To do this, a quick-reaction missile was needed. Planners discarded the liquid fuel style of rocket like the German V2 because its highly volatile propellent had to be stored outside of the missile and loaded immediately prior to launch. This was a cumbersome demand that a successful SAM system could not tolerate. The answer lay in a two-stage rocket, with a more stable solid-fuel first stage boosting a liquid-fuel warhead stage on its way to a successful intercept. The upper stage could be pre-loaded with hydrazine as propellant and jet fuel as the oxidiser – a new and viable way to create a standing force of liquid-fuelled rockets. The ability to handle and store this mixture was within grasp.[167]

The need to guide such a warhead to the proximity of an inbound enemy bomber required rapid, yet practical computing by 1945 standards. The answer lay in using the US Navy's ageing shipboard Mk 33 fire control director in concert with radars. Although this system had known limitations, it proved functional for the SAM system being designed. A ground launch team used the appropriated Mk 33 fire control director to monitor the movement and positions of the target aircraft and the outbound missile, and compute updates in course for the SAM that could be effected with radio commands for deflection of control surfaces on the weapon.

The first iteration of the missile system, called Nike, was mature enough for flight testing in 1951. The missile produced a subscale test explosion 57ft from the target QB-17 flying at 33,000ft some twelve miles downrange at the White Sands complex.[168]

Below and oveleaf: Sometimes, even the vaunted Flying Fortress succumbed to the damage it received in missile testing over the White Sands/ Holloman Missile Range complex, as the mangled wreckage of this QB-17 downed by a Nike SAM in 1952 indicates. *AFHRA*

The system was viable, but still in need of refinement and repeatability, leading to many more target drone QB-17 flights over the White Sands area. And while the US Army perfected Nike in the skies over New Mexico, the USAF concurrently employed drones like the QB-17 to validate AAMs that would support its obligations in the defence of the US. Those Flying Fortress drones occupy a special place in history.

F-82 Twin Mustang – almost a drone

The whole concept of droning full-scale aircraft because they are at risk of destruction calls for a balance between risk and reward, or cost and benefit. Proponents of target drones in the USAF knew the sting of parsimonious budgets. Their quest for drones to support a wide array of programmes had to be carefully couched in terms of cost and benefit that showed good stewardship of the budget, and of the airframes available. Aircraft earmarked for one-time-only flights, by nature, could not amortise their expense over multiple sorties as could recoverable drones.

The 3200th Drone Group looked at available obsolescent USAF aircraft that could be used for one-time drone flights at the lowest cost. The critical limiting factor, from an availability and expense perspective, was the autopilot. Three styles were considered usable in droning – the Minneapolis-Honeywell C-1, Sperry E-4 and Bendix-Pioneer F-1. These autopilots were in critically short supply in the USAF system, and no longer available for new aircraft installations. But parts for them were available, making the presence of one of the approved autopilots in an existing aircraft a plus for inexpensive droning.

The 3200th researched a list of aircraft and their autopilots. While acknowledging that a specific fighter had 'severe mechanical maintenance requirements', the report concluded the best available aircraft for one-time droning would be North American F-82F, G and H Twin Mustangs. A research report produced by the unit in 1951 found the Twin Mustang to be 'the only aircraft type that presents an immediate solution to the one-time-flight drone configuration'.[169]

The report lauded the F-82 series for quick one-time droning because it was being withdrawn from frontline service, and 17 Twin Mustangs were expected to be available in early 1952. These aircraft used the acceptable Bendix-Pioneer F-1 autopilot. Remote flight controllers compatible with this autopilot were already available from the US Navy. The report continued:

> 'The overall cost of its drone conversion is estimated to be the least expensive of all aircraft considered. The aircraft is substantially free from unsafe take-off characteristics, is very stable in flight, and has a wide speed range.'

So it seemed like the drone advocates had found an ideal match for the one-time-flight needs of the USAF. However, the report added:

> 'The F-82 aircraft presents severe mechanical maintenance requirements which, along with the scarce availability of spare parts, compromises its success as a drone to a large extent.'[170]

So instead of seeing twin-fuselage QF-82s dropping from the sky over New Mexico in a dirty pall of smoke and debris, the USAF continued with QF-80 Shooting Stars, and later jet fighters, plus low-time B-17Gs retrieved from desert storage.

How many QB-17s?

By the end of 1951, the 3205th Drone Group was equipped with 20 QB-17 drones and 17 DB-17 directors, along with two QF-80 drones and five DT-33 director aircraft. At that time, 11 QB-17s were at the modification depot, as were five QF-80s. The USAF had programmed a total of 80 QB-17 and 30 QF-80 drone conversions. Of five projects requiring USAF drone support, the Nike and Falcon missile efforts at White Sands received the largest single batch – eight drones.[171]

At the end of 1951, the 3205th Drone Group tabulated the expected needs for the primary drones of the era – QB-17s and QF-80s – by all of the service branches over the next two years:

A gaggle of director B-17Gs on the ramp at Holloman on 16 October 1951, including 44-83684 with the letter F on its tail. This aircraft was later obtained by Ed Maloney's Planes of Fame Museum, and it has appeared in film and television productions. *USAF*

Target Drone Requirements for 1952–53

PERIOD	TYPE	USAF	ARMY	NAVY	TOTAL
Jan-Mar 1952	QB-17	5	9	1	15
	QF-80	2	2	3	7
Apr-Jun 1952	QB-17	5	7	5	17
	QF-80	2	2	6	10
Jul-Sep 1952	QB-17	5	12	5	22
	QF-80	2	3	8	13
Oct-Dec 1952	QB-17	5	13	5	23
	QF-80	2	3	12	17
Jan-Dec 1953	QB-17	30	37	6	73
	QF-80	10	9	18	37
TOTAL	**QB-17**	**50**	**78**	**22**	**150**
	QF-80	**18**	**19**	**47**	**85***

(*maths discrepancy in QF-80 total numbers – should probably be 84)

What this table leaves unexplained is whether these numbers reflected expected attrition, or merely the total number of required drone sorties, which is more probable. With frugal use of drone resources, multiple flights could be gained from each drone, making the total number required less than the astounding tally of 150 QB-17s. These were just the targets – the group identified its two component units as either the drone squadron or target drone squadron, since some of the other droned aircraft were for hazardous sampling missions and test work where they were not actually targets. The 3205th Drone Group characterised the difference this way in early 1952:

> 'Drone Squadron would furnish drone support to the Atomic Energy Commission and civilian agencies. Target Drone Squadron would furnish target drone support to the Department of the Army, Navy, and Air Force.'[172]

On 25 October 1951, members of the drone group and other interested USAF parties met to discuss items like standardisation of QB-17 and QF-80 drones. The need for a self-destruct mechanism was emphasised. Early test drone missions sometimes included armed piloted fighter aircraft tasked with the responsibility of downing an errant drone if required for safety. Another topic was the efficacy of radio control systems based on the Minneapolis-Honeywell C-1 autopilot, where the briefing presenter said it was basically sufficient, but not good for manoeuvring in missile tests at high altitude, and not adequate for use with radar control operations.[173] Future testers would revel in developments that allowed 8g manoeuvres with PQM-102 drone versions of the Convair F-102 Delta Dagger jet fighter. The state of the art continually builds on earlier accomplishments.

Four bent propellers only stopped turning after hitting the ground when QB-17 44-85575 belly-landed. With a limited number of Flying Fortresses available as more and more were consumed, reparable drones like this one were likely to be rebuilt. *AFHRA*

In November 1951, the USAF faced several urgent shortages affecting its drone programme. Trained personnel were in short supply and QF-80 production was insufficient to meet both USAF and US Navy needs, so the former informed the latter that a limited number of QB-17s would be made available instead.[174]

On 15 November, Det 1 at Holloman flew its first operational QB-17 drone mission in support of the Falcon development programme in which a ground-launched example of the AAM was fired. The primary QB-17 drone (44-85573) had a call sign of 'Bullseye' or 'Bullseye One', while the secondary drone (QB-17 44-83695) was 'Bullseye Two'. The primary drone functioned and was safely recovered for future missions. North American F-51 Mustangs provided chase aeroplane service.

Five days later, Det 1 launched its second mission. As with the first mission, take-off and landing were accomplished by control pilots in Jeeps, while airborne control was furnished by crews in two mother ship B-17s. Radar plotting and controlling put the QB-17 in the right location for the missile shot within test parameters. The drone was directed to its assigned test target altitude of 12,700ft. Delays in the launch time instigated by the missile team necessitated the landing and refuelling of one of the chase aeroplane F-51s.

At 1300hrs on 27 November, QB-17 44-83603 made its NULLO take-off for a Nike SAM test firing. For the third operational mission flown by Det 1, the F-51 chase aeroplanes were replaced by North American F-86 Sabres. The drone survived, and during its descent through 14,000ft, the radio control pilot's efforts to increase the QB-17's manifold pressure produced no results. The mission after action report noted:

> 'All attempts by both directors and ground control units to increase throttle failed and the radio control pilot in Able Director landed the drone in the emergency landing area. The drone suffered no damage and was flown back to Holloman AFB approximately (2) hours later.'[175]

As this episode clearly proves, the level of redundancy and capability in the USAF QB-17s of 1951 far outstripped the rustic wartime *Aphrodite* drones of seven years earlier.

QB-17 44-83603 went aloft over White Sands again on 4 December – the fourth such mission for Det 1. A Nike passed near the drone but did not strike it. At that precise moment the QB-17 began a shallow left turn. Both director B-17s attempted to control the errant drone to no avail, and the bomber twisted into a spin and crashed into the sparse desert about six miles from the radar station.

Mission five launched QB-17 44-85573 on 11 December in support of Nike. Handing off from ground control pilots to director B-17s to radar-directed ground pilots allowed mission accomplishment by placing the QB-17 within the needed airspace for the SAM shot. At 1423hrs the drone was at 28,000ft over the White Sands Proving Ground under radar plot control. The Nike approached the QB-17, passing without causing damage to the drone. Testers requested keeping the drone aloft for a second SAM shot to be made about 30 minutes later, and the USAF agreed to this frugal use of assets. By 1643hrs the QB-17 was back on the ground, safe after being targeted twice by SAMs in the same sortie.[176]

16 December saw QB-17 mission six at White Sands/Holloman. At 0903hrs the throttles were advanced on the NULLO takeoff drone, and two minutes later a director B-17 took control. A Falcon missile shot was registered at 1001hrs – the drone was unharmed and had safely landed by 1027hrs.[177]

As previously noted, the post-war drone efforts of the USAF were enmeshed in declining manpower rolls, shrinking budgets and new demands from a host of agencies. All of this made it difficult for drone advocates to find enough of everything they required to meet the service's needs for ever-more-capable remotely-piloted full-scale targets and research aircraft. In the midst of these struggles, a plaintive observation from one unit historian at the end of 1951 spotlighted the bureaucratic morass that rapidly changing and chronically understaffed units faced in the background:

'During the first quarter we were known as the 3201st Air Base Support Squadron; during the second quarter we were known as the 3200th Air Base Squadron; and now pursuant to the authority contained in Headquarters Air Proving Ground General Order 22, dated 29 October 1951, effective 1 December 1951 we were redesignated as the 3205th Air Base Squadron.'

'All these changes have been on paper only, but they have made necessary great mountains of paperwork. Special orders must be cut transferring all personnel, entries made on all personnel records and R&Rs notifying all service units on the main base must be typed and delivered.'[178]

So, while striving to be the best drone organisation they could be, the elements of this Eglin-based unit reeled from repeat unit name changes that created bureaucratic paperwork they had to perform.

This single frame of test film with inset stopwatch shows the destruction of a striped QB-17. Some drone paint schemes did not include national insignia on the wings. *AFHRA*

Wingtip QB-17 cameras

In November 1951, workers from the Douglas Aircraft Company arrived at Holloman AFB to instal Firing Error Indicator (FEI) equipment – wingtip camera pods – on QB-17 drones used in Nike missile tests. The first aircraft so modified was QB-17G 44-83603. The need to use the limited number of QB-17s at Holloman on other tests like Falcon missile firings that did not require the wingtip camera pods led to some removals and replacements of the modified Flying Fortress wingtips depending on the mission requirements.[179]

QB-17 emergency procedures

By the end of October 1951, Det 1 at Holloman had compiled a standard operating procedure for handling emergencies occurring in QB-17 drones. Illuminating common practices of the era, it defines a safe area as an 'area where a drone aircraft may be crashed with the probability of damage to personnel or property being at a minimum'. The range safety system is defined as 'a separate electronic system, with its own power supply, that can be used to turn the aircraft, disengage the auto pilot and cut the engines'. Chase aeroplanes are 'fighter aircraft used to shoot down a Drone aircraft if necessary'.[180]

The operating procedure describes what to do if there is autopilot failure that involves control surface oscillation. At that point the aircraft is to land immediately. If there is a complete failure of the autopilot, with the 'plane performing unpredictable maneuvers, the drone will be dumped' referring to the QB-17 safety system or fighter aircraft. If a malfunction of radio control makes it impossible to extend the landing gear on the drone, it 'will be landed on the runway by Ground Control'. If the QB-17 is unable to retract its gear for a Nike mission it will be cancelled, because the drone would not be able to reach the required mission altitude. If the QB-17 gear will not retract for a Falcon missile mission, the latter will continue.

If there is a complete loss of all types of turns the drone 'will be dumped'. With a complete loss of radio control, the 'R/C [radio control] pilot will attempt to land Drone on White Sands area using range safety system'. A complete loss of radio control and the separate safety system is cause for the drone to be dumped. If the drone received systems damage, control of its flight would be returned to the director aircraft as quickly as possible. 'In the event of other structural damage to Drone, director will descend Drone over Safe area. Decision as to possibility of safe landing at Holloman will rest with Ground Control Team. At no time will the Drone be deliberately flown over a populated area, and headings in the direction of these areas will be held to a minimum'.[181]

The loss of an engine, without fire, was to be resolved by having the ground control team land the QB-17 at Holloman. In case of fire on the drone without complete radio control loss, 'the Drone will be vectored to Safe Area, with Director aircraft controlling descent. If possible Drone will be landed by Director in White Sands area'. If at any time the Director crew deemed the burning drone's continued flight to be dangerous, 'the Drone will be dumped. After the command has been given to the chase aircraft to fire at the drone aircraft, the responsibility for the drone aircraft belongs to the fighter detachment'. Radar plots could be used to direct the fighters to the site of the drone if it was not in visual range.[182]

This photograph, taken in the first quarter of 1952 at Eglin, shows the Plexiglas-enclosed office of a DB-17 director remote pilot, complete with hooded television monitor and 'beeper' control panel to the right. *AFHRA*

During 1951, the decision was made to instal two one-pound blocks of high explosives to separate the right wing from QB-17 drones as a range safety destruct mechanism. Modification of all drone Flying Fortresses to accommodate this was begun that year. Earlier, the range safety system aboard QB-17s consisted of a separate electronics package with its own power supply, enabling the control pilot to turn, disengage the autopilot and cut the engines. This was also the era in which armed fighter aircraft were launched during White Sands drone missions for the purpose of downing the QB-17 if other means of recovery failed.[183]

On at least some QB-17s, the range safety destruct system components were installed in a Flak-proof case bolted inside the tailwheel compartment. This could conceivably make the destruct system survivable in the event of a missile strike that did not destroy the ability of the QB-17 to fly. An AS-150 antenna was mounted outside the tail gunner's enclosure to receive signals from the control pilot. The system included the use of microswitches in the main landing gear wells that would only allow activation of the system when the undercarriage was retracted. This provided another level of safety against inadvertent ground activation of the destruct system.[184]

Drones gather test projects in 1952

By the first quarter of 1952, the 3205th Drone Group's target drones were aligned with test programmes for the US Army, US Navy and USAF. These included Falcon (USAF AAM), Nike (US Army SAM), SAM-N-6 Talos (US Navy SAM), SAM-N-7 Terrier (US Navy SAM) and AAM-N-5 Meteor (US Navy AAM). Nike and Falcon were accorded the highest priority for support by the group. Support was also furnished for USAF suitability tests of the F-86D Sabre and Lockheed F-94C Starfire jet fighters, which were deemed to be of second-highest importance for the group.[185]

The salt flats at White Sands saved more than one drone when landing on the paved Holloman runway was considered too risky, since a mishap could tie up the runway. This QB-17, nicknamed *PUG*, will need a replacement for its missing Plexiglas nose plus other repairs before starting the Wright Cyclones and ferrying the manned bomber back to Holloman in 1952. *AFHRA*

Before the suspension of Talos flights at White Sands in the first quarter of 1952, QB-17s had flown twenty NULLO flights in support of the programme, losing two drones and recovering two more with damage. The support of F-86D and F-94C testing amounted to modification of three QB-17s to be shared between the two interceptor types, but missions were not expected until May 1952.

Terrier support was expected to start in August 1952, with a USAF detachment established at Point Mugu. Firings of Terriers would be made at sea by USS *Norton Sound* (AVM-1), a seaplane tender modified for an extensive career as a missile and armaments test bed. Terrier launches would feature both dummy and actual warheads, implying the expected loss of some of the QB-17s.[186]

The 3205th's roster of assigned aircraft in January 1952 included nineteen QB-17s, eighteen DB-17s, one TB-17, five DT-33s, two QT-33s and five B-29s. The latter typically were employed in non-drone test projects. Anticipating the need for more drones, the group forecast the arrival of seven QF-80s and DT-33s between February and August, and eleven more QB-17s between June and August.

On 22 January 1952, Det 1 at Holloman launched a QB-17 for a Nike support sortie, mission seven for the unit. The chase aircraft assigned for potential destruction of the drone should it become errant was an F-82 Twin Mustang. One Nike firing was accommodated and a second was cancelled due to delays with the missile, and the QB-17 returned to base.[187]

Mission eight, on 24 January, at Holloman was also delayed when an onboard destruct system in the QB-17 required fixing. An F-51 Mustang was assigned as a chase aeroplane just in case. When the mission did finally take place, the Falcon missile under test approached the QB-17 from the rear and struck the right outboard engine, knocking off the propeller and cowling. As a director aircraft approached the drone, smoke and fuel could be seen streaming from the stricken Number Four engine. Radio control was working well, so the QB-17 was landed on the salt flats of the White Sands Proving Ground about fourteen minutes after impact, with no further problems.[188]

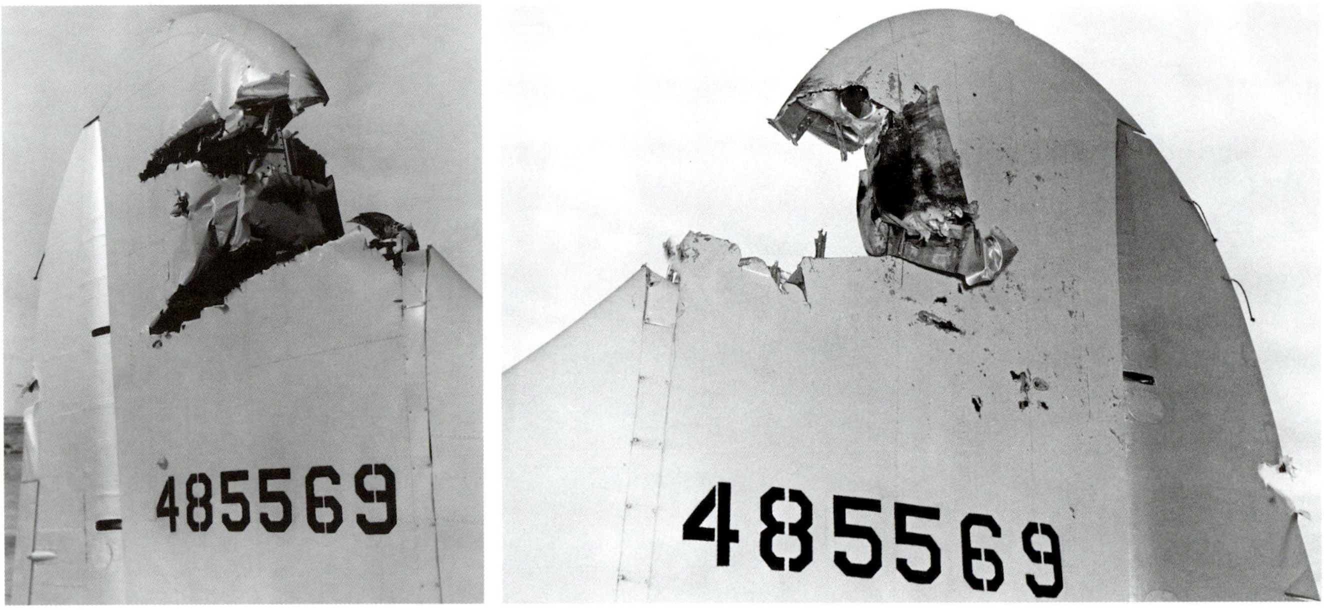

A Nike missile impact caused this damage to the vertical fin of a Holloman-based QB-17 in 1952. Although missiles fired in tests were sometimes inert, if they impacted the drone the results could range from mild to catastrophic. *AFHRA*

Mission nine served the Talos programme on 27 January. Chase aeroplanes for this US Navy test were F6Fs, which had different communication radio frequencies that would have required testers to switch to the Military Emergency Channel had they needed the Hellcats to swing into action.[189]

29 January was a brisk desert winter day at the White Sands/Holloman complex – just above freezing, and ready for drone mission ten, in support of the US Army's ambitious Nike SAM programme. The first of two available drones cranked its four Wright R-1820 radial engines into life, with a popping settling to the powerful characteristic rumble that had been heard so many times at wartime airfields in England years earlier. This time, a single F-51 provided chase support. Radar plotting for final positioning of the QB-17 provided the accuracy needed, and testers were able to squeeze two separate missile firings in before the drone returned to base unharmed at 1558hrs.[190]

Mission eleven on 5 February sent a QB-17 aloft over White Sands for the benefit of another Nike launch. A brace of F-51s provided chase services as needed. At 1408hrs the missile made physical contact with the QB-17, impacting the right elevator and stabiliser. Skid control was lost, but the drone was still controllable, and the radio control pilot in the Able Director Flying Fortress guided the drone to a safe landing on the salt flats of White Sands.[191]

Operations were frequent, and mission twelve came two days later, again in support of Nike. A single F-51 provided chase support. The mission switched to the second available SAM when the first experienced problems before launch. That first missile was later pronounced ready for flight, so a second pass was made by the QB-17 to give the Nike team an opportunity to fire again. This time, the SAM veered off course and was intentionally exploded. Neither missile struck the QB-17, which made a safe recovery.[192]

Mission thirteen on 19 February saw the first prepared Nike bow out with problems before launch. A second was scored as a miss – the programme was still experimental, and such events were considered part of the system maturation process. An F-86 and an F-51 provided chase support. This was Leap Year, so one more February drone mission could be scheduled on the 29th. Mission fourteen again served the Nike programme. Two Mustangs and a Sabre provided chase. The drone employed a manoeuvre system to simulate violent evasive action. It reached a top speed of 205mph IAS and lost 1500ft in a dive, before gaining 1800ft in the climb-out that followed. All of this effort counted for nothing, however, as the Nike's guidance system failed before reaching altitude and the missile was destroyed as a safety measure.[193]

On 4 March Det 1 launched a QB-17 on a Nike mission over White Sands. It was mission fifteen for the organisation, and a cloud deck kept the maximum safe operating ceiling at 19,000ft. The SAM struck the QB-17 near the waist window at an angle, exiting the fuselage forward of the tailwheel. The Flying Fortress drone gamely continued flying, and it was descended by controllers to the designated safe area for a landing. Radio control performed normally before missile impact, but afterwards the drone manifested an oscillation that could not be stopped, possibly caused by damaged control cables. The aircraft's weakened fuselage buckled when the drone landed, after which the QB-17 burst into flames.[194]

Plumes of billowing black and white smoke mark the end of a QB-17 drone on the salt flats at White Sands on 4 March 1952. *AFHRA*

A TB-25 set up in a ground rig and fitted with special underwing racks was used as an early test launch platform for Falcon AAMs at White Sands in 1952. Several more Mitchells fulfilled the role of host airframes during the air-to-air firing phase of the missile's development. The weapon seen here is the Falcon in its original Project MX-904 configuration. *NARA*

The loss of its tail section following a missile strike spells the end for this QB-17 over the desert. *AFHRA*

Three days later mission sixteen took a QB-17 aloft for Falcon AAM support. The missiles aborted, and all aircraft returned to base. Mission seventeen again supported Falcon testing on 8 March. Delays and aborts on the missile side of the operation led to no firings, and the aircraft landed.[195] A B-25 Mitchell twin-engined bomber was used as a host airframe for early Falcon testing.[196]

Mission eighteen on 11 March again endeavoured to pit two air-launched Falcons against a QB-17 drone. The approach of a frontal weather system with high winds and dust storms caused a prudent retreat by the drone, which landed safely. Mission nineteen came two days later. A pair of F-51s provided chase aeroplane support. Success was logged when the first Falcon registered a near-miss, passing about 15ft from the QB-17's right wingtip. The drone director crew inspected the bomber after the first missile shot and pronounced it sound for a second Falcon to be fired in its direction. This weapon spiralled off the launcher and missed the drone by a great distance.

A Douglas B-26 Invader used for photography of the mission landed on the runway for which drone controllers were set up to receive the QB-17. A blown nosewheel tyre on the Invader blocked the runway, causing the drone ground control stations to be moved quickly to another airstrip. Testers agreed in the future to keep other aircraft away from the drone runway until after the QB-17 was recovered.[197]

Mission twenty on 28 March was briefed to include enough target passes for two Nike launches. Both missiles were detonated before approaching the QB-17, however, when efforts at starting the drone's smoke generator failed, possibly due to radio frequency problems that caused the aircraft to revert to an emergency flight system.[198]

Between April and June 1952, Det 1 had six QB-17s damaged, including two destroyed, during missile firing tests. Mission twenty-one pitted QB-17 44-85569 against a Nike missile with a live warhead on 2 April. After several holds imposed by the SAM launch team, the missile reached the location of the QB-17 at 1500hrs. Collateral damage occurred, the extent of which was not evident until the remote pilots set up the Flying Fortress for landing. Flaps could not be lowered, so a no-flap landing was performed. On landing, brakes were ineffective and the bomber rolled off the downwind end of the runway into the desert.

A subsequent inspection of the QB-17 revealed its brake lines had been severed beneath the co-pilot's position, rendering braking inoperative – later, some QB-17s would be fitted with an arresting hook to bring the drone to a halt on the runway. A list of needed repairs for 44-85569 included replacement of the Plexiglas nose, replacement of the right outer wing panel, replacement of the flap mechanism linkage, replacement of two main and three Tokyo tanks in the right wing, extensive airframe sheet metal repairs, replacement of some cockpit glass and more. What the list does not infer is how much of the damage was from the Nike, and if any occurred during the drone's rollout into the desert. Before counting the sheet metal work, it was estimated repairs to the drone would use 3000 man-hours.[199]

A Falcon mission on 3 April was number twenty-two for the Holloman detachment. The TB-25 wielding the missile made five test passes before the intended live fire pass was aborted due to problems with the Falcon. Mission twenty-three, the following day, was another Falcon support effort. The test bed TB-25 carrying the AAMs made one test approach followed by a hot missile run at mid-morning over White Sands. The Falcon went astray and was logged as a miss. Another hot run resulted in an aborted Falcon. Much remained to be learned about the Falcon, and how to make it viable. Mission twenty-four on 8 April – another Falcon flight – was terminated early due to high winds and blowing dust in the desert.[200]

QB-17 44-83658 was groomed for a Nike support sortie (mission twenty-five) on 10 April. It would have been easy to presume this would be another excursion over the desert followed by a routine drone landing at Holloman. However, 44-83658's take-off roll at 1248hrs would be the aircraft's last. A cloud ceiling kept the target altitude around 20,000ft, instead of the briefed 28,000ft. The drone responded as it should, and presented itself to the first Nike at 1400hrs – the weapon missed the QB-17.

A second SAM launch 42 minutes later hit the drone squarely in the bomb-bay area. Black smoke punctuated the impact as the fuselage broke into two pieces just aft of the wing. Debris, some flaming, was seen raining down over the desert after the main wreckage had hit the ground. At the time of impact, some cloud cover was lower than the drone, and a crewmember aboard a director DB-17 watched the stricken QB-17 disappear into the undercast.[201]

The next NULLO B-17 flight at Holloman, Mission twenty-six, was in support of Falcon testing on 22 April. The missile-carrying TB-25 launch platform released one AAM at 0750hrs. It was rated a very near miss. A second Falcon fired at 0815hrs tumbled from the launcher and did not recover in time. It was scored a clear miss. The early timing of this mission was followed by a second QB-17,

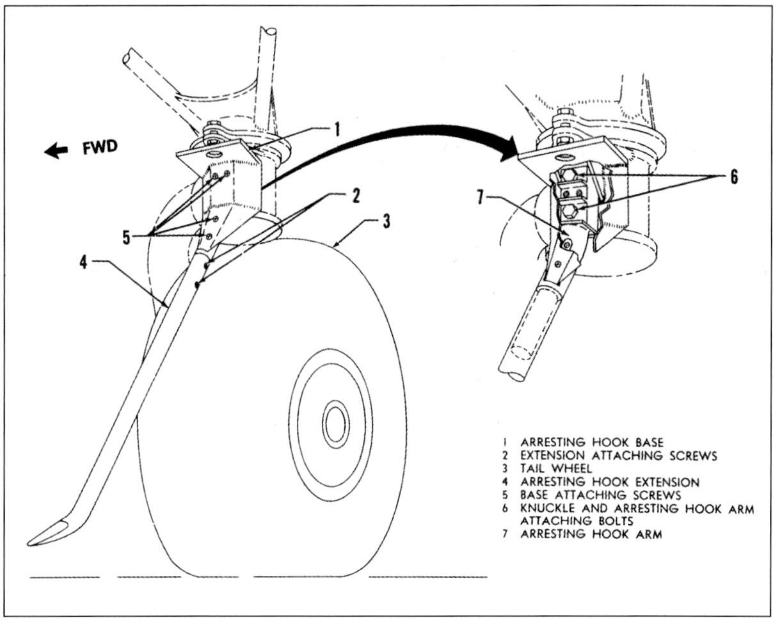

Some QB-17s were fitted with a tailhook mounted to the tailwheel strut just ahead of the tyre to keep drones from running off the end of the runway should any braking control anomalies crop up. *Author's collection*

Right: QB-17 44-85573 landed on unpaved ground at the White Sands complex after taking a direct hit from a Falcon AAM in the spring of 1952. *NARA*

Below: A close up of the damage caused by the Falcon missile hit on the tail of QB-17 44-85573. *AFHRA*

mission twenty-seven, planned for launch at mid-morning that same day. Two more Falcon firings from the TB-25 were planned. Although problems with the missile caused the effort to be aborted, the day's activity showed the detachment's ability to mount more than one drone mission in a day.[202]

Mission twenty-eight on 24 April was briefed as another flight that would provide opportunities for two separate Nike launches. Both SAMs had warheads, and the risk posed to QB-17 44-83738 was understood. Radar issues prompted the use of one of the airborne DB-17 directors for final control of the QB-17. Cloud cover again blocked the intended altitude of 28,000ft, and the drone climbed to only 9000ft. The first SAM, fired at 1344hrs, missed. Some accounts state that 44-83738 was relocated to 10,500ft for the second missile shot, which launched at 1426 hrs. A direct hit sent the QB-17 earthward, streaming flames until it struck the desert floor about ten seconds after impact with the Nike. The broken drone made little lateral travel in its final plunge.[203] April 1952 had been an expensive month for Det 1.

Holloman QB-17 mission twenty-nine, on 6 May, was another attempt to have a smooth launch with the finicky Falcon AAM from a TB-25 test aircraft. The first missile firing was cancelled when batteries failed just before the intended launch, and a second Falcon was scrubbed due to a servo failure in the weapon. The TB-25 landed to load a third Falcon, took off again, and then scrubbed the mission due to yet more unspecified problems with the missile. Two days later, mission thirty again presented a QB-17 drone to the Falcon team as a target. A miss, and problems with a second Falcon, caused delay, and then the QB-17 began losing radio control signal capability with both of the airborne DB-17s.

The very real possibility of a total radio control failure prompted the immediate landing of the QB-17 on the salt flats. As described in an after action report of the mission, 'A letdown was started at 0945[hrs]. A pattern was set up and an excellent landing was made with the drone by Capt Proctor'. The empty QB-17 sat on the desert floor with its engines running until a member of the drone team arrived by helicopter to cut them. An inspection verified the drone was in good condition, and it was flown off the salt flats and back to Holloman later that day. A radio control receiver in the drone was found to be operating intermittently, leading to the prudent cautionary landing on the salt flats.[204]

Mission thirty-one on 17 June was another Falcon NULLO sortie. Two AAMs were fired, and while the first missed, the second hit the QB-17, prompting a precautionary salt flats landing of the Flying Fortress. Mission thirty-two, flown on 23 June, supported the ground-based Talos SAM. A miss was scored, and the drone returned to base. Three days later, a QB-17 again flew for the Falcon AAM team. This time, the missile damaged the drone, which was summarily landed on the salt flats. With help from Holloman AFB base operations, someone was at the idling drone within eight minutes to shut its engines down.

The next day (27 June) saw another QB-17 sortie to support Falcon testing. A hit was scored against the drone, but its controllability led the team to recover it back at Holloman instead of the salt flats. Ground control pilots successfully brought the QB-17 back to base, where it joined three other damaged QB-17s in the repair workshop – some were expected to return to service the following month.[205]

In July, Det 1 relocated on Holloman AFB and acquired the use of a hangar large enough to shelter two B-17s and several T-33 or F-80 jets. This was a significant benefit to the maintainers, who could now work on aircraft in the shade of the hangar instead of in the blazing sun on the ramp. Maintenance on aircraft parked outdoors in the summer had required mechanics and technicians to report for work at sunrise to tackle jobs before the extreme heat made aircraft skin and tools too hot to touch.[206]

On 3 July, for mission thirty-five, a QB-17 was the object of a Talos missile shot that failed to hit the drone. Between 8–22 July, a variety of proficiency and test flights took place. The Holloman team practiced a new pattern that would present the drone QB-17 at a 90-degree angle for side attack Falcon firings from the test bed TB-25 flown by missile manufacturer Hughes.

Graphic and gritty, this photograph captures the life and violent end that awaited many QB-17 drones. ***AFHRA***

With a clearly punched-in entry hole at the Cheyenne tail turret and an exit point under the right stabiliser, this QB-17 was damaged by a Falcon AAM hit on 27 June 1952 over the White Sands/Holloman Missile Range complex. *AFHRA*

Mission thirty-six was flown on 24 July in support of the Falcon programme, as was mission thirty-seven the next day. On the 24th, the first Falcon failed to launch, the second flew and was scored as a miss and, after reloading, the TB-25 launched a third AAM that did minor damage to the QB-17 when it hit. The following day's mission saw a Falcon fired without striking the drone.[207]

Mission thirty-eight flew on 8 August as a Nike NULLO. Two missiles were fired and no hits resulted. Mission thirty-nine on 15 August was a Nike NULLO flight. Again, two SAMs were fired and no hits made. As the QB-17 rolled out on landing, the pin securing the tailwheel sheared, allowing the drone to ground loop. No damage occurred, and steel shear pins were installed from that time onward to reduce the likelihood of a repeat experience.[208]

Mission forty was a Nike NULLO flight on 19 August. One missile fired and no hit was scored. On 21 August missions forty-one and forty-two were mounted as Falcon NULLOs. Mission forty-one was the first to see a Falcon AAM fired at a lower altitude of about 3000 ft above ground level. No hit was scored. Mission forty-two saw the drone get airborne, but the mission was cancelled due to bad weather. Missions forty-three and forty-four were undertaken on 22 August, supporting the Falcon. The primary drone did not check out for mission forty-three, so the ever-ready reserve QB-17 took over. This was a low-level mission, and the one Falcon fired scored a hit on the right wing of the Flying Fortress. Radio controllability of the damaged QB-17 was good, so the decision was made to land it at Holloman instead of a rear area. The landing worked well. Mission forty-four was a high-altitude Falcon effort, with the first of two missiles failing to fire and the second AAM missing.[209]

Mission forty-five did not take place until 16 September, and again it was a drone flight in support of Nike. There followed a lull in target missions, during which Det 1 flew training and testing sorties, including Nike beacon checks on the jet drones up to 35,000ft. 18 September's mission forty-six was a Falcon NULLO, which hit the QB-17.

Nothing but scrap metal remains of this QB-17 after it was intercepted by a Falcon over White Sands in 1952. Range specialists say the debris from old wrecks is picked up so as to avoid confusion with newer test drones or devices that may come down on the range and need to be located. *AFHRA*

The converted bomber began an uncommanded descending turn to the right which control pilots were unable to correct. The damaged Flying Fortress crashed and burned about 20 miles north-west of Holloman in the expanse of the New Mexico desert. The DB-17s landed, refuelled and took off again for another QB-17 Falcon NULLO that day. Two missiles were fired and neither hit the drone.

Mission forty-eight on 19 September was a drone flight in support of the Falcon programme. The QB-17 took a hit in the tail section. Good radio control was maintained, and the drone was landed back at Holloman. Six days later, mission forty-nine supported Nike tests. The DB-17 directors were spaced many miles from the drone, and a DT-33 was aloft as well to provide fast interception of the QB-17 if needed.[210]

Missions fifty and fifty-one supported the Talos SAM on 1 October 1952, as did mission fifty-two six days later. No hits were logged. Mission fifty-three was flown on 16 October to support Falcon testing. One AAM missed and the second missile had a malfunction, bringing the mission to a close. Mission fifty-four the following day was another Falcon NULLO. Again, one AAM missed, but the second hit near the tail. The DB-17 crew entered formation with the stricken drone and determined no elevator or rudder control was available. The QB-17 was flying in a skid, left wing low. The 'air-beeper' pilot tried to hold the left wing up, but the skid remained. With only partial throttle control and some aileron use, he did his best to guide the QB-17 to the broad salt flats at White Sands. The skid induced the left main gear to fold back on landing, badly damaging its attachment point.[211]

21 October saw mission fifty-five flown in support of the Nike programme. The first of two SAMs damaged the QB-17, although ground stations could not immediately see that. The second weapon missed, and when the director caught up

Damaged but controllable, this QB-17 was landed on the salt flats at the White Sands/Holloman Missile Range complex in the New Mexico desert. This was a precaution to avoid the possibility of having a mishap on the active Holloman runway that could be detrimental to other aircraft operations. Repairable drones were fixed and flown off the salt flats and back to the main base. (*AFHRA*

to the drone, damage from the first Nike was evident. Good radio control ability still remained with the drone, and it was landed uneventfully at Holloman. Mission fifty-six on 30 October was a Falcon NULLO, plagued by problems with the TB-25 launch aircraft that led to mission cancellation.

The next day saw mission fifty-seven launched as a Falcon NULLO. The first AAM missed, and when the second could not be fired the mission was ended. The excitement was not over for the day, however, as the QB-17's tailwheel would not extend for landing. Plans were made to recover the drone at Holloman with the tailwheel still retracted. Arriving in the traffic pattern, the drone had its tailwheel extend on its own. The landing proved uneventful, despite the errant wheel having actually only partly extended. Following this incident, Det 1 decided that all future NULLO B-17 flights would have the fuse on the tailwheel retraction motor pulled before take-off, leaving the tailwheel fully extended throughout the mission.[212]

Mission fifty-eight at Holloman was a Nike NULLO early in the morning of 6 November. The plan called for the firing of four Nike SAMs, and this happened during the course of 56 minutes. None struck the QB-17, although near misses were logged. Two weeks later, a Nike drone support sortie was flown as mission fifty-nine. Two missiles were launched, resulting in near misses. Mission sixty, on 26 November, is noteworthy for that fact that a QF-80 NULLO supported the Nike tests over White Sands. Mission sixty-one on 4 December reverted to a QB-17 for a Nike NULLO. Four SAMs were fires and no hits recorded. Mission sixty-two, on 9 December, was another jet Nike NULLO. Mission sixty-three ten days later closed out Det 1's drone sorties over the White Sands/Holloman area for 1952. It was a Nike NULLO, with two missiles fired at the QB-17. Near misses were logged and the drone landed safely at Holloman.[213]

As the Flying Fortresses continued to age, in the summer of 1952 Det 1 reported shortages of B-17 turbosuperchargers and tyres and tubes. Efforts to keep the QB-17s airworthy included sheet metal repairs to three drones that had been hit by missiles over White Sands. A spare B-17 wing was flown in from Eglin to repair QB-17 44-85573 and a bomb-bay centre section arrived from Eglin to rebuild QB-17 44-85617, which had been out of service for three months. To make them more effective at mimicking enemy aircraft for missile tests, two QB-17s had chaff dispensers installed and tested during the second half of 1952 at Holloman. In August of that year, Det 1 ramped up its training for, and use of, jet drones like the QF-80.[214] The USAF recognised the need for drones faster and higher-flying than the reliable old QB-17s, and the QF-80 was a step in this direction. Nonetheless, QB-17s would remain in use into 1959.

Starfire and Sabre Dog targets

A test project starting on 18 June 1952 used a drone flying from the Eglin complex out over the Gulf of Mexico, where it was to be the target of rocket launches from F-86D Sabre Dog (the common nickname for the D-model Sabre) and F-94C Starfire jet fighters. The object of this project was to determine the firing accuracy of the E-4 Fire Control System (F-86D-5) and the E-5 Fire Control System (F-94C).

QB-17s 44-83589 and 44-83605 share ramp space at Eglin in the early 1950s. *USAF*

Mission one saw an F-86D release six 2.75in Mk 4 Folding-Fin Aerial Rockets (FFARs) on each of two passes while on a heading to avoid having the weapons aimed toward land. Miss distance was calculated as 150ft for the first firing pass and 100ft for the second. One Sabre Dog aborted for intermittent radio problems, and no instrumented data was recorded due to problems aboard the F-86D interceptor. Mission two was launched later that same day, with similar results due to problems with the interceptors. No rockets were fired on the second mission. The drone operators' after action report included the pointed recommendation that no further NULLO flights be expended on this project 'until further assurance is gained that all required equipment will function properly'.[215]

Mission three, on 24 June, saw the spare drone employed when the primary QB-17 experienced instrumentation problems. Tense moments ensued as the spare drone became airborne, nosing up until airspeed bled off from 115mph to a sluggish 78mph. The ground control elevator pilot was unable to achieve elevator control and called for the DB-17 director to take over. When the director also found it impossible to control the drone's down-elevator response, the master director aircraft, called 'Overdriver Lima', saved the day and brought the errant QB-17 under control. One rocket firing pass was made by the F-86D, loosing six rockets with a calculated miss of 90ft. A second fighter aborted shortly after takeoff, and the F-86D project officer cancelled the rest of the mission.

The darkest day for post-war USAF drone operations came on 25 August 1952 when an F-86D pilot fired inert FFARs at, and hit, a manned DB-17 director aircraft instead of the drone QB-17 involved in the test at Eglin. The stricken Flying Fortress plunged into the Gulf of Mexico in flames. This day's mission had called for direct firing at the drone, instead of offset firing as had been done with earlier F-86D sorties. The object of this flight was to hit the drone with inert warhead rockets, record the hits on film and, if possible, safely land the QB-17 for further analysis and interpretation of the hits. A USAF report on the mishap said:

A Falcon missile peeled open the wing of this QB-17 at White Sands on 22 August 1952. *AFHRA*

'Authority for this mission had been directed by HQ USAF to determine as quickly as possible the kill capabilities of the F-86D because of "D" production schedules."[216]

An RF-80 photo-reconnaissance variant of the Shooting Star and a camera-equipped B-26 Invader were aloft to record the action. A North American B-45 Tornado crew had observed earlier portions of the activities, and a second director B-17G, typical for such missions, was also aloft. After the mishap, at least one pilot participating in the operation commented about the large number of aircraft in the sky during the live-fire test.

The team planning this mission moved the DB-17 twice as far from the QB-17 as had been originally planned, and it was believed the radar image of the two Flying Fortresses would indicate which one was the drone by its placement in the loose formation. Furthermore, the yellow panels on the drone were considered to be sufficiently visible to give the Sabre Dog pilot an adequate visual cue that it was the target, instead of the all-silver DB-17. Those drone markings would come up for stark revision in the wake of the incident.

The drone was set to fly at 15,000ft about 100 miles south of Eglin. The first F-86D of the day missed the drone in its firing pass. The second fighter pilot broke off passes four times following a visual check of his target after he had found that his radar showed him locked on to either the drone director or the B-26 photo aircraft instead of the QB-17. When the second pilot fired at the drone, he missed. The pilot of the third, and last, F-86D said he made a number of efforts to lock on to the drone and *not* other aircraft, and was convinced of the appropriateness of his target when he fired the rockets.[217]

The FFARs hit the DB-17 near the junction of the left wing with the fuselage, and pieces of the bomber could be seen coming off after impact. Fire issued from the damaged DB-17 almost immediately, and the stricken aircraft began spinning to the left within a minute, disintegrating as it fell. Of the eight men aboard DB-17 44-83680, two in the waist section successfully bailed out, one free-falling down to about 3000ft before opening his parachute. Within 22 minutes of radio calls indicating the downing of the DB-17, the first of eight B-17s was aloft to search the Gulf of Mexico for survivors. The two men who bailed out were the radio operator and electronics technician, and they spent the night in a life raft in choppy waters before being rescued the next day by a US Navy vessel.

The QB-17 drone was recovered at Duke Auxiliary Field No 3 near the town of Crestview, Florida, where strong crosswinds pushed the Flying Fortress off the runway, inflicting slight damage. For six days, B-17s made low-altitude sea searches looking in vain for other survivors from the DB-17.[218]

Following the mistaken identity tragedy, directors were told to remain three miles from drones, with a 2000ft altitude separation. One very visible outcome of this mishap was the change to QB-17 paint schemes to include complete coverage in bright yellow paint, with three-foot-wide black stripes on each wing and on the fuselage, to make them stand out more from silver DB-17s. USAF insignia were to be applied to the fuselage only. The rich yellow colour specified was Army/Navy Aeronautical (ANA) orange yellow lacquer No 506, which equates to the later Federal Standard colour FS13538. The broad, angled black stripes were ANA jet shade No 622. In the months following the

The separated left main gear strut assembly on this QB-17 made landing on the White Sands salt flats prudent to avoid blocking the main runway. *AFHRA*

crash, two drone missions were cancelled because the aircraft were still being painted with the new bolder markings.[219]

Even with this dazzling drone paint scheme, a USAF history document noted that a repeat of the mishap could occur if the fighter pilot 'is completely absorbed in his radar scope and forgets to make continuous and positive visual checks throughout his aiming run. Therefore, an unarmed pacer aircraft accompanies the armed fighter aircraft to make positive visual identification prior to firing'.[220]

Drone overwater guidance

In April 1952 the USAF established some rules for specific project QB-17 drone operations out of the Eglin AFB complex in the Florida panhandle when drones were flown remotely to overwater target ranges. Point of origin for the Flying Fortresses was Duke Auxiliary Field No 3. The QB-17s would take off and traverse the distance to and from the sea range area at an altitude of 1000ft or less. This was to minimise the potential for hazards in the community if a drone went rogue. The rationale was succinct – 'An altitude of 1,000ft would minimize the area that the drone would crash'. And all of the drones were to have a functioning remote-control destructor mechanism on board.

Even with this onboard destruction system, the drones would have fighter chase aeroplanes that could intercede and down the drone if need be. An explanatory letter from the 3205th Drone Group on 24 April 1952 detailed the operation:

> 'The drone and the director aircraft will be at an altitude of approximately 800ft with the escort fighter aircraft flying a criss-cross flight path approximately 1,000ft above and in firing position behind the drone.'

The drone was to remain at an altitude of about 800ft within eight miles of shore, outbound and inbound.[221]

With many small airstrips located on the Eglin complex, the pierced steel planking runway at Range No 52 was authorised as the emergency landing strip for drones experiencing problems that could preclude a safe landing back at Duke Auxiliary Field No 3.

Since the Eglin complex often had multiple and unrelated test missions in the air simultaneously, a cautionary note was added in the communications involving the low-level drone ingress and egress flight path:

> 'A time lag exists in drone maneuverability due to the activation of controls through the remote linkage. Pilots of manned aircraft must be alert and give way to all NULLO drone flights.'[222]

A drone rudder controller watches the approach of a QB-17 to ensure that it lands in the centre of the runway's width. Mounted binoculars will help him observe the behaviour of the landing Flying Fortress far down the runway as brakes are applied. *AFHRA*

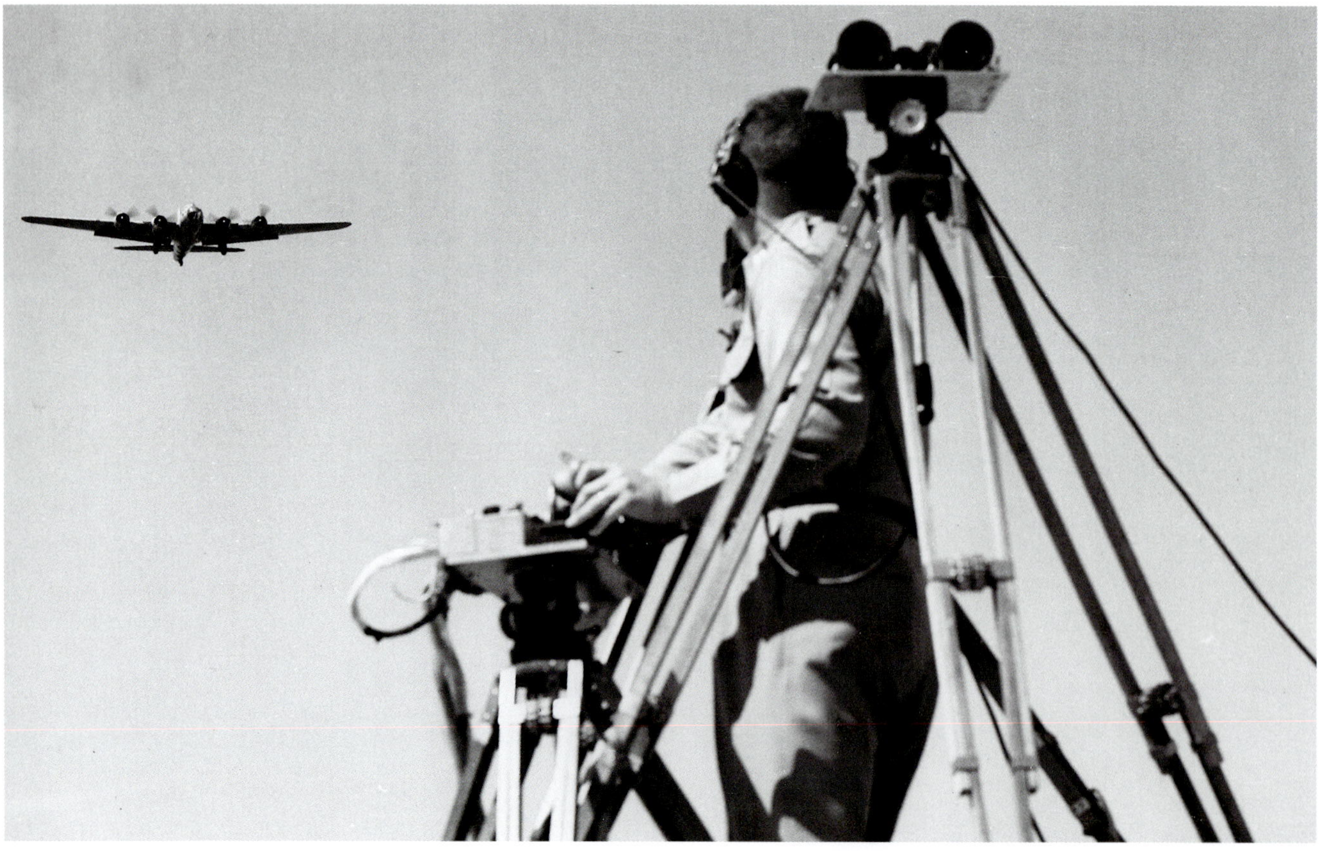

QB-17 stand-in for Matador

The 3205th Drone Group provided a manned QB-17 drone during March 1952 to validate a radar control operation at Patrick AFB, Florida, for remotely-piloted SSM-A-1 Matador surface-to-surface cruise missiles. Success of the project relied on some quirky adaptation in the QB-17. The ground radar station beacon used a double tone system for signalling drone movement and the QB-17 used an incompatible single tone system for its autopilot controls.

The radar operator aboard the QB-17 could receive light signals at a special light installation in the drone. These signals, sent from the ground radar station, indicated the intent of making a right or left turn of a particular number of degrees. The radar operator in the drone relayed these light commands to the QB-17 pilot, who executed them. In this way, the ground radar operators could watch the plot of the QB-17's movement, and make desired heading changes that were visible to the onboard radar operator, who relayed the information to the QB-17 pilot for action. It may have been rustic, but it enabled radar validation to be made that supported Matador missiles.[223]

That same month, photographers on the ground at White Sands/Holloman found it difficult to find, and photograph, B-17 drones flying at high altitude. They suggested installing smoke generators on the Flying Fortress drones, and the 3205th Drone Group aircraft maintenance section duly fabricated some that were successfully used by the QB-17s.[224]

High mission tempo

In January 1953, the 3205th Drone Group was busy flying missions from Eglin, Holloman and Point Mugu. The size and importance of the ongoing drone operations at Holloman resulted in Det 1 becoming the 3225th Target Drone Squadron as of 1 January 1953.[225]

Even as the 3205th embraced QF-80 jet fighters as the emerging drone technology, the need for B-17s continued to satisfy the growing demand for such aircraft. Fortunately for the USAF, it still had pockets of stored Flying Fortresses that could be quickly refitted as either drones or directors. On 10 May 1953, four crews left Duke Auxiliary Field No 3. Their destination was Hill AFB, Utah, where they took delivery of three B-17s from storage to ferry to Brookley AFB in Mobile, Alabama, for modification for their new duties.

'Musical chairs' with B-17s on 2 June saw two crews ferry a pair of Flying Fortresses from Mobile to Davis-Monthan AFB, Arizona. From there, the crews flew commercially to Utah to pick up two more B-17s from Hill AFB storage to drop off at Mobile. Thirteen days later, three crews from Duke Auxiliary Field No 3 went to Hill to ferry three more stored B-17s to Mobile for conversion.[226] Despite the USAF having rapidly modernised far beyond the use of B-17s as bombers, a small but active community within the service took advantage of the availability of late-model Flying Fortresses still in the inventory.

The mission tempo for drone flying from Duke Auxiliary Field No 3 in 1953 was lower than it had been in previous years. On 17 March, a practice QB-17

At a 1953 Duke Auxiliary Field event, 3205th Drone Group QB-17s were on display, as were control pilot consoles for inspection. As the QB-17 in the distance moved down the runway, visitors could see its control panel televised. ***AFHRA***

NULLO mission over the Gulf of Mexico gave intercepting fighters the opportunity to exercise their skills. Three days later, a proper QB-17 NULLO flight – the first of the year – settled on an altitude of 5000ft over the Gulf to enable the fighters to approach from at least 7000ft without being obscured in overcast. With an F-84 serving as the chase aeroplane, an F-86D made two 'wet passes' (in the vernacular used by the drone group) with FFARs firing, as opposed to 'dry passes' with no rockets being launched. The drone remained under control and was returned safely to Duke Auxiliary Field No 3. 24 March saw another NULLO mission over the Gulf, with less than optimal results blamed on the fighters firing 'bent weapons'![227]

3 April saw another NULLO flight at 10,000ft to support F-86D rocket launches, again with the historical note of failure due to 'bent weapons'. The Sabre Dogs returned to Eglin and quickly re-armed, after which they caught up with the QB-17 and downed it with a volley of FFARs.[228]

Finless 100lb practice bomb casings held a grouping of M-18 smoke grenades that could be activated to provide positive identification of a QB-17 drone, versus a manned DB-17 mother ship. *AFHRA*

Efforts were made in the first half of 1953 at Duke Auxiliary Field No 3 to prevent any recurrence of the accidental downing of the manned DB-17 that had occurred in August 1952 over the Gulf of Mexico. QB-17 drones were now equipped with underwing 100lb practice bombs containing smoke grenades that could be remotely activated in flight. Their plume gave positive identification of the aircraft as a drone. M-18 smoke grenades were fitted within the thin skin of a lightweight empty practice bomb. Two practice bombs were mounted under each wing of a QB-17.[229]

Holloman QB-17 sorties in 1953

The newly-created 3225th Target Drone Squadron in the New Mexico desert at Holloman AFB had a busy schedule supporting missile programmes by providing QB-17 and some QF-80 drones in 1953. QB-17 NULLO mission sixty-four on 6 January supported Nike. Mission sixty-five two days later was another QB-17 Nike effort, while mission sixty-six on 15 January saw a QF-80 sortied in support of the SAM programme. Mission sixty-seven on 20 January was a QF-80 flight for Nike, while Mission sixty-eight two days later supported SAM testing with a QB-17 drone. Mission sixty-nine was a QF-80 NULLO flown on 29 January for Nike, while mission seventy on 3 February, which was to have involved a QB-17 targeted by a SAM, was cancelled prior to the weapon being fired. Mission seventy-one nine days later was another QB-17 Nike effort, with one missile fired and no hit scored.[230]

Falcon AAMs were the object of missions seventy-two and seventy-three on 20 February against QB-17s. The first mission aborted due to problems with the TB-25 launch aircraft and the second saw a firing that missed. The 12 March mission seventy-four tasked a QB-17 as a target for the Falcon programme. No missiles were fired. Mission seventy-five took place the following day, again for the benefit of the Falcon. Problems led to dry runs only, and after four hours aloft, the QB-17 ran out of allowed NULLO time and landed. Mission seventy-six on 17 March was another QB-17 Nike effort. When ground control radar for the SAM experienced difficulties that kept the QB-17 orbiting for a long time, the drone had to land to refuel. Four Nike SAMs streaked through the New Mexico skies that day, and they all missed.[231]

This bomb shackle mounted to the underside of a QB-17 wing was used to hold a smoke generating device. The stencilled sign (which reads *REMOVE CLAMP FROM CAMERA STORE CONDUIT BEFORE REMOVING OUTER WING PANEL*) to the right of the shackle indicates that this is a drone aircraft. *AFHRA*

1 April saw a QB-17 Falcon effort for mission seventy-seven. Eight runs were made but no AAMs fired. Mission seventy-eight the following day was another QB-17 sortie for Falcons, with two AAMs scored as misses. Mission seventy-nine on 3 April again saw a QB-17 being targeted by a Falcon, with one missile fired and scored as a miss. Three days later, QF-80 missions eighty and eighty-one supported nuclear tests in Nevada in *Upshot–Knothole*. 16 April saw QB-17 mission eighty-two for Nike. Six missiles were fired, three with the drone Flying Fortress at 10,000ft and three with it at 15,000ft. All six were scored as misses.

Mission eighty-three on 20 April saw a Nike achieve a hit for the first time in many months. Once the QB-17 had been struck all control of it was lost, with the drone crashing in the desert. With no means to save the aircraft, 'the Range Safe System was activated to see if it would perform under actual conditions', a USAF history noted. 'The charge was set off, but it did not blow off the wing as was expected'. Suggested relocation of the explosive charge was forwarded to the 3205th Drone Group headquarters at Eglin.[232]

Mission eighty-four on 21 April was supposed to see a QB-17 being targeted by a Falcon, but when no action was logged after four hours of NULLO time, the drone was landed. Three days later, mission eighty-five was a QB-17 NULLO Falcon support effort – conflict with an unrelated Matador missile test put the drone on hold for an hour. The first Falcon fired at 1134hrs tore the tailwheel from the Flying Fortress and the second AAM of the mission, at 1314hrs, found its mark and struck the right wing of the QB-17. The drone entered a tight spiral to the right and crashed two minutes later. A Falcon was the beneficiary of QB-17 mission eighty-six on 27 April 1953. One Falcon was launched but no hit was scored. Two days later, mission eighty-seven was a Falcon QB-17 NULLO flight. Two AAMs were fired and no hits registered.[233]

On 8 May two more Nevada *Upshot–Knothole* QF-80 missions, numbered eighty-eight and eighty-nine, were logged for the squadron. Mission ninety did not come until 19 June, and was a QB-17 Talos effort. Radar station issues led to cancellation of the flight. The next day, mission ninety-one was also mounted for Talos. One missile was fired at the QB-17, but no hit was scored. Mission ninety-two, flown on 23 June, was a Nike QB-17 mission. This was a lower-level effort flown at 6600ft. Although the first Nike was a miss, the second was a direct hit, and the 'air-beeper' pilots were not able to keep the drone under control. It crashed just before noon. Mission ninety-three came on 29 June and supported Falcon with a QB-17 early morning launch. After holds and dry runs, the Falcon team cancelled this mission. Mission ninety-four was also flown on 29 June for Falcon. The one AAM fired was a miss. Mission ninety-five closed out June on the 30th in support of Falcon. One missile was fired and the QB-17 escaped unscathed.

Broken solid aluminium Hamilton Standard propeller blades and a damaged cowling tell the story of a missile hit at White Sands. Photo legend referencing project MX-904 on the original print indicates the QB-17 was hit by a Falcon test missile. The wingtips behind the propeller are stock Flying Fortress rounded tips that could be replaced on a QB-17 with special camera pod wingtips. *AFHRA*

For the first half of 1953, the Holloman squadron had logged 1253 flying hours with its QB-17s and DB-17s. The gain of seven Flying Fortresses was offset by the loss, through transfers and crashes, of six QB-17s.[234]

Missions ninety-six and ninety-seven on 2 July were Falcon NULLO flights. One missile was expended during the first mission after nine dry passes and no AAMs were fired on the second sortie. Mission ninety-nine (mission ninety-eight, and other mission numbers that are missing from this sequence, was a QF-80 drone sortie, as detailed in Chapter 7) on 21 July supported Talos with a QB-17 drone. Unusually, a US Navy F6F Hellcat drone was also involved, flying at a lower altitude than the USAF Flying Fortress. Only one Talos was fired, and logged as a miss.

The squadron undertook its 100th mission on 22 July with a Falcon QB-17 NULLO. This proved to be a memorable sortie, for the lone Falcon fired scored a direct hit, sending the Flying Fortress into a flat spin that demolished it upon desert impact. Missions 101 and 102 came on 28 July as Falcon NULLOs. No fewer than seven AAMs were fired at the QB-17 and all missed. Mission 103 on 13 August was a Nike QB-17 mission that saw two SAMs fired. Both missed.

A Talos NULLO two weeks later was mission 105. As the QB-17 was climbing through 22,000ft, its No 1 engine outboard on the left wing began to smoke and burn. The control pilot immediately began descending the QB-17 toward the salt flats for an emergency landing. Living up to the wartime legends of Flying Fortress durability, the aircraft remained aloft even after the blazing No 1 engine fell from the wing of the QB-17 two miles from touchdown on the salt flats. The control pilot continued with his approach, and the three-engined QB-17 force-landed with no further issues.[235]

On 1 September, during mission 106, two Falcons were fired and no hits scored. Mission 107 two days later saw five AAMs unleashed in the direction of the QB-17, and again no hits were logged. Mission 108 supported Nike on 17 September with a QB-17. Neither of two SAMs fired hit the drone. 2 October's mission 110 was for Talos, with the US Navy putting up a Hellcat drone below the Flying Fortress. When the first F6F went out of control and crashed in the New Mexico desert, a second Hellcat drone was launched, only for the Talos project to cancel the mission with no missiles fired. Mission 111 on 6 October was another NULLO Talos support flight, with the QB-17 flying at 13,500ft. Radar control was inoperative, so no missiles were fired. Mission 112 the following day was a QB-17 for Talos, with the drone being missed by the sole SAM fired.

8 October's mission 113 saw support for the Falcon project commence once again, with a QB-17 NULLO flight orbiting for two hours before the AAM team cancelled the operation with no launches due to missile problems. Mission 114 the following day also supported Falcon testing, with the solitary AAM fired missing the drone. The QB-17 experienced intermittent communication issues while descending to land, so it was parked on the salt flats as a precaution and then flown out of there within the hour without issue.

A Talos support sortie was flown as mission 115 on 14 October, with the USAF putting up a QB-17 and the US Navy contributing an F6F drone. One Talos was fired and declared a miss. Both Talos and Nike were supported with QB-17 drone mission 116 on 20 October. Nike fired first, resulting in a miss. Talos cancelled because of cloud coverage. As the Flying Fortress drone was returning to base, a dust storm and rain shower – products of unsettled desert weather – forced the controllers to keep the QB-17 aloft until the visibility cleared. Still, the drone had to be landed in adverse winds.[236]

A QB-17 burns in the desert, the victim of a Falcon missile shot on 22 July 1953. The valuable wingtip camera scoring pods appear to have detached and come to rest on the ground nearby. ***USAF***

Scars in the desert bear witness to the curved slide made by this QB-17 at White Sands on 21 October 1953. The flaming loss was dramatically captured on film. The righthand wingtip camera pod appears to have detached in the slide, while the left pod looks to be intact. *USAF*

21 October saw mission 117 for the Falcon AAM. Crews could be forgiven if they did not expect much to come of the day's work, given ongoing problems with early Falcon tests. Two missiles were fired at the Flying Fortress and the first one left what was described as a 'scratch' on the upper right side of the ample vertical stabiliser of the drone, leaving only minor damage (although photographs show it broke the skin). The second Falcon tore into the inboard section of the QB-17's right wing. As the bomber was descended to the safe area for a landing, the right wing exhibited flames and the No 3 engine fell earthward. The right main landing gear also extended. Upon contacting the salt flats, the aircraft ground looped and was consumed by fire.[237]

Talos and Nike were both scheduled to take advantage of mission 118 the following day. One example of each missile was fired at the QB-17 and missed. Mission 119 on 27 October was another joint Talos and Nike venture facing a QB-17 drone. In execution, only the latter weapon fired that day, resulting in a miss. The same took place two days later with mission 120, only this time the only missile firing was the Talos, again resulting in a miss.[238]

The NULLO flights of November and December 1953 were all Falcon efforts. Mission 121 came on 4 November, when two Falcons fired at the Flying Fortress missed. Mission 122 was flown the following day. While in the target pattern, electronics problems crippled the QB-17, which could only respond to a right skid command instead of normal turns. An emergency landing in the salt flats was followed by the left landing gear collapsing, causing a damaging ground loop.[239]

QB-17 43-39362 after it burned out on the White Sands range on 21 October 1953. This Flying Fortress may have been an SB-17 search-and-rescue aircraft prior to becoming a drone. *USAF*

The gutted hulk of QB-17 43-39362. *USAF*

Mission 123 on 2 December saw two Falcons fired at the QB-17, with both missing. Mission 124 the following day and mission 125 on 4 December rounded out a busy year for the drone unit. That final mission saw the QB-17 lose ground radar control, so the director aircraft took over. When problems with turns persisted, the QB-17 was returned to base. On long final for Holloman, skid control went erratic, and the crew decided to guide the QB-17 to the salt flats for an emergency landing. The problems continued to mount en route when directional control was lost. Shortly after the director pilot put the QB-17 into a climb to clear terrain all remaining control of the drone was lost, and it crashed into an uninhabited part of the mountains.[240]

As good as drone operations were becoming, gremlins still lurked that could throw a droned B-17 out of control, when it might have been kept under control if manned.

Point Mugu and San Nicolas Island for QB-17 drones

As part of the 3205th Drone Group's establishment of Det 2 at Point Mugu on 1 July 1952, a site survey clarified the relationship between the airfield's runway on the coast of California and the US Navy's airstrip just offshore on San Nicolas Island. The 3205th reported:

> 'The terrain at Point Mugu makes R/C operation impracticable at this base. The most logical and practicable station for such operation is on San Nicholas Island, which is fifty miles south of Point Mugu. This facility was inspected and found satisfactory. It has a hard surface runway 6000ft x 150ft, with good approaches. The ground adjacent to the runway is of sufficient hardness to support a B-17, which is an asset. Buildings are at a minimum on the island, but we were promised such shelter as we require. A small detachment is maintained on the island, and they will assist us in any matter possible.'[241]

The issue with the main Point Mugu runway was its east–west orientation dictated by prevailing westerly winds. While this orientation was suitable for piloted aircraft, the approaches used with QB-17 drones could not be accomplished due to a 1500ft mountain peak two-and-a-half miles from the eastern end of the runway. The QB-17s would need to be ferried as piloted aircraft to the airstrip on San Nicolas Island. The remoteness of the latter meant the USAF would need to leave a set of remote control rudder and elevator stations permanently on the island. Electronics specialists went to San Nicolas Island 24 hours ahead of scheduled NULLO missions and operating crews arrived aboard mission aircraft four hours ahead of drone take-off time. Ground equipment maintenance problems arose due to the moist salt air at San Nicolas Island.[242]

Later, in August 1955, the USAF and the commander of the Naval Air Missile Test Center agreed that NULLO QB-17s could actually take off from and land back on the main Point Mugu runway. The USAF brought equipment it had needed on San Nicolas Island back to the mainland. Missions launched and recovered at Point Mugu required no pre-positioning flights, as had been the case for San Nicolas Island operations. This saved about five hours of flying time each mission. Maintenance aspects of USAF drone operations became easier when the remote strip was no longer necessary.[243]

Following Det 2's formation on 1 July to support US Navy target drone needs for missile tests, three QB-17s and three B-17 directors were flown from Eglin to Point Mugu on the 18th of that same month. Interservice quirks of consequence soon cropped up. The USAF radios used in the air and ground stations were ARC-3 variants – the US Navy used ARC-1. In the era of ground crystals for radio frequencies, the two types were incompatible, and the USAF had to use a limited supply, rotated between aircraft as needed.[244]

In addition to tests by the US Navy with Terrier missiles, scheduled to begin in 1953, the QB-17s of Point Mugu were made available to Hughes Aircraft for more Falcon AAM testing. In October, the US Navy obtained permission to employ USAF QB-17 drones in testing of the AAM-N-2 Sparrow I AAM. On 18 and 26 November, Sparrow I launches from a Douglas F3D Skyknight gave satisfactory results despite failing to achieve any direct hits on the QB-17. On 3 December, a Sparrow I clipped the QB-17's No 1 propeller after deflecting from a wing hit. On the downwind leg for landing at San Nicolas Island, the QB-17 issued fire from the No 1 engine nacelle, which the US Navy's fire department on the island quickly subdued. Late that month, negotiations were underway to have a repair team from Norton AFB, in southern California, fix the marooned QB-17 on San Nicolas Island.

QB-17 44-83649 survived the loss of part of its left horizontal stabiliser to a Sparrow I AAM. It finally succumbed to a Sidewinder AAM over Inyokern on 18 February 1954. This photograph shows the bolt-on arrester hook ahead of the tailwheel. *AFHRA*

The US Navy gave the 3205th a list of requirements for the intended drone sorties. Altitudes would range from 5000ft to 32,000ft, and ground speed was desired to be 200 knots. Headings should have an accuracy within two degrees, and altitude maintenance within 100ft was called for. Maximum mission duration was placed at four hours.[245]

Fourteen QB-17 NULLO test support flights were made by USAF Det 2 at Point Mugu/San Nicolas Island in the first half of 1953. Eleven of these sorties supported the US Navy's Terrier SAM and the rest were for the Sparrow I AAM.

The Point Mugu detachment was also given responsibility as of 8 May 1953 for supporting US Navy Sparrow I and Terrier tests at China Lake/Inyokern, in eastern California. With only one set of ground control stations available to Det 2, the units on San Nicolas Island had to be transported by sea to Port Hueneme, and thence by truck to China Lake/Inyokern. Of the nine Inyokern QB-17 support missions that were undertaken, one, on 21 May, saw the drone land early with an engine out. It was determined that extended duration flying at an altitude of 30,000ft that day required high power settings, leading to the engine failure.[246]

Det 2's input to the 3205th Drone Group history for January–June 1953 described the intricate aerial ballet that the director pilots had to perform at China Lake/Inyokern to keep out of the danger zone for missiles:

> 'Two firing patterns were utilized during the Inyokern operations, both of which required the use of two director aircraft. Both the closing and 90° crossing patterns required the primary director to follow the drone around an elliptical race-track pattern and break one hundred degrees at three minutes before firing to reach a safe area. The distance and position of the primary director with respect to the drone precluded efficient control during the remainder of the firing run and drone recovery following missile launch. The secondary director aircraft in an orbit on the non-firing side of the launch site assumed control of the target drone at H-3 minutes and effected recovery after launch. Radar vectoring was required to steer the primary director from its position at time of launch to the secondary director and drone formation. The fact that two director aircraft were essential to each operation made it mandatory that a spare director in addition to a spare drone be available for immediate flight.'[247]

The US Navy waived the requirement for explosive self-destruct systems on the QB-17s at Inyokern. Fighters supplied by the US Navy, sometimes reported as McDonnell F2H Banshee jets, would be aloft to shoot down any errant QB-17s should that become necessary. The US Navy designated certain restricted and populated areas where the drones could not overfly in the China Lake vicinity. Controllable missile-damaged QB-17s could be landed at Armitage Field, the main base for testing. Alternately, a dry lakebed twenty miles south of China Lake/Inyokern in the Mojave Desert was designated for emergency director-controlled QB-17 landings. This was a last resort measure, as its remoteness in the desert would have an effect on manually cutting the drone's engines after landing. The subsequent repair and recovery of the aircraft from the lakebed would also be something of a logistical nightmare for Det 2.

During the first half of 1953, Det 2's QB-17 drone missions supported US Navy missile tests at Point Mugu/San Nicolas Island as well as alternating to China Lake/Inyokern. No Flying Fortresses were lost during this period.[248]

From July through to December 1953, the squadron (Det 2 became the 3235th Target Drone Squadron on 1 July 1953) conducted eleven NULLO flights for US Navy missile development programmes. These served Point Mugu and *Norton Sound*, as well as China Lake/Inyokern. Five of the missions supported Sparrow I and four in October were for Terrier. On the fifth Sparrow I test from San Nicolas Island, the QB-17 took a hit on the upper surface of the left wing just outboard of the No 1 engine, causing serious damage. Still controllable, the drone was brought back to the airstrip on San Nicolas Island, catching fire while on final approach – a safe landing was still made. A civilian crew from Norton, working without the benefit of the sheltering confines of a hangar, had the QB-17 repaired on San Nicolas Island in about four months.[249]

The two remaining NULLO flights for US Navy support were Sidewinder tests in the desert at Inyokern in December 1953. The sorties involved a tail chase approach, with the Sidewinder launch aircraft closing on the QB-17 from below and behind.

During the second half of 1953, USAF electronics technicians built a second set of ground controls, relieving the substantial problem of moving a set between San Nicolas Island and Inyokern. Also during this period, the three QB-17s assigned to the Point Mugu squadron were sent to Norton to be painted yellow, with diagonal black bands.

On 9 January 1954, with USAF QB-17 operations still serving the Inyokern test facility, QB-17G 44-83566A received substantial damage to the underside of its right wing outboard of the No 4 engine when it was struck by a Sidewinder AAM. The damaged Flying Fortress made a safe recovery. 21 January saw an Inyokern QB-17-versus-Terrier flight, with the latter scoring a miss. The first outright loss of a QB-17 flying from the California test facilities in support of the US Navy occurred on 18 February at Inyokern when QB-17G 44-83649 ran afoul of a Sidewinder. The Flying Fortress quickly caught fire and exploded, showering the desert floor with aluminium debris. The radio control pilot successfully salvoed the wingtip camera pods that were held in place with explosive bolts prior to the crash.[250]

This photograph of a QB-17 landing at Eglin in 1954 was provided with a detailed explanatory caption. 'A B-17 drone of the 3205th Drone Group is seen crabbing in for a cross-wind landing during remote control operations. From his control station, rudder controller Captain Charles L. Coons will kick the drone straight just before it settles to the runway. Elevator and power controls are handled at a similar station near the side of the runway. Take-offs are made by the same ground control team. Airborne control is commanded from a director aircraft that accompanies the drone to the mission area. The control truck to the left transmits the radio control signals to the guidance system of the drone. Observing the drone is Mr. Lynn Hall (left), representative of Sperry Gyroscope Corporation.' *AFHRA*

23 March saw a QB-17 tasked to provide target service for both a Terrier test and a Sidewinder launch. A practice run was flown for the benefit of the Terrier crew, but scheduled missile firing passes were aborted by the test conductor, who deferred the shots to a later date. Sidewinder testing included three firing passes, with a launch on the last one scored as a miss. On 20 April QB-17G 44-83674 took a Sidewinder hit within the propeller arc of the No 3 engine, clipping about three inches from the aluminium tip of the bomber's Hamilton Standard propeller on that engine. The damage was only discovered when the drone was parked. It was cleared for a one-time ferry flight to Point Mugu, presumably for repairs.[251]

On 1 May, a Point Mugu/San Nicolas Island QB-17G took a solid hit in its No 1 engine from a US Navy Terrier SAM fired by *Norton Sound*. Both engines on the left wing were damaged, as was the wing structure. Nonetheless, a practiced crew of drone pilots safely landed the crippled drone.

The year unfolded with results similar to earlier Nike and Falcon missions at Holloman, where far more misses than hits were recorded, and numerous fail-to-fire scenarios developed as the new missiles were undergoing growing pains. 18 May saw QB-17 44-83674 take a hit from a Terrier missile in its left wing. Fire accompanied the strike. The QB-17 remained controllable for a few moments before rolling and diving at faster than 400mph indicated airspeed from 10,000ft into the ground in a destructive impact.

An aggressive operational tempo had seen eight QB-17 drone missions mounted in April–May to serve US Navy customers In California. However, a lull in Point Mugu/Inyokern use of USAF QB-17 drones in mid 1954 led to the establishment of ground control pilot stations at Marine Corps Auxiliary Air Station Mojave, California, for proficiency training. The ground control stations were temporarily relocated from Inyokern to Mojave.[252]

State of the Art – 1954

In the first half of 1954, the 3205th Drone Group included briefing papers in its unit history that gave a succinct set of metrics for drone accuracy:

> 'Exacting standards of positioning can be met with the present equipment. The specifications of the AEC [Atomic Energy Commission] for their "Zero Hours" limited the time and space tolerances to 450ft horizontally, 200ft vertically and one to one-and-one-third seconds in time. These limits applied to both jets and QB-17s.

A passing missile tore a hole in the starboard wing of this QB-17 and clipped off part of a propeller blade at White Sands in 1954. The tough old bomber was safely landed. *AFHRA*

All flights made against these requirements were within limits.'[253]

The clumsy days of *Aphrodite* were becoming ancient history as USAF operations honed the skills of the 'air-beeper' pilots and their ground-based equivalents.

By the end of 1954, the regularity of use for QB-17 drones was making their operation almost – but never fully – routine. Crews knew what to do, what to look out for and how to fix problems in the drone control system, and the event of taking off and landing an unmanned Flying Fortress was now old hat. Still, the occasional issue would crop up that was harder to detect and fix with no one on board.

Into 1955, the operational tempo of ongoing exposure of QB-17s to missiles, and to drone flight in general, meant the 3205th had Flying Fortresses in need of repair at places like China Lake/Inyokern and San Nicolas Island/Point Mugu.

On 4 January a China Lake/Inyokern QB-17 sortie supported the AAM programme code-named Bird Dog, later to become Genie. Developed by Douglas, Genie was a nuclear-tipped missile intended to destroy inbound bombers. Its large radius of lethality made precision guidance unnecessary. Only one actual Genie nuclear detonation occurred, on 19 July 1957, in the Operation *Plumbbob John* test when an F-89J fired a missile over the Yucca Flats test site in Nevada.

Bird Dog and Genie development launches were made with inert missiles. The QB-17 would loiter at 18,000ft, giving the Bird Dog's launch aircraft the opportunity to use its fire control system to establish proper parameters for missile launch.[254] Following the first mission on 4 January the drone landed seemingly unscathed, as would be expected for an inert missile whose lethality relied merely on being within a large area in the general direction of the target. Post-flight inspection revealed some damage to a remote control receiver antenna mounted above the QB-17's cockpit – more research was needed to confirm if the inert missile had passed that close to the drone.[255]

In subsequent operational use, pilots of interceptors armed with Genies were told to turn abruptly after launch to avoid being consumed by the missile's nuclear blast.

On 5 January a QB-17 went aloft at China Lake/Inyokern, presenting itself to a total of three Bird Dog missile firings before the drone returned to base. The next flight, on 13 January, was a San Nicolas Island QB-17 mission to enable *Norton Sound* to fire two Terrier SAMs at the drone. The undamaged QB-17 landed uneventfully.

A 21 January Bird Dog effort at China Lake/Inyokern placed the QB-17 at 28,000ft over the Mojave Desert. Four were sent on their way toward the drone, apparently missing it. The QB-17, however, immediately went into a hard right banking turn – the remote pilot determined the Turn and Skid control functions were not working. The drone, with an inoperative range safety system since earlier in the mission, had by now drifted 36 nautical miles south-southeast of Inyokern, although it still remained over sparsely populated desert terrain. The mission commander opted to have the QB-17 make a wheels-up landing in the desert. Shortly after the forced landing, fire was visible in the waist of the drone, and it ultimately consumed all but parts of the bomber's tail section and engines.[256]

Days later (probably 24 January) another Bird Dog mission at Inyokern resulted in two missiles being launched, but no hits. On 4 March a QB-17 again went up for Bird Dog tests, and a salvo of two AAMs did no damage to the drone, which recovered safely. Another Bird Dog assignment was undertaken five days later. The missile-firing aircraft that day was an F-86E. The first of two firing passes was scored as a miss. On the second pass, the inert missile hit the drone and caused substantial damage to the front spar, skin and landing light on the QB-17's right wing. The drone remained controllable and landed safely. Another QB-17 mission that same day was again flown for the benefit of Bird Dog. One firing pass was made and one missile launched, scored as a miss.[257]

The close proximity of the director B-17 and striped QB-17 drone represents a landing approach when the television system between the drone and the ground station is inoperative, and the director aircraft furnishes vital airspeed and altitude information to the ground control pilots. *AFHRA*

This striped QB-17 was brought down by a Bird Dog AAM during a test flight from China Lake on 16 March 1955. *AFHRA*

On 16 March, with the QB-17 at 18,000ft, the intercepting fighter made three firing passes, launching one, two and two Bird Dogs on those passes. Recovery of the drone appeared normal up to approach, when the rudder station pilot could not get the right turn function to operate properly on short final. After a go-around, the next landing approach felt normal almost to touchdown, when a spurious down-elevator movement dropped the QB-17 in on its main gear with sufficient force to break off the left mainwheel and send the wingtip camera pods launching away from the bomber. Application of full power and full up elevator got the damaged QB-17 airborne again to an altitude where full control authority was checked and confirmed. A belly landing was made, adding to airframe damage that was estimated to require several thousand manhours to rebuild.

Once the damaged QB-17 debris was cleared from the China Lake/Inyokern runway, the day's second NULLO mission went aloft for Bird Dog. The Flying Fortress reached its 8000ft assigned altitude and waited for a chase fighter that could down the drone to join the flight. Two missiles were launched on each of two firing passes. The Bird Dogs of the second pass looked as if they hit the QB-17's right wing with a puff of smoke. The drone spiralled to the right, out of control, until it hit the desert floor. Both wingtip scoring pods were salvoed from the stricken aircraft as it fell.[258]

23 March saw a mission scrubbed when the Bird Dog carrier aircraft experienced communication problems. The QB-17 landed. The following day a QB-17 faced a Bird Dog salvo of two missiles on one pass and one on another. No damage was inflicted and the aircraft landed safely. Later that day a second mission was mounted, with take-off delayed when the master director DB-17 developed a fuel siphoning issue due to a broken seal. Another salvo of two missiles followed by a single firing resulted in no damage to the drone, which was safely recovered.

A 29 March test (this date is extrapolated from a blurred microfilm image) saw the QB-17 fly against an F-86E launch aircraft at 8000ft, then climb to meet an F-86D at 28,000ft. The lower level flights yielded two tail chase passes with one launch each. The high-altitude F-86D experienced a launch system malfunction and the remainder of the mission was cancelled. When the QB-17 returned to land, a 35-knot crosswind at a 20-degree quartering angle presented a challenge for the ground station pilots, who made a faster no-flap landing.[259]

Not all drone operations were conducted at altitude. On 1 April a QB-17 took off from San Nicolas Island at 500ft and descended to only 200ft over the waves of the Pacific Ocean, where a Sparrow I threaded its way between the Nos 3 and 4 engines on the right wing, inflicting repairable damage to the right wing leading edge. A safe NULLO landing was accomplished, and the damage was noted for rectification during the drone's normally scheduled periodic inspection. Later that day, after temporary repairs had been made to the QB-17's wing and the cameras reloaded, it was sent out on another 200ft overwater drone flight. One Sparrow I was launched, and a miss was recorded.[260]

Back to Bird Dog sorties at China Lake, on 2 April the QB-17 had to hold at 10,000ft for more than an hour while problems with the shoot-down chase aircraft were sorted out. Then it was up to 18,000ft, where the Bird Dog launch aircraft sent a total of three missiles hurling toward the drone, all scored as misses. The QB-17 was safely on the ground again just before 1100hrs. On 12 April, a salvo of three Bird Dogs resulted in at least one fatal hit on QB-17 44-83766, which left controlled flight and spun in from 18,000ft. The Flying Fortress was consumed by the impact and subsequent fire. Both Douglas-built wingtip camera pods were salvoed and descended beneath their parachutes, sustaining minor damage.[261]

A Bird Dog sortie downed QB-17 44-83766 on 12 April 1955 on the China Lake range complex. After at least one Bird Dog hit the Flying Fortress, the aircraft spun in from 18,000ft, ejecting its wingtip camera pods on the way down. Impact and fire consumed the QB-17. *AFHRA*

A mission likely dated 21 April saw a total of six Bird Dogs fired at a QB-17 during four passes. The undamaged drone landed safely. The Bird Dog mission from China Lake/Inyokern eight days later yielded only one firing out of seven passes, resulting in a miss. Another no-flap landing was performed in a stout crosswind. On 10 May a QB-17 sent aloft from China Lake/Inyokern for a Bird Dog mission landed after seven passes by the missile-equipped aircraft, with no launches.

One week later, a QB-17 was tasked with helping development testing for the US Army's Project *Porcupine* – one of several potential answers to the need to upgrade low-level anti-aircraft protection. Considering one type of enemy target to be fighter-bombers flying at altitudes from 6000ft down to only 50ft, *Porcupine* was supposed to engage at ranges between 3000–6000ft. A *Porcupine* battery was to consist of 64 launching tubes for 2.75in unguided rockets that could be fired at a measured rate of 6000 per minute. No complete *Porcupine* system had been built by the time the project was terminated in February 1956.[262]

On 17 May 1955, a QB-17 was kept at 3800ft MSL (800ft above the terrain) in support of *Porcupine*. As no wingtip camera scoring pods were required for this mission, standard rounded wingtips were fitted back onto 44-83605. On the lone firing pass, a salvo of 24 2.75in unguided rockets yielded several direct hits on the drone, causing a large explosion. Thereafter, a diving left turn from only 800ft above the ground demolished the QB-17 when it hit the terrain.[263]

One week later, another QB-17 undertook a *Porcupine* flight, this time clearing the terrain by only 600ft. The salvo of 24 2.75in unguided rockets again hit the low-flying drone, which suffered an explosion and fire immediately. The stricken bomber then rolled into a steep left turn and descent to its destruction barely five seconds after being hit by the rockets.[264]

Meanwhile, Bird Dog support missions continued on 20–21 May from China Lake/Inyokern when a QB-17 initially set up for crossing runs in front of the launch aircraft, followed by a tail chase that led to a missile firing on 20 May. The next day, the pattern was repeated. Cloud cover limited altitude, and the mission was concluded at the request of the project. The drone landed undamaged after both missions.

In early June, QB-17 44-83556 was on a China Lake/Inyokern Bird Dog test mission, climbing through 19,000ft, when its No 3 engine failed and a fire broke out in the wing behind it. The drone was safely landed, the fire was extinguished and an estimate of 400 manhours was given to repair the damage. That same day, after taking 50 minutes to clear 44-83556 and its debris from the runway, QB-17 NULLO mission 104 took off from China Lake/Inyokern and faced one salvo of two Bird Dog missiles, scored as misses, before landing. The mission was ended because the available range time expired – an occupational hazard when there were many tests, finite ranges and unavoidable mishaps and delays.[265]

Down but not out, this QB-17 was belly-landed and saved for repair, probably at China Lake, during Bird Dog tests. *AFHRA*

14 June saw QB-17 drone 44-83589 make its last take-off from China Lake to support the Bird Dog effort. The first missile firing may have struck the right wingtip camera pod, which inadvertently jettisoned from the aircraft and was not immediately found. About three minutes later, the left camera pod detached from the drone – the cause of this was noted to be 'under investigation'. A second firing pass destroyed the QB-17. The Bird Dog appeared to be gaining in contact lethality, for on 25 June the airborne QB-17, possibly 44-83704, was hit. Fires erupted in the inboard engines (Nos 2 and 3) on either side of the fuselage and the stricken Flying Fortress plunged earthward in a vertical dive, exploding on contact with the desert.[266]

A 29 June flight from San Nicolas Island put a QB-17 in harm's way for an AAM-N-6 Sparrow III (the semi-active radar homing version of the weapon, as opposed to the radar beam-riding Sparrow I) test. One firing pass garnered a single missile from the launch aircraft. The Sparrow III hit the propeller of the drone's No 4 engine and also caused sheet metal damage to an oil cooler duct fairing and the right horizontal stabiliser. A safe NULLO landing on three engines was made back at San Nicolas Island. The drone was only expected to be out of service about a week.[267]

By mid-1955 the 3205th Drone Group planned on the phase-out of QB-17s as drones by 1 January 1958; reality would take the Flying Fortresses into 1959. In 1955, the USAF cancelled efforts to create a formation drone system based on QB-17s and DB-17s, citing the end of their service lives as a primary reason. The 3205th also embraced the future of purpose-built drones like the Q-2A Firebee, which was now entering service in increasing numbers. But QB-17s were still viable and finite resources in 1955. As an example of their continued importance, on 6 October that year a US Navy F6F-5K Hellcat drone lost control on the ground at Point Mugu and seriously damaged the aft fuselage of a QB-17 it collided with. The USAF went to the trouble of shipping a B-17 aft fuselage section from Eglin to Point Mugu, where a team from Norton rebuilt the damaged drone for future use.[268]

Sampling the sorties flown by QB-17 operators at Holloman in the last half of 1955, two missions (294 and 295) on 6 July saw the drone present a target for an F-102 carrying Falcon AAMs. One was fired and missed on the first mission, while fire control issues precluded the expending of any missiles during the second sortie of the day. Two QB-17 missions on 7 July served Talos at 26,800ft and Nike at 16,000ft. One of each type of missile was launched and scored as a miss.[269]

A US Navy Talos SAM approached a QB-17 in 1954, making lethal contact evident by a streak of smoke and flame captured on film by a long-range tracking camera. Squared wingtips are visible on the drone, indicative of the presence of scoring camera pods. *AFHRA*

After a number of QB-17 sorties at Holloman that either scored misses or were cut off early for technical problems, on 14 July mission 303 saw a drone climb up to 37,000ft where it was subjected to stern attacks, with a Falcon fired on each of two passes. One AAM severed about three feet off the bomber's vertical fin, while the second Falcon may have grazed the left wing of the QB-17. The clipped drone landed uneventfully at Holloman. The following day, a Falcon shot – the third of the mission – made a direct hit on the QB-17, which jettisoned its wingtip recording pods while raining debris on the range as the stricken drone fell to earth.[270]

It was a perfect storm of calamities on 8 September during mission 324 over the White Sands complex. A Nike SAM found a QB-17 at 19,000ft, with a direct hit in the radio compartment of the Flying Fortress severing all radio communications between the drone and its controllers. The chase fighter earned its pay that day, shooting down the rogue QB-17 over the safety of the range.[271] Another Flying Fortress met its end over White Sands on 23 September during mission 332 when a solitary Falcon fired by an F-89 Scorpion tore into the radio compartment and sent the bomber crashing out of control. On 5 December, mission 349 continued the destruction of ageing QB-17s as a Talos head-on attack brought down another Flying Fortress on the restricted range area.

Sometimes missiles left traces of encounters with the drones that were not identified until the QB-17 was back on the ramp, with mechanics inspecting it closely for telltale signs of contact. Such was the case with a 15 December flight in which a Nike was initially thought to be a miss until post-mission inspection revealed trace fragments in the right wing of what was believed to be a spotting charge carried by the SAM.

On Christmas Eve a bright red QB-17 flown by the 3225th Target Drone Squadron released 500 chocolate candy bars over Holloman as a treat for the children of families living on base.[272] Although not referenced in the historical summary of the flight, it should be expected that the man-rated QB-17 had an onboard crew that day.

Two months earlier, USAF reports started calling director Flying Fortresses DB-17P and drones QB-17L, instead of using the bomber's original as-built suffix letter 'G'. Two main variations of Flying Fortress drones ensued, both based on the B-17G airframe. The QB-17L transmitted information via television and the QB-17N used telemetry to send data.

A US Navy F6F-5K drone ran amok at Point Mugu on 6 October 1955, smashing the tail of a red QB-17 and damaging the Hellcat's left wingtip camera scoring pod, which can be seen here dangling uselessly from the port wing. The USAF shipped the aft fuselage of a Flying Fortress from stocks at Eglin to California and a crew from Norton AFB rebuilt the QB-17. *USAF*

During the course of 1955, the drone contingent at Holloman succeeded in getting a salient change made to the procedure employed by the armed chase fighter that was tasked with shooting down an errant drone if it could not be reliably controlled by any means. The original procedure called for the fighter to be airborne as the drone took off, but drone operators argued this low-altitude positioning for a shoot-down could 'spray fifty caliber bullets over the Wherry Housing Area, or one of the other areas on the base, then have the impact of the drone to contend with'. The amended procedure had the fighter pilot standing by on the radio during NULLO take-off.

Late in December 1955, a DB-17 crew spent time at Patrick AFB in support of expected XIM-99 BOMARC (Boeing Michigan Aeronautical Research Center) SAM activity to come.[273]

QB-17 wingtip camera pods

Douglas was no stranger to the B-17, having built about 3000 Flying Fortresses under contract during the Second World War. Later, when the USAF wanted accurate ways to quantify the performance of anti-aircraft missile shots, Douglas designed wingtip camera pods for QB-17 drones that could be bolted on in place of the standard rounded wingtips, and unbolted as needed for a return to stock tips. The pod wingtips shortened the B-17's wingspan from about 103ft 9in down to an even 102ft.

The Douglas apparatus was called Kinescore. Each pod housed four Bell and Howell 16mm Filmo motion picture cameras, aimed to provide good coverage of the likely approach and departure paths of missiles. An electronic time generator clocked when the action took place. Each camera's wide angle lens covered 142 degrees of arc. At any given time, two cameras were filming the missile when it neared the drone Flying Fortress. Photogrammetric analysis enabled precision measurements of the missile's path and nearness.

The cameras were modified to operate at 200 frames per second, which was considerably faster than a normal 16mm movie camera's rate of 24 frames. Each camera in the pod was supplied with 100ft of film (sometimes Kodachrome colour film), which was considered a sufficient quantity to activate for several missile passes. The pods had originally used Fastex cameras running at 1000 frames a second, but the 200 frame rate proved adequate and consumed far less film – a finite resource aboard an airborne drone.[274]

The camera lens was such that it left a portion of each frame available for simultaneous recording of time to within one millisecond accuracy. Neon lamps in the camera pod provided synchronised time images and another lamp indicated the instant of missile detonation based on ground instrumentation. Since many of the missile shots were deliberately made with dummy warheads, this timer was a crucial component in analysing the efficacy of each missile shot. Some dummy missiles were fitted with a small pyrotechnic that produced a puff of smoke at intended detonation time, and this was recorded on the film.[275]

Douglas used the Fletcher 145-gallon drop tank as a basis for the Kinescore camera pod, and built versions suitable for both QB-17s and QF-80s. In the event of a missile striking the QB-17, that impact would trigger explosive bolts to detach both wingtip pods for parachute-braked landings, hopefully far from the crash site of a stricken drone. The explosive bolts released a teardrop cylinder containing the cameras from the rest of the adapted wingtip structure. A parabrake slowed the camera pod's speed while a timer let it free fall for 15 seconds before its main parachute deployed.

The interchangeable wingtips on some QB-17 drones allowed for use of scoring camera pods to measure incoming missile effectiveness. *Author's collection*

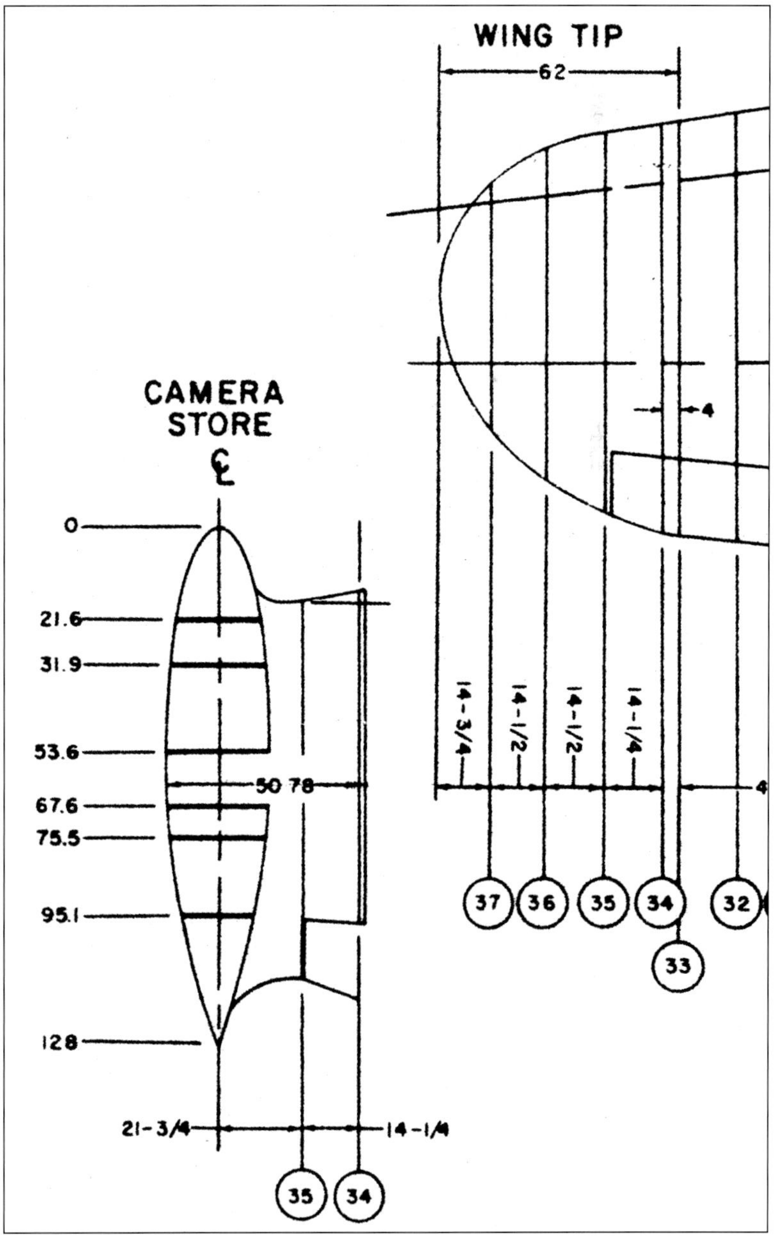

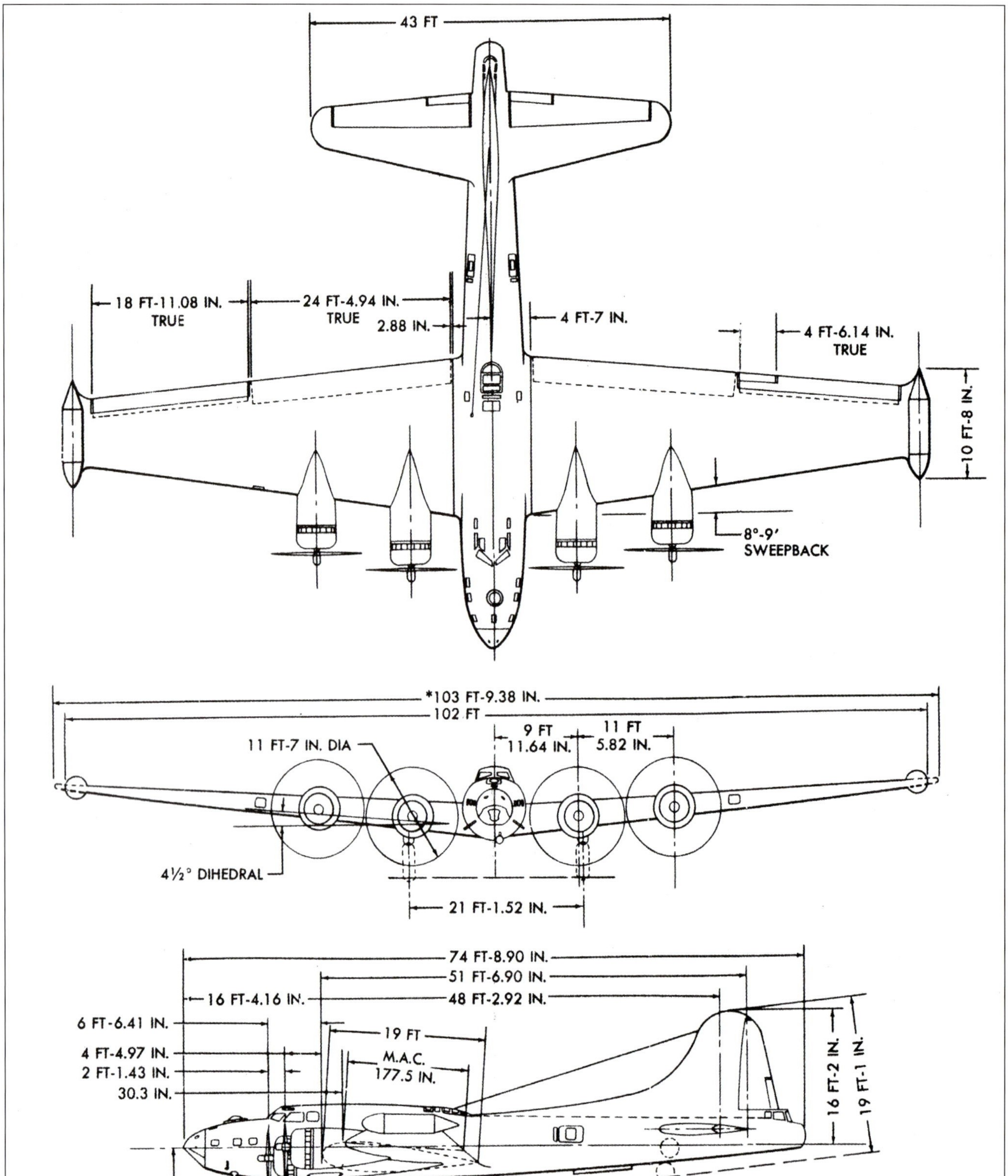

This three-view drawing of a QB-17 shows different wingspans for drones with camera pods. Wingtips on a stock Flying Fortress could be replaced by pods containing cameras – the pods had explosive bolts to allow them to detach in flight if needed. *Author's collection*

QB-17N 43-39508 was the final B-17G built by Boeing at its Seattle plant, the aircraft being rolled out on 9 April 1945. Converted into a drone post-war and issued to the 3205th Drone Group, it was lost while flying a sortie from Patrick on 21 October 1958.

There is a special poignancy in this view of bellied-in QB-17N 43-39508 when one realises that it was the last Flying Fortress built by Boeing in 1945, ending a ten-year construction run at Seattle. The aircraft was lost on 21 October 1958 in a flight from Patrick AFB. *AFHRA*

That deployment was another sequencing marvel of the day, as four more explosive bolts expelled the forward part of the pod and allowed the main parachute to extract while initially remaining reefed and not yet fully opened. This precluded abrupt deceleration for the equipment inside the pod, and tended to promote a more nearly vertical descent without drifting – something that could make it easier to locate the pod on the expanses of the test range. After a predetermined time had elapsed, the reefing line was cut and the parachute fully deployed.[276]

And the technology for saving the cameras and film did not end there. Deployment of the recovery parachute also tugged on lanyards that extracted two flotation bags from the pod and inflated them with CO_2, which could prove crucial for tests over the Pacific Ocean.[277] The usefulness of a flight test that destroyed a costly QB-17 drone could come down to the ability to preserve and recover the film in the wingtip pods.

The Kinescore pods were the brainstorm of Wolfgang Klemperer, an Austrian engineer who emigrated to the US in 1924. When the Kinescore drone camera pods were built, he was head of the applied physics section of Douglas' guided missiles division. [278]

BOMARC pounces on QB-17 from above

The BOMARC SAM had the ability to reach an altitude of 100,000ft, using rocket and ramjet propulsion to launch vertically on short notice. In testing circa 1957, a BOMARC XIM-99 (which became the CIM-10 in operational service) gave clues to its capabilities when it flew a 100-mile mission and was guided toward a QB-17, with the SAM flying at 60,000ft – an altitude more than the Flying Fortress could accommodate. In the literature of the era, mention is made of the BOMARC's ability to reach its target at Mach 2.5 on high, before diving for the final intercept. It successfully hit the distant QB-17.[279]

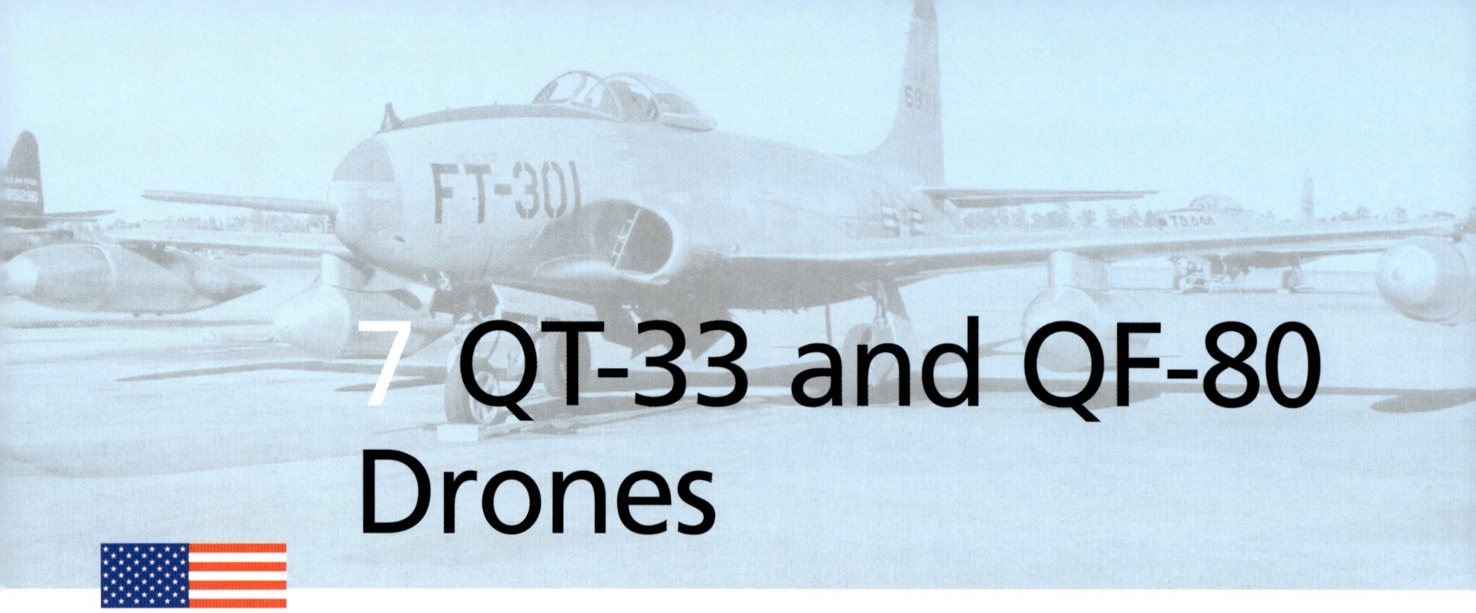

7 QT-33 and QF-80 Drones

The F-80 Shooting Star's nose gun bay, formerly home to six 0.50-calibre machine guns and hundreds of rounds of ammunition, lent itself to becoming an easy-to-service electronics compartment following droning. In 1948, civilian radio control engineer Richard W Hill from Wright-Patterson services the drone equipment in this early-conversion aircraft. *USAF/NARA*

The P-80 (F-80 from June 1948) Shooting Star and its two-seat trainer derivative the TF-80 (T-33 from May 1949) served the USAF well in a variety of roles. The Shooting Star was the first viable American jet fighter, with the XP-80 prototype having made its maiden flight on 8 January 1944. Although reaching USAAF units too late to see action in the Second World War, F-80s were heavily committed to combat from the very start of the Korean War in June 1950.

The lengthened T-33 trainer first flew on 22 March 1948, with more than 5600 examples subsequently being built by Lockheed in a production run that continued until 1959. Some 1715 single-seat F-80s also rolled out of the Lockheed Burbank plant in California between 1945 and 1950. Although the Shooting Star was soon considered obsolete as a fighter following the introduction of the swept-wing, transonic F-86 Sabre from 1949, its availability and reliability made the aircraft ideal for droning. In addition to serving as trainers, T-33s were ubiquitous throughout the USAF as utility jets. The aircraft's second seat made it useful as a DT-33 drone director, with the drone pilot in the back. Other examples became QT-33 drones.

Just as some pre-war US Navy biplane drones had been modified with tricycle landing gear for ease of remote operation, the USAF generally droned tricycle gear aircraft, with QB-17s being the salient tailwheeled exception. The nosewheel configuration of the F-80 and T-33 was found suitable for drone operation. As early as 1947, a drone P-80 was tested at Muroc before being returned to Wright Field. A further evaluation in 1952 pointed the way to more capable systems for QT-33s and DT-33s as the state-of-the-art of droning moved forward.

The first examples of the pioneering Lockheed jet had in fact been converted into drones the previous year when a batch of Shooting Stars were fitted with Sperry components and redesignated QF-80As. In 1952, and lasting in to 1954, the USAF used an evolved Sperry drone control system in Project *Bad Boy*, which saw the droning of more single-seat Shooting Stars for hazardous test and target use. The

Yellow paint adorned this director F-80 undergoing flight-testing with Air Materiel Command at Wright-Patterson AFB on 5 May 1948. ***USAF/NARA***

work was accomplished at the depot at McClellan AFB near Sacramento, California. The *Bad Boy* Shooting Stars were collectively labelled QF-80Es, regardless of which model they had been as fighters. A number of them went to Holloman, where they served as airborne targets for the development of the Falcon AAM.[280]

Bad Boy II was a major production effort at droning Shooting Stars, which would be redesignated as QF-80Fs. Improved radio guidance capability, the use of UHF instead of VHF command radio, telemetry, a built-in smoke system and the use of centreline-mounted rather than underslung wingtip fuel tanks made by Fletcher were all hallmarks of the QF-80F series. The wingtip tanks were compartmentalised to hold both fuel and scoring cameras. Possibly as many as 125 QF-80Fs were delivered from 1955 through to 1962.[281]

Something has caught the eye of the pilot of this drone director DT-33 as he straps into the cockpit of the aircraft on the Eglin ramp. *AFHRA*

DT-33/QT-33 crew qualifications

By 1951, with several real-world drone operations already completed, the 3200th Drone Group at Eglin had produced a training syllabus that outlined minimum requirements for director pilots and airborne radio control pilots in DT-33 director jets. Director pilots needed at least 50 hours of jet aircraft pilot time, and they were required to have at least five hours of ground training in basic remote control equipment operations and capabilities. Their syllabus at that time required 15 hours of training in remote control drone landing from a flying DT-33.

Air controller pilots who would fly in the back seat of a DT-33 to control either QT-33s or QB-17s received metal stick training in Flying Fortresses, operating the drone controls they would use in a DT-33 while aboard a QB-17. They also received metal stick training aboard a DT-33.

Ground-based radio control pilots for T-33s were required to have performed 100 ground-controlled QB-17 take-offs and landings, as well as being rated pilots with 25 hours of jet time. They would also receive metal stick training for take-offs, landings and go-arounds.[282] The requirements and specialties of USAF drone pilots in 1951 reflected its reliance on B-17 and F-80/T-33 aircraft.

Teapot QF-80s

For the 15 April 1955 *MET* shot of the Operation *Teapot* atomic tests at the Nevada Test Site, three QF-80s were subjected to airborne blast effects. The *Teapot* final report described the effort as follows:

> '[It] was planned to investigate the response of aircraft structures in flight to the blast effects from a nuclear explosion. In particular, it was desired to experimentally verify the inputs necessary to produce lethal damage to the aircraft and the responses of the aircraft to their destructive loads. Measurements were planned to secure structural behavior data in the post-buckling range to determine the phenomena and progression of structural failure. This would provide a check for theoretically calculating lethal volumes for aircraft.'[283]

Theoretical calculations predicted an overpressure gust load of 3.8PSI (pounds per square inch) would

The elevator and power control pilot carefully brings a QF-80 drone in to land at Eglin. The jet's progress is being closely watched by a handful of onlookers. *AFHRA*

be sufficient to cause structural damage to the aircraft in flight. Accordingly, planners figured a way to have the three QF-80s fly in locations where one would receive less overpressure at 2.8PSI, another would receive 3.8PSI and the third jet would receive 4.8PSI as a way of bracketing the predicted lethal load. The anticipated failure location was expected to be the jet's horizontal stabilisers. Cameras and sensors were aligned to capture deflections in the stabilisers, wings and vertical tail of the QF-80s.

'The drone aircraft were positioned at preassigned altitudes by airborne radio and ground radar control and were timed to arrive directly above ground zero at shock arrival', the report explained.[284]

The research sought to determine lethal airframe damage that would terminate flight, and disregarded radiation exposure since, as testers explained, a pilot might receive a lethal dose of radiation yet live long enough to complete a mission. For so many reasons, only drone aircraft could be involved in such research. The testers noted:

> 'The F-80 was selected as a test aircraft for Project 5.1, since it was the only available proven jet drone. An analysis was then made of the F-80 aircraft that indicated that the horizontal stabilizers were the critical structural components.'

Several F-80 horizontal stabilisers were subjected to laboratory failure testing to quantify the loads that could be expected to cause failure. With known data for the F-80, it was believed formulas could be derived to predict structural failure in other aircraft types.[285]

The test was arranged in an effort to create a nuclear shockwave at altitude in free air, without reflected shockwave issues. This was intended to provide meaningful data on the amount of shock required to destroy aircraft for anti-aircraft purposes. 'However', the test report explained, 'problems involving timing and coordination of delivery eliminated the possibility of using an air burst for this test, and a surface burst of adequate yield could not be used at the Nevada Test Site because of off-site fallout limitations. There remained the possibility of a low tower shot, which would be satisfactory only if the reflected wave merged with the incident wave to form a single-peak shock wave'. Each QF-80 drone was required to be directly above Air Zero at the time of shock arrival.[286]

Since the purpose of this test was to determine lethal mechanical destruction loads on aircraft, it was expected that some or maybe all three of the QF-80 drones would not be recoverable. Therefore, the report explained:

> 'It was necessary to provide a system through which the recorded data could be recovered, even though the aircraft were lost. This was done by means of a jettisoning system. All recording equipment was housed in two jettisonable pods under the wings and in the jettisonable cockpit canopy. The jettisoning system could be operated by remote control from the director aircraft and was arranged to effect automatic jettison in the event of either remote-control carrier failure or a primary power failure.'[287]

The elevator and power control pilot prepares to launch a QF-80 at Eglin in the first half of 1954. Out of view is a similar rudder control station to assist with the take-off. Behind the QF-80 is a manned DT-33 director aircraft that will assume control of the QF-80 on climb-out. *AFHRA*

The background research and testing that went into the whole concept for the *Teapot* blast test took time and cerebral fortitude in order to have any chance of producing meaningful results. Engineering savvy produced the special underwing pods for the QF-80s, plus the airframe-mounted sensors and cameras capable of quantifying nuclear blast effects on the jets in flight.

The project received four bare-bones QF-80s in March and May 1954. As described in the *Teapot* final report:

> 'Four QF-80 drone "shells" were delivered to the contractor's plant at Orlando, Florida, in March and May of 1954. These aircraft were modified and instrumented for participation in Project 5.1 of Operation TEAPOT. The instrumentation of the first drone was completed at Orlando on 19 October 1954 and the modified canopy and bomb pylon fairings were installed. It was immediately flight tested in Orlando to determine the effects of the modifications. The drone was then ferried to Eglin AFB and delivered to the 3215th Drone Squadron of the 3205th Drone Group who had been given charge of aircraft operation for the test program.
>
> 'On 20 and 21 October 1954 the 3215th Drone Squadron made further flights to determine the flight characteristics of the drones after the dummy pods were added. Considerable aileron buffet was experienced at high speeds with the dummy pods and fairings installed. By redistributing the weights in the pod to more closely duplicate the actual equipment weight distribution and by redesigning the pylon fairing, the buffeting was reduced to a negligible level. There were no adverse effects other than increased cockpit noise level from the modified cockpit canopies. The three remaining drones were delivered to the 3205th Drone Group by 2 December 1954.'[288]

The world of droning was entering an age where the actual modification and operation of aircraft as drones was understood and increasingly easy to accomplish. But the modification of bare-bones drones for specific scientific purposes was still a cut-and-try process of hand-made prototyping.

While at Eglin, tests of the QF-80s' instrumentation packages and dry runs of their mission were accomplished. Since the jets were slated to fly directly over the nuclear explosion, another modification was made while they were at Eglin. The lower surfaces of the QF-80s received a special coat of white paint that was highly reflective and heat resistant. Called High Altitude White PV-100, it was specially developed by the Vita-Var Corporation and carefully applied to a proper effective thickness.[289]

In February 1955, the QF-80 drones, support equipment and personnel took up residency at Indian Springs AFB, about 45 miles north-west of Nellis AFB in Nevada. Many sequences had to play out for the complex and expensive *Teapot* drone test to succeed. To ensure control of the QF-80s during the mission, two DT-33 director aircraft were assigned to each drone, providing redundancy. The DT-33s controlled the QF-80s until ground controllers using MSQ-1 radar assumed command of them and flew the drones over the blast site. Following blast exposure, the DT-33s again assumed

A 3205th Drone Group ground control team checks out control inputs before launching a QF-80 at Eglin in 1954. The rudder control pilot stands atop the truck, while the elevator and power control pilot is seated. Note the arrestor hook visible beneath the QF-80. *AFHRA*

The crew of the DT-33 in the foreground will control the QF-80 in the background after the ground control pilots effect its take-off. *AFHRA*

control of the (surviving) drones and flew them back to Indian Springs. The QF-80s also were assigned two chase aircraft to provide photographic coverage post-blast, and also to shoot the drones down should safety require this.[290]

On 22 March manned drone QF-80A 'Drone 301', which was assigned the No 3 position for the event, participated in *Teapot*'s *Bee* shot to determine the effects of a nuclear explosion on the propagation of telemetered signals and to serve as a general check on the drone instrumentation set-up. Testers were satisfied with the outcome. The subsequent *MET* shot had its share of drama as one drone crashed and another ran off the runway into the Nevada desert before becoming airborne. The test report chronicled the action:

> 'The primary test was scheduled for Shot 12 [*MET*], and preparations were made accordingly. In order to assure participation of the required three drones in the test mission, all four drones were completely prepared on D-1 day. At this time a complete inspection and functional checkout of the instrumentation and drone remote-control equipment was made. Cameras and recorder magazines were loaded as a final step of this checkout. Approximately two hours before takeoff time on D-day, another complete instrument check was begun. Airborne recorders were balanced for 1g flight loads on the basis of records from previous flights. Just before takeoff, the cockpit canopy and instrumentation pod jettisoning systems were armed.
>
> 'Since the telemetry ground station was located beyond a mountain range from the takeoff point, no reception of the signals could be made until a few minutes after takeoff. At this time receiver channels were rechecked for balances.
>
> 'Drone 1 made a successful takeoff but went out of control shortly thereafter and crashed. Drone 2 took off on schedule two minutes after Drone 1 and was followed by Drone 3, also on schedule. By this time the spare drone replacing Drone 1 was readied and started the takeoff run. Just before flying speed was attained the director flamed out on the runway. Drone control was transferred to the director for the original Drone 1, which was making a normal pickup approach behind the drone at an altitude of about 50 feet. The drone became airborne successfully, but not before it had veered off the runway, jumped a ditch, and traveled about 300 feet across the desert. The pods probably received severe bumps from protruding brush, rocks, or dirt during the run, since they were necessarily mounted low and the ground clearance was small.
>
> 'After takeoff, all drones were under complete control and entered the flight pattern satisfactorily.'[291]

The drones, one bearing scars from its desert excursion, made their way to the Frenchman's Flat area of the Nevada Test Site where the tower held the nuclear device. As the three QF-80s were navigated over the tower, a nuclear blast reckoned later to be 22 kilotons in strength sent its wave toward the underbellies of the drones. Despite the three QF-80s not being positioned correctly at the time of blast reception, testers nonetheless said they gained useful data from the effort.

Eglin-based DT-33 director aircraft at right will control the red-painted QF-80 after a groundcrew launches the drone. *AFHRA*

Due to the yield of the nuclear device being less than anticipated and the drones not being exactly over Air Zero when the tower-mounted weapon detonated, none of the three QF-80s was downed. All had some level of controllability as they departed the blast area, although airframe damage was evident.[292]

'Drone 1' (QF-80A 44-85311), farthest from the blast, had an actual slant range of 5386ft from the explosion and arrived overhead almost 300ft higher than planned. 'Drone 1' remained controllable, and hand-off from the DT-33 to a ground pilot for landing was normal. Touchdown looked good, but the QF-80 bounced several times back into the air until the jet collapsed its nose gear. The right main tyre blew, and the drone skewed off the right edge of the runway.

'Drone 1's' horizontal stabilisers showed only minor, non-fatal damage from blast flexing and the white paint had generally deflected heat. Its recorder pod and canopy were successfully jettisoned and recovered. Interestingly, the jet's telemetry pod departed the drone shortly after shock arrival, and testers speculated that this might have been due to weakened attachment fittings following the drone's overland desert excursion on take-off.[293]

'Drone 2' (QF-80A 44-85077) arrived overhead with a slant range of 4596ft from the blast, nearly 300ft farther away than planned, including 238ft higher. But this QF-80 was nonetheless closer to the blast than 'Drone 1', sustaining markedly more damage to its horizontal stabilisers and elevators as a result. When the DT-33 re-engaged 'Drone 2' after the blast, the QF-80 had dropped 150ft in altitude. Both wingtip fuel tanks were gone, and the horizontal stabilisers showed an unmistakable upward bend.

More than normal amounts of down elevator input were required to make 'Drone 2' descend, and the choice was made to land it on a dry lakebed emergency landing strip. Bouncing badly after touchdown, the drone veered to the right in a crash-landing that destroyed the special underwing instrumentation and camera pods. Some of the data from the latter was recoverable, however. Evidence of popped rivets from the blast deflection, and a hint of white paint blistering where it had become slightly dirty were other markers of this jet's closer proximity to the blast.[294]

'Drone 3' (QF-80A 45-8301) had a slant range of only 3885ft from Air Zero. The test report described this QF-80 as follows:

> 'Drone 3 also survived the blast but lost some altitude. When intercepted by the director [DT-33], both tip tanks were gone, the elevators, stabilizers and ailerons were damaged, and there was some heat damage evident on the drone lower surface. The horizontal stabilizers were seriously damaged.'

Efforts were made to land the damaged 'Drone 3' on Pork Chop Dry Lake, but altitude control had become difficult and the jet crashed. The underwing pods and the modified canopy were successfully jettisoned and retrieved. 'Drone 3' had the worst stabiliser bending, showed heat damage to the paint where other colours and shades had impinged on it, and bore evidence of structural tears due to blast effects.

The evaluation team provided an overview of the results of the test:

> 'In general, the drone damage was not as severe as was anticipated. Even though the horizontal stabilizers on Drone 3 were broken, and on Drone 2 were considerably damaged, the damage did not appear sufficient to be classed as destructive as applied to manned aircraft flight. Therefore, none of the drones were destroyed, and it is possible that all could have been flown to a successful mission, if not to a safe landing.
>
> 'This test did confirm the basic prediction that the blast effects were more severe than the thermal effects, and that blast was the critical factor. The horizontal stabilizers were proven to be critical structures, since they were the only components to receive significant damage. However, failure did not occur at the predicted station on the horizontal stabilizer. Failure actually occurred at Station 40-50, which was the secondary break station, and was thought to be less critical than Station 10-20, which was undamaged.

Two QF-80 drones and a DT-33A drone director await their participation in the Operation *Teapot* atomic tests at the Nevada Test Site in 1955. The aircraft in the foreground is QF-80A 45-8301, and it has been fitted with a single jettisonable pod housing flight recording equipment beneath each wing. Manned by a pilot, 45-8301 (flying as 'Drone 3') survived *Teapot*'s *Bee* shot on 22 March, only to fall victim to blast damage in an unmanned flight on 15 April during the *MET* shot. Data was recovered from the jettisoned underwing pods and the modified canopy, which also contained recording equipment. *National Nuclear Security Administration*

'The fact that the damage to the drones was less than anticipated can be attributed largely to the decreased gust velocities associated with the lower overpressure, for which there are several contributing factors. The bomb yield was lower than scheduled by about twenty percent, which would normally be expected to result in a decrease of overpressure of about twelve percent. The increase in slant range for Drones 1 and 2 would normally be expected to result in a decrease of overpressure of about ten percent. The increase in slant range for Drone 3 would be expected to result in a decrease in overpressure of less than five percent.

'It is therefore indicated that the total decrease in overpressure caused by these two factors would be about twenty percent for Drones 1 and 2 and about fifteen percent for Drone 3. These figures tally reasonably well with actual measured values.

'The fact that the stabilizers did not break in the predicted manner indicated that there is a considerable difference between response of the structure to a dynamic gust load of this type and to a static load as applied in the laboratory. This is also possibly a contributing factor to the drones not being damaged as much as predicted.

'It was evident that, in order to effect complete, immediate destruction of the aircraft in flight, considerably greater damage had to be sustained. In this test an attempt was made to destroy the aircraft by a bending moment failure of the stabilizers. Though the inputs obtained in Project 5.1 were less than planned, the primary structural members were broken and the stabilizers had considerable permanent set. However, the surfaces were still intact and were sufficient to provide stabilizing loads enabling the aircraft to continue straight-and-level flight. Tests made at MIT [Massachusetts Institute of Technology] with the recovered stabilizers revealed that even the most-severely damaged stabilizer was capable of carrying considerable load. It appears that it might be necessary to actually remove the lifting or control surfaces in order to guarantee immediate destruction of the aircraft.'[295]

Although no QF-80s were destroyed outright during the *Teapot* detonations, the hazards of the research conducted mandated the use of drones over the blast site.

Holloman Det 1 QF-80s

As Det 1 of the 3205th Drone Group sharpened its skills with QF-80s in addition to QB-17s at Holloman in the second half of 1952, the unit sustained two landing mishaps in November.[296] Although Shooting Stars would soon become available to weapons testers at White Sands, these incidents reveal that there were growing pains preceding this.

Det 1's first actual NULLO jet mission came on 26 November in support of the Nike programme. Two SAMs were fired, scoring near misses, after which the jet landed uneventfully. This was believed to be the first successful jet NULLO flown in the US – overseas nuclear tests had used NULLO jets on three missions, so the droning of such aircraft was still new.[297]

On 23 January 1953, EQT-33 jet trainer 49-927, with a drone letter 'Q' in its prefix, was being flown by an assistant engineering officer for the squadron at Holloman when its engine flamed out. The crash of the jet was severe enough to destroy it, although

Day-Glo orange QF-80 Shooting Stars sit on the Holloman ramp between missions. Buzz numbers on USAF drones sometimes had the drone-designator 'Q' added. *Gerald Balzer collection*

the pilot survived with only minor injuries. Six days later, a NULLO QF-80 served as the target for a Nike mission. One SAM missed, and before a second could be fired the QF-80 developed radar control issues and was safely landed. At that point, QF-80 Nullo missions were still far fewer than QB-17 sorties, although the jets made steady inroads in the first half of 1953 at both Holloman and Indian Springs. On 8 May, for example, two QF-80 sorties supported *Upshot–Knothole* from Indian Springs.[298]

It was not always about flying the drones. Sometimes it was about fixing them, like these QF-80 Shooting Stars in trouble at Holloman in the second half of 1952. *AFHRA*

This QF-80 at Eglin's Air Proving Ground in 1956 has had the letter Q added to its buzz number near the exhaust section of the fuselage. The single-seat Shooting Star fighter gave good service as a drone that could be ferried with a pilot aboard. *USAF/NARA*

Three months earlier, FEI camera pods had been installed on the wingtips of an RF-80 from the Wright Air Development Center (WADC) and test-flown with good results. The pods were then mounted to the wings of Holloman-based QF-80 45-8644, where they checked out properly in some aspects, but one of the pods, which also contained fuel, failed to feed. The pilot was forced to drop the unbalanced tank. In March, problems with carrier signal necessitated changes in the QF-80 antenna locations and styles. One of the squadron's QF-80s, accompanied by a DT-33, flew to WADC for proper mating and matching of antennas.

Mission ninety-eight on 17 July was a Nike QF-80 NULLO. The drone flew at 6000ft MSL (2000ft above ground level), which meant that a control Jeep, call sign 'Desert Inn', had to be located within the target area in case the below-the-mountains altitude of the QF-80 blocked other means of control. One Nike was fired and one miss scored.

When the director aircraft closed with the QF-80 after the firing pass, it was discovered that the drone's throttle had advanced to 100 per cent and would not respond to commands to lessen this setting. Altitude control remained locked on, so the director had no ability to descend the drone. Only navigational right or left turns could be made, so the QF-80 was orbited over a safe area in the desert while the director continued trying, unsuccessfully, to regain more control of the drone. Finally the Shooting Star ran out of fuel, stalled, and crash-landed on the desert floor in a rough belly landing that caused major damage. The electronic gear was salvageable, however.[299]

Mission 104 was a QF-80 Nike NULLO on 20 August, the jet operating at 30,000ft MSL. The one SAM fired was a miss. Mission 109 flown on 1 October again saw a QF-80 supporting a Nike, with the drone on station above 30,000ft. Two SAMs were launched, but the QF-80 survived undamaged.

Shooting Stars continued to enhance their usefulness in regimes not supportable by QB-17s, as on 1 July 1955 when a Falcon downed a QF-80 over the White Sands complex. Six days later, an unmanned Shooting Star flew at 40,000ft for one hour and forty-five minutes to support Sparrow I missile testing. The QF-80 was approached head-on by a US Navy Vought F7U Cutlass jet fighter with a closing speed estimated at 1020mph, its pilot firing two Sparrow Is that missed the drone. The latter then made a normal descent and landing.[300]

Mission 316 on 23 August 1955 pitted a QF-80 against a Falcon launch aircraft in several dry passes, followed by a launch run that sent a missile into the drone. The QF-80 crashed on the White Sands range. On 9 September a Falcon at 35,000ft severely damaged the left elevator of the QF-80 it was attacking. Despite its elevator being virtually useless, the drone was landed intact at Holloman – the first successful recovery of a damaged QF-80 at this site. In November, during mission 344, a Nike missile struck a QF-80 at 35,000ft, with the wreckage coming down on the White Sands range.[301]

A QF-80 meets a fiery end after being struck head-on by an XM3E1 Hawk SAM on 5 May 1958. This sequence of photographs was published in several DoD periodicals in 1959–60 to coincide with the introduction of the MIM-23 Hawk into service with both the US Army and the US Marine Corps. *US Navy*

8 Evolution of USAF Fighter Drones

The Cold War was a hectic time of military aeronautical developments that rapidly obsoleted recent aircraft types. The supersonic Century Series of jet fighters – aircraft with nomenclature starting at F-100 – were not immune to this fate, yielding several iterations of drones.

A development announced in 1955 sharpened the capabilities of drones and their operators. Sperry Gyroscope Company and the USAF's Air Research and Development Command began using radio and radar to keep the drone precisely under control for automatic take-offs and landings, as well as mid-mission manoeuvring. Should all signals be lost while the drone was in flight, after five seconds had elapsed an automatic pilot system on board the drone took control and set a power climbing turn to the left until a designated altitude was reached. At that time, altitude hold was engaged and the drone continued to orbit at 265mph until the signal was restored and the drone brought back to a landing.[302]

As the fielding of this new system shows, the 1950s were not just years of consuming surplus aircraft as drones in the same old way. Technology was improving, and being leveraged to make drone flight more precise.

QF-86E Sabres for the US Army

In the 1970s, the US Army forecast the need for full-scale drone aircraft to challenge several SAM and anti-aircraft gun projects. Some of these, like the FIM-92 Stinger, would have great success, while others would be shown in tests to be less than optimal for one reason or another. Flight Systems Incorporated (FSI) of Mojave, California, learned of US Army interest in a drone in 1973, and proposals

US Army QF-86E Sabre (formerly N74170) was sometimes nicknamed *Bessy*. Photographed at Holloman, this jet was said to have been shot down in 1980. *Mark Nankivil collection/Wayne Whited via Gerald Balzer*

Also part of the US Army's Sabre programme at the White Sands/Holloman Missile Range complex, this Sabre shows evidence of RCAF markings – the previous home of a number of the jets converted to drones for US Army missile tests. The white panel atop the jet's nose reflected the sun's heat away from electronics while the aircraft was parked on the desert ramp. *Mark Nankivil collection/Wayne Whited via Gerald Balzer*

and negotiations subsequently led to the company's creation of Sabre drones, designated QF-86Es, based on ex-Royal Canadian Air Force (RCAF) airframes built by Canadair. Some of the Sabres FSI acquired had previously received demilitarisation cuts in their wing structures that needed repair, which FSI accomplished at its Mojave facility.

The FSI rationale was to create an economical droning system for the Sabres that readily lent itself to keeping the QF-86Es man-rated for ferrying and low-risk test flying, but capable of being used as drones when required. The Sabres, to be flown from Holloman, would rely on the same ground control station as used in the QF-102/PQM-102 drone programme (detailed later in this chapter).

The FSI QF-86E soon proved itself to the US Army, and production of the drones was established at Mojave – the first delivery of operational QF-86Es from FSI was made in mid-1977.

For visual detection, the Sabres were fitted with a smoke tank in the right gun bay in the forward fuselage, with piping carrying oil to a spout that vented it into the exhaust trail. The smoke could be switched between a solid trail or a segmented puff. The QF-86Es were marked *US ARMY* and retained their Canadian serial numbers. It was estimated the FSI QF-86Es averaged about 25 flying hours in the drone programme before being shot down.[303]

The US Army employed QF-86Es as targets during testing of the Stinger, Roland II and MIM-104 Patriot SAMs and the M247 Sergeant York tank-mounted self-propelled anti-aircraft gun system. By late 1984, around 50 QF-86Es had been delivered to the US Army, which continued to use the drone Sabres until mid-1996. Some surviving aircraft that were not expended in tests made it into private hands for operation as warbirds.[304]

Simple US Army markings adorned this Sabre drone conversion at FSI at Mojave in January 1978. *Frederick A Johnsen*

QF-102/PQM-102

The F-102 Delta Dagger was a bold effort at making a supersonic delta wing jet interceptor in the early 1950s, with the original design by Convair having to undergo substantial reworking to achieve its aim. Although bested by newer designs and eventually put out to pasture by the USAF in the 1970s, stored F-102s had one last act to perform as supersonic drone targets. The end user was Aerospace Defense Command, which needed a high-altitude supersonic-capable afterburning droned surrogate for training its pilots over the Gulf of Mexico.

The Delta Daggers were picked for this programme because they were available and inexpensive, and had an afterburner signature desired by the user. Other aircraft were considered, and were possibly even better-suited for becoming surrogate MiG-21s, but the rows of F-102s at Davis-Monthan AFB's Military Aircraft and Storage Disposition Center (MASDC) made a powerful argument for their usage.[305]

Under Project *Pave Deuce* ('Deuce' was an affectionate nickname for the F-102 based on the word 'deuce' used to represent the numeral 2), Delta Daggers could operate as man-rated QF-102s that were capable of being ferried where needed, or non-man-rated PQM-102s that could be remotely launched, cruised and landed whilst participating in hazardous test sorties. The goal was to create a viable afterburning jet target capable of greater than Mach 1 straight-and-level flight, with 8g manoeuvring. Development and acceptance of the PQM-102 into the inventory as a drone system involved a detailed and exhaustive flight test programme.[306]

Starting with a contract in March 1973 followed by a programme directive that July, *Pave Deuce* included engineering development in Crestview, Florida, later that year. Engineering and flight test efforts were underway at Holloman from January through to 7 November 1974. From 8 November 1974 through to 31 January 1975, NULLO flights of droned Delta Daggers supported missile-firing missions as *Pave Deuce* matured.

Sperry Flight Systems of Phoenix, Arizona, developed the droned Delta Dagger. First, three F-102s were converted to basic QF-102 man-rated drone configuration. This allowed tests of the flight control stabilisation system (FCSS), visual augmentation smoke system and anti-skid brakes, among other features. Following development and benchmark flight testing at Holloman, the QF-102/PQM-102 was officially accepted as a target system on 1 April 1975.[307] However, the first PQM-102 to be shot down had actually fallen on 11 December 1974 during AIM-9L trials over the White Sands/Holloman Missile Range complex.

The Delta Dagger drone system consisted of two variants. As explained in the *Pave Deuce* final report:

> 'Once an F-102 is converted into a PQM-102 it becomes de-man-rated and is no longer used with a pilot unless it is re-man-rated for ferrying purposes. The QF-102 is a manned version of the PQM-102 and is used for captive presentations, crew training and system checkout. Both vehicles are modified to carry the following subsystems:
>
> Flight Control Stabilization System
>
> Airborne Command/Control and Telemetry System
>
> DIGIDOPS Scoring System
>
> Anti-Skid Brakes
>
> Smoke Visual Augmentation System
>
> Destruct System (PQM-102 only)
>
> Various Antennas (DIGIDOPS and Telemetry)'[308]

The *Pave Deuce* mobile ground station employed tracking radar with a maximum range of fifty nautical miles. If this system failed to track the drone, a back-up radar with a ten-mile range could be used. The mobile ground station was a large van fitted with a top-mounted work station for conducting drone Delta Dagger flight operations. The system also had a fixed ground station with a 200-mile range using AN/FPS-16 radar. The latter was also equipped to receive telemetry information during a test operation.[309]

The FCSS was contained in a pallet installed in a compartment behind the cockpit in man-rated QF-102s and mounted to the ejection seat rails in non-man-rated PQM-102s. By the time both variants had been developed, FCSS capability significantly enhanced the operation of droned Delta Daggers. The system's flight reference computer was the basis of the flight control computer. Aircraft sensors and an air data computer's inputs to the flight control computer included aircraft attitude, rate and normal acceleration parameters. The air data computer furnished barometric altitude, Mach number and calibrated airspeed. Programmers for low and high altitude could command that specific manoeuvres be performed by the drone F-102.[310]

The distant and grainy demise of a PQM-102 Delta Dagger is a spectacle that validates the effectiveness of the missile fired at it. *USAF*

The PQM-102's primary control system used electrical inputs for activating control surfaces, while the back-up system relied on mechanical inputs.

The mobile ground station carried redundant power generators in the event of a failed system. The non-man-rated PQM-102 was fitted with a pair of lead-acid 24-volt 36 amp-hour batteries that could provide enough power to allow recovery of the PQM-102 in the event of a complete AC and DC power failure aboard the drone. The stakes were high with these costly and limited-in-quantity jets, and power recovery options enhanced the likelihood of saving a drone to fly another day. In a further safety measure, the F-102's original wheel

This incredible sequence of photographs features the first interception of a PQM-102 drone following its conversion into a target in the *Pave Deuce* programme. The aircraft was hit by an AIM-9L fired from an F-4D Phantom II while flying over the White Sands/Holloman Missile Range complex on 11 December 1974. *USAF/Maj William A Turchick via Rob Turchick*

When able to be manned, as seen in this photograph, the Delta Dagger drone became a QF-102. When not pilotable from the cockpit, it would be a PQM-102. *USAF*

brakes were replaced with an anti-skid system and the hardware required to make it operate properly. The *Pave Deuce* report explained:

> 'In order to obtain satisfactory braking action on the PQM-102 aircraft, the basic F-102 brake system had to be modified. Additions included wheel speed transducers, solenoid shut-off valves, brake relay valves, a servo valve and a control box containing electronic circuitry.
>
> 'Braking action is accomplished by the initiation of the brakes-on command via the normal command system. The system applies the wheel brakes in a manner which slows the aircraft at a constant rate of deceleration while continually compensating for any erratic rates of deceleration (skids) after touchdown. Stopping distances utilizing this system are typically shorter than that obtained by manual braking action. While each wheel individually senses changes in deceleration rates, a composite command is sent to both brakes to provide proper braking.

PQM-102s on the ramp at Tyndall in September 1978 retained their serial numbers on their vertical fins, plus three-digit drone inventory numbers on their aft fuselage. Corrosion-control touch-up paint treated chronic weathering issues on the dorsal fuselage surface of some of the Delta Daggers. *Frederick A Johnsen*

Delta Daggers selected for the drone programme included a handful of two-seat TF-102s, readily visible by cockpit outline changes. The TF-102 at the right formerly served with the New Mexico ANG. ***Frederick A Johnsen***

> 'The system does not compensate for small variations in braking effectiveness of the individual brakes, and minor steering corrections (via command system) are required to maintain a constant heading.'[311]

To enhance visual acquisition of a drone Delta Dagger in flight, a smoke generation system was installed. The *Pave Deuce* report described this system as follows:

> 'The [smoke] generation system is installed in the QF/PQM-102A. The system consists of a 50-gallon oil storage tank, cradle assembly, hydraulic pump, shutoff valves, vent valves, check valves, drain valves, nozzle assemblies, associated plumbing and electrical system.'

The oil capacity for the smoke system in production PQM-102 aircraft was reduced to 28 gallons.[312]

The PQM-102 featured an aircraft destruct system that approached the problem of an otherwise unrecoverable Delta Dagger drone in two ways. Typically at altitudes of 1500ft or less, the drone's flight could be terminated by issuing a control command for a hard nose-down manoeuvre that would fly the jet abruptly into the ground. At higher altitudes, an explosive device was installed for PQM-102 destruction. This consisted of a Mk 48 explosive warhead. Its wiring system included a weight-on-wheels sensor that would only allow the explosive destruct command to proceed when the aircraft was not sitting on its landing gear, thus precluding a catastrophic accidental ground detonation.[313]

The Mk 48 warhead destruction device was tested in an F-102 airframe on the ground. The test proved conclusively that its warhead would sever the aircraft, causing termination of flight. Debris from the explosion was found as far as 235ft from the aircraft.[314]

A tattered-looking F-102 undergoes drone conversion at Litchfield Park in January 1980. ***Frederick A Johnsen***

A red-tailed former Wisconsin ANG F-102A faces a Pennsylvania ANG Delta Dagger at the Sperry Litchfield conversion facility in January 1980. *Frederick A Johnsen*

The PQM-102 was equipped with a commandable fail-safe system. When the fail-safe mode was on, the fast destruct timer (preset from one to thirty seconds) automatically activated in the event of loss of carrier (LOC) or loss of all DC or AC power. The drone Delta Dagger employed the ability to enter a safe orbit if uplink LOC occurred, as described in the *Pave Deuce* report:

> 'A preprogrammed climbout/orbit maneuver is initiated after 1.5 seconds in the event of uplink LOC. If the fail-safe mode is OFF, the orbit maneuver is continued until expiration of the 1 to 15 minute time (preset), at which time the target self-destructs. A ground abort program is initiated which shuts the aircraft down and inhibits the explosive destruct if the aircraft should experience LOC while on the ground.'[315]

Clearly, the PQM-102 effort yielded a sophisticated drone that had several options for recovery or destruction to maximise both utility and safety.

The Delta Dagger drone's command control/telemetry system gave the jet a 200-nautical-mile control distance under positive control from take-off to landing.

The three F-102s converted into QF-102 man-rated targets at Crestview to support the Sperry Flight Systems' development engineering, systems interface and initial flight performance goals were ferried by the contractor to the government test site at Holloman. One of the aircraft (FAD 601) was subsequently converted into a non-man-rated target at Holloman and flown successfully against AIM-9J and AIM-9L AAM firings during January 1975.

Five additional Delta Daggers were converted to PQM-102 targets at Crestview, and two of them

F-102A 56-0987, formerly of the Florida ANG, undergoing conversion to drone configuration at Sperry's facility in Arizona in January 1980. *Frederick A Johnsen*

were bought by the US Army for the Stinger SAM programme. All five PQM-102s were ferried to Holloman by the contractor for final re-configuration to pure PQM-102 targets. The developmental test programme ran into November 1974.

The first NULLO QF/PQM-102 flight took place on 13 August 1974 over the high desert ranges of New Mexico. The jet's control system was sophisticated enough to permit both automatic take-offs and runway aborts. Early testing showed the *Pave Deuce* drone system could not rely on pilot-supplied pitch trim changes, since a remote pilot lacked adequate cues to apply alterations in a timely manner. Automatic pitch trim in the FCSS was necessary.

A curious phenomenon early in the programme negated the effectiveness of the smoke visualisation system when the jet was in afterburner. As explained in the *Pave Deuce* report:

> 'The smoke system functioned very well at military power and below; however, the oil used to generate smoke would burn during afterburning operation, producing no smoke. Several modifications to the nozzle were tried but would not provide satisfactory results for both afterburner and non-afterburner operation.
>
> 'The system was modified by adding an afterburner nozzle assembly which received oil and mixed it with the engine bleed-air before spraying it into the afterburner exhaust stream. When the target was not operating in afterburner, the oil was directed to the primary nozzle. The nozzle was positioned to direct the oil stream to impinge on the engine exhaust gasses which produced the smoke trail.'[316]

Since the non-man-rated PQM-102 variants were subjected to extremely high manoeuvring G-loads (as high as 8g), the Ram Air Turbine (RAT) that provided emergency systems power on the F-102 in the event of other power system failures was prone to uncommanded deployment under high load factors. The fix was to remove the RAT and secure its door on PQM-102s.[317]

During the course of testing *Pave Deuce* aircraft over the White Sands/Holloman complex, the highest a drone flew was 56,870ft MSL and the lowest was 392ft above ground level. *Pave Deuce*'s intended top speed of Mach 1.35 at 35,000ft was not attained during the test programme, with the fastest speed recorded being Mach 1.3 in September 1974. The White Sands complex was a mixed blessing for the QF/PQM-102 test programme, as noted in the Pave Deuce report:

> 'The greatest appeal of the White Sands Missile Range was the accuracy of its optical data and the sophistication of its data acquisition system. Its shortcomings were its relatively small size (approximately 35 x 135 miles) and its complexity, both of which affected its ability to support flexible requirements of the PQM-102 Target System.'[318]

Holloman AFB, adjacent to the White Sands complex, had a long history of drone support. It featured a drone runway (Runway 21) separate from the base's main runway. For QF-102 missions, the chase aircraft took off on Runway 21, two minutes before drone launch, entered a closed pattern and called for drone launch about 30 seconds out, arriving abeam of the drone on take-off.[319]

A PQM-102 drone mission could involve two remote pilots in a ground station. One handled pitch and power chores, while the other concentrated on roll and yaw. Take-off could be

F-102A/PQM-102 56-1446 was downed by a missile over the Gulf of Mexico on a target drone flight on 17 March 1982. This photograph was taken during its conversion at the Sperry facility at Litchfield in January 1980. *Frederick A Johnsen*

fully automated, or the ground pilots could control the jet. Once airborne, the ground pilots navigated the PQM-102 to a radar-equipped range where another remote ground-based pilot took the drone through its mission before sending it back to the drone runway and control of the first two pilots.[320]

The three-year development and test programme for the *Pave Deuce* QF-102/PQM-102 target drone conversion yielded a remarkable supersonic afterburning jet that could sustain 8g manoeuvring. However, *Pave Deuce* was more than just the latest jet fighter drone conversion. It represented new thinking and technological applications that set the PQM-102 apart from earlier drone programmes.

Where typically a droned aircraft required airborne director aircraft such as T-33s to control it after take-off and before landing, the PQM-102 could be controlled entirely by operators on the ground, removing the need for costly director aircraft. The non-man-rated concept for the PQM-102 versions saved costs since items like the ejection seat did not need to be carried or maintained once the aircraft was redesignated. Similarly, systems like oxygen did not need to be serviced or maintained in the PQM-102. Testers said the non-man-rated PQM-102 could be overstressed without invoking the need for the same level of safety inspection required of manned aircraft, further saving money. Such savings would be impacted if the PQM-102 ever needed to be ferried to a different location, thereby demanding the costs and effort of re-man-rating it.[321]

Completion of the *Pave Deuce* test and evaluation programme at White Sands/Holloman was cause for the relocation of the jets and support equipment to Tyndall AFB, Florida, which would be the primary operational location for the Delta Dagger drones, in February 1975. This included QF-102/PQM-102 aircraft, support equipment and spares. Two PQM-102s needed to be re-man-rated for ferrying from New Mexico to Tyndall. Details on how this was done were included in the *Pave Deuce* report:

> 'To re-manrate the PQM-102 aircraft, the following general tasks were accomplished:
>
> (1) The FCSS pallet was removed.
>
> (2) Provisions for emergency and normal landing gear systems were installed.
>
> (3) The ram air turbine, control stick, seat and egress system, and flight and navigational instruments were reinstalled.
>
> (4) Miscellaneous drone peculiar hardware were secured and the cockpit cabin was sealed for pressurization.
>
> (5) Various affected aircraft systems were operationally checked in accordance with standard F-102 Technical Orders and an abbreviated functional check flight was completed on both PQM-102 aircraft.
>
> The above tasks required approximately 260 manhours per aircraft and were completed in 11 work days.'[322]

The final *Pave Deuce* test flights at White Sands on 31 January 1975 saw PQM-102 FAD 607 downed by an AIM-9L. That afternoon, FAD 601 was damaged by another AIM-9L and destroyed when controllers attempted to land the stricken PQM-102.[323] This rigorous debut of the Delta Dagger as a supersonic target drone system over White Sands subsequently led to years of use at Tyndall. The aircraft entered drone service typically in whatever paint and markings they had last carried as operational jet fighters before being placed in storage. High visibility orange panels were duly applied to make visual acquisition of the drones easier.

On 21 April 1977, a pair of PQM-102s flew in close formation at White Sands, presenting a target for a US Army Patriot missile test and proving their ability to fly in proximity to each other as drones.[324]

The last use of a PQM-102 was in 1986.[325] It has been said 153 Delta Daggers were taken out of storage at the MASDC for conversion to drones.

On 20 July 1982, F-102/PQM-102 56-1259, formerly of the Texas ANG, was shot down over the White Sands/Holloman complex. This photograph was taken during its conversion at the Sperry facility at Litchfield in January 1980. *Frederick A Johnsen*

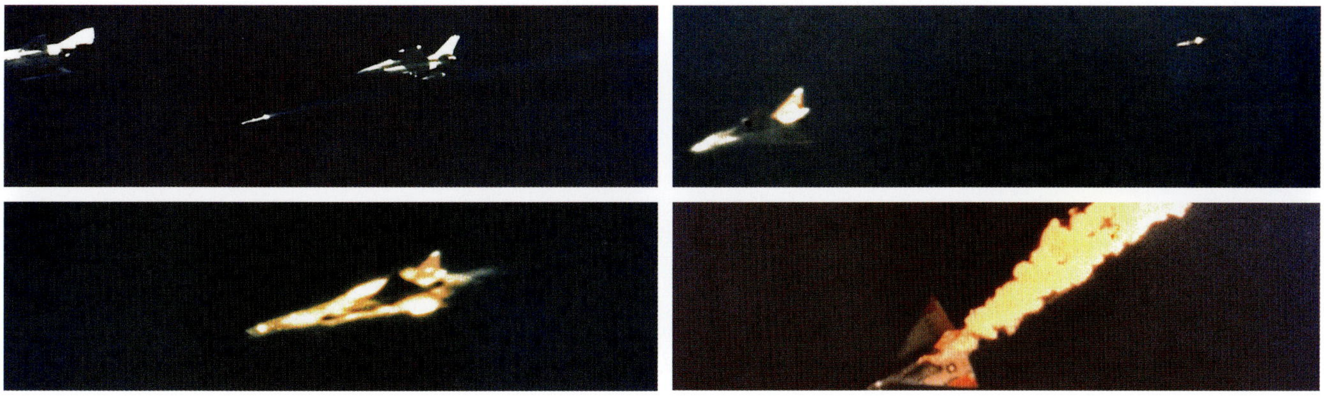

The reach of long-range tracking cameras catches the launch of an AIM-120 AMRAAM from an F-16 Fighting Falcon, and its ultimate destruction of a PQM-102 drone over White Sands in 1982. This marked the first successful kill by an AMRAAM in testing. *NARA*

The designation PQM-102B has been used to distinguish a number of Delta Daggers said to have low-level capabilities superior to earlier PQM-102s, and possibly the ability to be optionally piloted, according to some accounts.

QF-100 *Pave Hun*

The North American F-100 Super Sabre, unofficially embraced as the 'Hun' in an abbreviated use of 'Hundred', is acknowledged as being the first production fighter capable of achieving supersonic speed in level flight. The aircraft later earned plaudits for its role as a fighter-bomber in South East Asia. As F-100s were replaced with newer aircraft in the USAF, they found utility with a number of Air National Guard (ANG) units. Eventually, a large number of surviving Super Sabres were converted into QF-100 drones to supplant the PQM-102. If *Pave Deuce* was the programme name for droning the F-102, *Pave Hun* was a natural tag for the QF-100 effort.

The USAF identified about 325 F-100s in storage at Davis-Monthan for use in *Pave Hun*, intending to yield at least 300 flyable drones.[326] Ultimately, 312 Super Sabres are tallied as going into the drone programme.[327] The first YQF-100 flight at Tyndall AFB was made in January 1981, and Super Sabre drones served until 1998.[328] Some survivors of the QF-100 programme became static display aircraft.

A drone QF-100 emits smoke from a pipe feeding oil to a vent at the engine exhaust. *USAF*

F-100D 55-3610 from the Missouri ANG was an early conversion project at Sperry. The incomplete removal of Spraylat white protective coating left ghosting around the forward fuselage. This photograph was taken in January 1980. *Frederick A Johnsen*

QF-100D 56-3135 featured numerous blotchy paint touch-ups, including an orange star instead of US national insignia, while its painted-out canopy indicated that manned flights were over for the aircraft. This aircraft was converted into a drone by Sperry Flight Systems in 1987.

Acres of F-100s under a threatening sky at Davis-Monthan in January 1980 will yield hundreds of Super Sabres for drone conversion under project *Pave Hun. Frederick A Johnsen*

Controllers look through the smoky curtain generated by a a QF-100 drone about to take off at Tyndall during *William Tell 1984. USAF/NARA*

At a time in the development of the AIM-120 Advanced Medium-Range Air-to-Air Missile (AMRAAM) when congressional support was in question and the weapon was experiencing some production issues, the USAF pulled off a spectacular test on 4 May 1990 over the Gulf of Mexico ranges used by Eglin, employing four QF-100 drones against a single AMRAAM-armed McDonnell Douglas F-15 Eagle. The latter faced its quarry in a head-on, look-down, shoot-down scenario that challenged the abilities of the fighter and the missiles to lock on to their targets. The task was further complicated by the presence of electronic countermeasures (ECM) jamming aircraft intended to thwart the AMRAAM-armed F-15.

The Eagle was in level flight at 15,000ft and 0.9 Mach when the first two QF-100s presented themselves at 10,000ft and Mach 0.85, with a lateral displacement. The second pair of QF-100s approached at only 5000ft and Mach 0.85 – these aircraft also carried ECM jamming gear, and they were assisted by four other similarly equipped aircraft in the immediate vicinity.[329]

A QF-100 *Pave Hun* drone during fighter weapons meet exercise *William Tell 1986*. External plumbing for smoke oil is visible running along the upper side of the fuselage. *USAF/NARA*

Eighteen QF-100 drones line the ramp during *William Tell 1986*. Full-size aerial target programmes can benefit from economy of scale if large quantities of an aircraft type are available for droning. *USAF/NARA*

Drone operator Dick McKibben keeps a light touch on the control column as he operates a QF-100 drone at Tyndall during exercise *William Tell 1986*. The black panel at his fingertips is specifically labelled QF-100. *USAF/NARA*

QF-100D 55-3727 suffered damage to its port infrared wingtip pod possibly during a *William Tell 1986* live fire target drone flight. *USAF/NARA*

The F-15 successively fired its four AMRAAMs, all of which achieved kills. Three of the missiles, without warheads, struck the QF-100s and the fourth passed within an operationally lethal distance of its drone target. One of the QF-100s was unrecoverable and crashed in the Gulf of Mexico, and at least one of the others landed with damage severe enough to result in a collapsed left undercarriage leg and other tearing of sheet metal.[330] AMRAAM subsequently went on to achieve aerial victories in combat, its success being due in no small part to the availability of QF-100 target drones for realistic testing.

Riveted patches touched up with spray paint for corrosion control cover the 20mm cannon troughs on the underside of the nose of this QF-100. The aircraft was photographed idling on the drone runway at Tyndall prior to flying a *William Tell* mission in October 1988. *USAF/NARA*

Technicians ready QF-100Ds 56-3135 and 56-3307 at Tyndall AFB for *William Tell* flights on 5 October 1988. It looks like fresh and liberal spray applications of olive drab and orange high-visibility paint have obscured USAF insignia on both fuselages, resulting in them being replaced with orange stars. The Plexiglas canopies have been sprayed over as well, and the wingtips are capped with infrared pods. *USAF/NARA*

The damage to this QF-100D, while not fatal, was nonetheless spectacular, and put an end to its career as a target drone. The Planes of Fame Museum in Chino, California, has preserved the torn aircraft as it was received. *Frederick A Johnsen*

A QF-106A Delta Dart is readied for its final act as a drone.
Mark Nankivil collection via Gerald Balzer

QF-106 Delta Dart

The epitome of Convair's deep exploration of delta-wing jet fighters, the F-106 Delta Dart equipped USAF active duty and ANG units from 1959 until 1988. An all-weather interceptor, the F-106 was famous for setting speed records that exceeded 1500mph. For many years, F-106s stood alert as part of North American Aerospace Defense Command's commitment to block hostile bomber attacks on the continent.

Shortly after retiring from service as interceptors, Delta Darts emerged as QF-106 drones – 184 airframes were converted.[331] Used as Full Scale Aerial Target (FSAT) drones from 1990 to 1998, QF-106s flew from Holloman and Tyndall. The droning programme converted mostly F-106A single-seaters, although approximately 30 two-seat F-106Bs were also modified. Flight Systems undertook the initial QF-106 drone conversions at Mojave in a programme known as Pacer Six, with American Electronic Laboratories also modifying aircraft in East Alton, Illinois. Heat sources suspended on pylons beneath the wings of QF-106s aided testing of infrared seeking missiles.[332]

The last QF-106 was expended at Holloman in February 1997. By then, the aircraft had supported development of a number of missiles including the AIM-120 AMRAAM. Some drone QF-106s survived, including one used by the National Aeronautics and Space Administration (NASA) in towed tests at Edwards AFB in 1997–98.

This QF-106B shows the rudder paint scheme of the 49th Fighter Interceptor Squadron, a former user of the jet. Since droned jet fighters had to be expendable, money was not used on refinishing and painting the entire aircraft. Bright orange visibility panels overpainted existing paint and markings, which otherwise were left as-is. *Mark Nankivil collection via Gerald Balzer*

9 Remote Phantom Phlyers

The McDonnell Douglas F-4 Phantom II attained cult status as a fan favourite amongst aviation enthusiasts during its decades of service, including time spent equipping USAF, US Navy and US Marine Corps squadrons. The longevity of the Phantom II was such that in the 1970s, while new F-4s were still rolling off the production line in St Louis, Missouri, early US Navy Phantom IIs were being painted bright orange and flying as drone QF-4s at Point Mugu.

As early as 1974, US Navy documents show efforts at droning F-4B Phantom IIs. Four were converted by September of that year at NADC in Pennsylvania, with two more on the way. A contractor study commissioned at this time by the US Navy said the expense of keeping QF-4Bs man-rated would likely be less than the expected loss rate for purely non-man-rated versions of the aircraft, especially when the baseline overhead was figured for either variant. The lure of cheap drone conversions that were not man-rated was seductive, but hard to achieve. Test flights of piloted drones could reveal recoverable problems that would lead to the loss of a non-man-rated drone, the study posited, suggesting a piloted option was actually frugal.[333]

The *GREAT PUMPKIN* was one of two QF-4B man-rated drones on the line at Point Mugu in January 1978, joining a QF-86H and two DF-8 drone director aircraft. *Frederick A Johnsen*

The droning of F-4B Phantom IIs by the US Navy gave the service a Mach 2 full-scale adversary for missile development and proof testing. Ironically, as QF-4Bs entered the drone pool at the end of their service lives, new F-4 models were still under construction at McDonnell Douglas in St Louis. *Frederick A Johnsen*

A QF-4B Phantom II drone at Point Mugu in January 1978. *Frederick A Johnsen*

The discussion about creating non-man-rated US Navy QF-4s included the possibility of lifting them by helicopter between Point Mugu and San Nicolas Island, since at that time drone take-offs from Point Mugu were prohibited. But the US Navy's drone Phantom IIs were to be man-rated. *US Navy via NARA*

The US Navy continued to use QF-4s for a number of years, consuming later-model F-4Js (including examples that had been upgraded to F-4S standard) and F-4Ns, which were upgraded F-4Bs.

The USAF's 309th Aerospace Maintenance and Regeneration Group (AMARG), the current organisation responsible for the thousands of military aircraft stored at Davis-Monthan, listed 318 F-4 Phantom IIs regenerated from that boneyard for service as drone FSATs.[334]

Like US Navy Phantom IIs, the USAF's QF-4s were also man-rated, and flew as unoccupied drones when mission danger dictated. As with other drone systems, an explosive destruct device would be installed to down an errant unmanned QF-4 before it could possibly reach a populated area. USAF QF-4s superseded QF-106s, with initial Phantom II operational status being attained in 1997. The QF-4 could achieve Mach 2 (1600mph) and had a ceiling listed at 60,000ft. The USAF described QF-4 operations as follows:

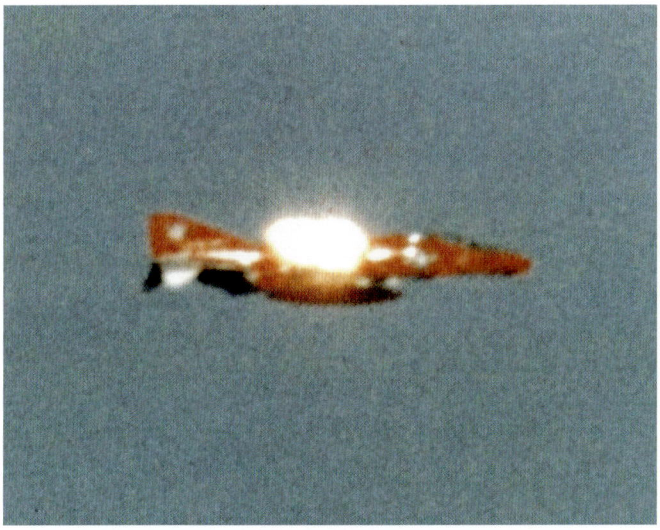

An AIM-9 Sidewinder hits a QF-4B mid-fuselage on 31 January 1974 during a live-fire mission from the US Naval Missile Center at Point Mugu. *US Navy*

The destruction of this US Navy QF-4B drone was accomplished by an AIM-54 Phoenix missile in 1983. *US Navy*

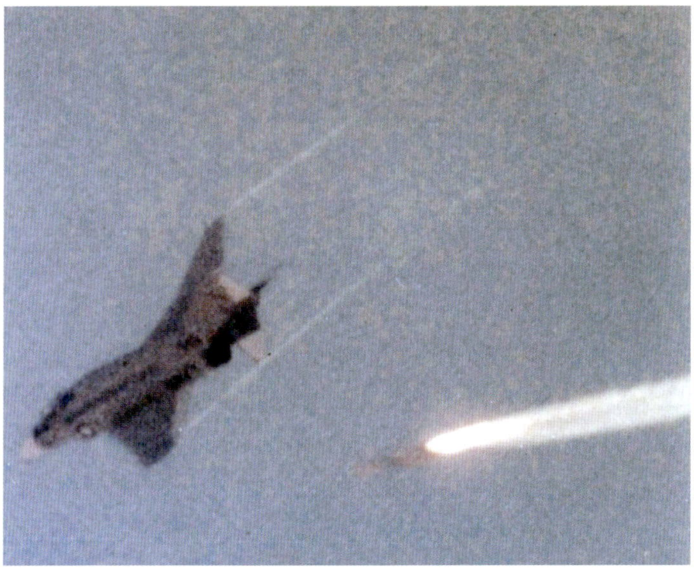

A QF-4E manoeuvres in the near-vertical aspect, revealing its high-visibility drone markings on the tail, wings and horizontal stabilisers during a training mission from Tyndall on 18 November 2008. *USAF*

Crewed by a solitary pilot, a QF-4E returns to Tyndall following a training mission. The Florida base's dual runways can be seen in the background. *USAF*

> 'The QF-4 is equipped to carry electronic and infrared countermeasures to fully evaluate fighters and weapons flown and fired against it. Full-scale aircraft can be flown totally by computer, or controlled manually during takeoff and landing using a mobile control station located at the runway. As a safety precaution, a chase plane trails the QF-4 during critical periods of flight.'[335]

The precautions taken with drones such as the QF-4 – flying them over sparsely populated areas and installing destruct mechanisms in them – were observed for a good reason, as the following anecdotal examples illustrate.

On 7 February 2001, USAF QF-4G 69-0237 crashed shortly after take-off from Tyndall. As a take-off crash, the drone Phantom II was full of fuel that fed an intense fire. No injuries were reported.[336] In September 2004, a QF-4E over the White Sands/Holloman Missile Range complex failed to respond to commands from its controller. The drone Phantom II exceeded its flight limits and stalled. Neither the QF-4E's autopilot nor inputs from the controller could regain normal flight, so the out-of-control jet was intentionally destroyed over the range. The Phantom II's destruction was valued at $1.5 million.[337]

Twelve QF-4 drones line the ramp at Holloman – the storied host of so many classic USAF drones since Nike SAMs challenged QB-17s of the early 1950s. When this photograph was taken in the summer of 2012, these legacy aircraft still had several years left to winnow their ranks before the final Holloman QF-4 launch in December 2016. *USAF*

Above: Civilian contractors prepare a QF-4E for take-off on the drone runway at Tyndall on 12 May 2015. Later that day, the NOLO Phantom II was used as a full-scale target for a pilot from the New Jersey ANG's 177th Fighter Wing (FW) participating in Exercise *Combat Archer* – the air-to-air component of the 53rd Wing's weapons system evaluation programme. *USAF*

Left: Ground controller Lt Col Thomas Mudge (Ret) remotely pilots a QF-4 during a *Combat Archer* mission on 12 May 2015. *USAF*

On 10 August 2006, a QF-4E had just lifted off when it went out of control near the western end of Holloman runways 22 and 25, impacting the desert and issuing a rising pyre of black smoke visible for miles. Up to its departure and crash, this QF-4E was under control of a ground pilot within the White Sands Missile Range complex. Unsure if the Phantom II's onboard destructive explosive charge had detonated in the crash, clean-up crews were forced to wait 24 hours before approaching the wreckage.

By the last half of 2005, it was apparent to Department of Defense (DoD) planners that the only current FSAT, the QF-4, had finite numbers and would require replacement. A report on the issue noted, 'The use of drone versions of the F-4 aircraft as our single full-sized airplane target will end in the foreseeable future as we run out of usable platforms. A replacement vehicle is needed'.[338]

The DoD study included an eloquent explanation of the need for FSAT drones, because missile targeting systems responded differently to full-size aircraft than they did to sub-scale drones:

> 'Full-scale targets are a necessary part of our test target inventory, because certain aspects of an engagement by a missile depend on geometric and signature details that can be captured only by a large airframe. One example of this is related to the final guiding and fuzing of a radar-guided missile where glints from overlapping returns from different areas of an extended target will affect the performance of the missile differently from that associated with a small, compact target. In general, miss distance will increase towards the end of the engagement, particularly for today's high performance missiles that employ fast response times.
>
> 'Another example is the lethality of the missile: how effective is the blast pressure, the warhead fragments (along their relative velocity vectors to various locations along the extended target) and the missile body contact, if achieved, in bringing down the target. While static tests against replica vehicles can play a partial role in examining the combination of missile warhead effectiveness and target vulnerability, it is not until all elements of the missile are brought together – warhead, fuze, closing velocity and end-game geometry – and tested against full size targets that we gain the necessary confidence. This is particularly true today as we go to smaller and smaller warheads and depend increasingly on direct hits or lethality enhancers.[339]
>
> 'We are projected to run out of the inventory of our single full-scale target, the QF-4, a drone version of the F-4 aircraft, about 2011. A decision on a replacement aircraft is needed soon to avoid a gap in full-scale target availability. The Task Force recommends the development of a drone version of the F-16 aircraft because it can provide a substantial supply of surplus aircraft for many years to come. A competing view is to try to continue with F-4 aircraft even though the F-4 variants now available will be increasingly costly to modify into drone vehicles.'

In 2005, the DoD estimated how long the QF-4 would be available based on drone conversion and consumption. 'The available inventory of QF-4 targets will be depleted by about 2011 at the current usage rate of 25 per year and the current production rate of about 20 per year.' The DoD study acknowledged the presence of foreign F-4s as potential drones after consumption of the US airframes. 'Apparently there are many F-4 variants in existence around the world but these variants would generally be more expensive to modify. The "good" F-4s are quickly being used up.'[340]

The QF-4 outlived the 2005 predictions. BAE Systems still had USAF QF-4 deliveries on the books into 2013, and delivered the 300th QF-4 to the service the previous year. BAE Systems rolled

A contractor maintainer directs an unmanned QF-4C down the drone runway for take-off on 12 May 2015 at Tyndall. This Phantom II was used as a full-scale target by the 82nd ATRS and was shot down by an F-16 pilot from the 177th FW during *Combat Archer*. *USAF*

A QF-4E performs the 82nd ATRS's last Phantom II NOLO take off, in afterburner, from Tyndall on 27 May 2015. This marked the end of almost 20 years of Phantom II drone operations from the Florida base. *USAF*

Phantom IIs into and out of a 123,000 square foot hangar at Mojave, in California, where around 100 employees with varying technical specialties labored over each airframe for about six months to refurbish and convert it for drone use.[341]

In actuality, the last QF-4 mission at Tyndall came on 27 May 2015, when two drones took off at around 1015hrs and were despatched about thirty minutes later by F-15s firing AIM-120s and AIM-9s. QF-4s remained in service in New Mexico for a further eighteen months, with the last USAF Phantom II flight at Holloman being a ceremonial stand-down on 21 December 2016, when four manned QF-4s flew both subsonically and supersonically for an appreciative crowd. These aircraft were expected to be consumed on the nearby White Sands ranges as ground targets since museums had access to plenty of unmodified F-4s for display purposes.[342]

The last active-duty USAF pilot to fly the F-4 Phantom II, Lt Col Ron 'Elvis' King (right), commander of the 82nd ATRS's Det 1, talks with former QF-4 pilot Maj (Ret) Eric 'Rock' Vold (centre) and QF-4 pilot/controller Lt Col (Ret) Jim 'WAM' Harkins after they completed the squadron's final military flight with the jet at Holloman on 21 December 2016. Lt Col King flew QF-4E 74-1638, parked behind them, as the lead aircraft in the four-ship Phantom II farewell formation. *USAF*

10 US Navy Jet Drones

QF-9

Grumman and the US Navy embraced the same basic aircraft designation – F9F – for the straight-wing Panther and the later, closely related, swept-wing Cougar. The Panther proved its merit in heavy use throughout the Korean War, where it was the main jet type flown from carriers by US Navy units and ashore by the US Marine Corps. As they were replaced by faster, more modern fighters from the mid-1950s, some F9F-5s were ripe for conversion to drone status. The US Navy's pre-1962 nomenclature rationale used the letter 'K' to designate drone aircraft, and suitably modified Panthers were initially called F9F-5Ks. Surviving Panther drones in 1962 became QF-9Ds following the introduction of the Tri-Service aircraft designation system on 18 September 1962. Director aircraft for the Panther drones were drawn from F9F-5 stock and were designated F9F-5KDs in the old system, before becoming DF-9Es from 1962.

Similarly, swept-wing Cougars commenced US Navy drone operations as they departed regular unit service. The F9F-6K became the QF-9F in 1962, with the improved F9F-6K2 being redesignated the QF-9G. The F9F-6PD was a drone director Cougar that had been a photo-reconnaissance variant in frontline service. It became the DF-9F in 1962. F9F-6Ds were directors modified from F9F-6 fighters, the first model of the swept-wing Cougar. They, too, became DF-9Fs in 1962.

QF-9 drone formation

In November 1964, the US Navy at Point Mugu marked a first when a pair of QF-9G Cougars inaugurated two-aircraft drone formations to enhance the anti-aircraft problem presented to ships at sea. With ground controllers using television to help them guide the two QF-9s, the drones made a run at the sea test range near San Nicolas Island. In the terminology of the day, the QF-9 drones were identified as Master and Slave. Using the televised view from a pod carried beneath the wing of the Master drone, air and ground controllers worked together to place the Slave QF-9 in proximity to the Master.[343]

The F9F-6K Cougar drone, an example of which is seen here in June 1958, stepped up the performance envelope over earlier US Navy drones. *AFFTC/HO*

The last bit of attention to ensure that a Cougar drone had a straight send-off was the manipulation of the nosewheel on the runway. *US Navy*

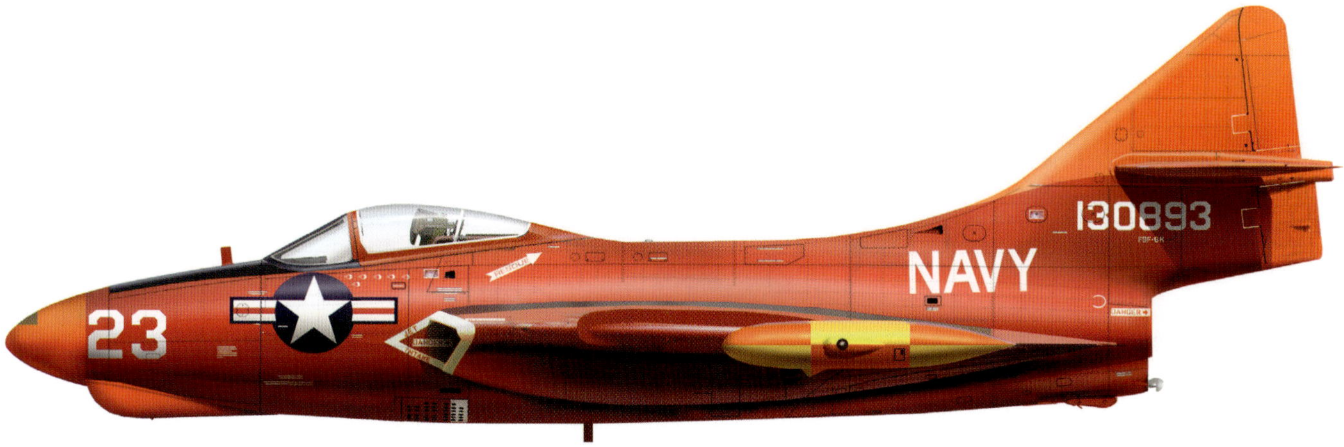

F9F-6K Cougar BuNo 130893 drone was converted into a target in 1958. Fitted with wingtip camera scoring pods, the aircraft also featured six mission markings beneath the cockpit.

The television signal from the Master QF-9 was received on San Nicolas Island and relayed with the help of microwave technology to Laguna Peak, near Point Mugu. From there the signal was picked up by Lt Sam Doran, operating the Slave drone.[344]

Four years later, in another first for the US Navy, a QF-9J became the first single-seat jet fighter drone to be fitted with a fixed forward-looking video camera. Its installation proved to be hugely beneficial for the ground-based drone pilot, enhancing his situational awareness especially during take-off and landing. The camera enabled a single pilot to handle all aspects of the mission, instead of handing off between airborne and ground-based remote pilots.[345] This was a breakthrough moment in American droning operations, and such cameras would be widely employed on programmes like the US Navy's extensive use of F-86s as targets.

QF-9G drone's longevity

The US Navy maintained target drone operations from Naval Station Roosevelt Roads in Puerto Rico for fleet anti-aircraft defence training. Utility squadron VU-8 flew QF-9G drones in the early 1960s, when average life expectancy of the targets at Roosevelt Roads was pegged at just two low-altitude missions. However, one of the Cougars, identified simply as 'No 65', racked up 17 successful missions that earned it coverage in the March 1964 issue of monthly periodical *Naval Aviation News.*

An F9F-6K Cougar drone with orange over red high-visibility paint and wingtip camera scoring pods. *Bill Swisher via Gerald Balzer collection*

Middle: F9F-6K2 Cougar drones at Point Mugu on 22 April 1961.
Bill Swisher via Gerald Balzer collection

Right: An F9F-6K2 Cougar drone in fresh Day-Glo orange paint that would soon fade to patchy shades in the sun at Point Mugu in April 1961. *Clay Jansson via Gerald Balzer collection*

Scratched shiny red paint suggests a Cougar drone well used. This F9F-8K was photographed at Point Mugu in April 1961. *Clay Jansson via Gerald Balzer collection*

The ships targeting Cougar drones as part of their training were expected to aim for near misses to prolong the useful lives of the QF-9s. However, hits were inevitable, hence the rationale for using drones to undertake such missions. On seven of its flights, 'No 65' was targeted by Terrier SAMs while the jet was at an altitude of only 50ft, or lower, above the wave tops. As the QF-9G racked up sortie after sortie, the squadron painted its nose white, onto which 17 drone mission symbols were added. The aircraft's final fate remains unrecorded.[346]

This 'ferocious' Cougar drone featured multiple mission symbols that attested to its longevity. It was photographed in March 1967. *Clay Jansson via Gerald Balzer collection*

In January 1973, this orange QF-9J was photographed at Point Mugu. A number of US Navy drone paint schemes added a white border around the national star insignia. *Dave Stern via Gerald Balzer collection*

One of the US Navy's DF-1C Fury drone director jets operated by Utility Squadron VU-8 at Naval Station Roosevelt Roads in 1963 shepherds a QF-9G drone until control of the aircraft was assumed by personnel aboard the ship that would fire upon the Cougar. At that point, the Fury director would loiter at a safe distance, ready to resume control of the Cougar if the drone survived the live-fire sortie. *National Naval Aviation Museum*

Fury directors

A series of carrier-based US Navy jet fighters in the 1950s paralleled USAF F-86s, but with design changes intended to make the naval variants more suited to carrier operations. These similar-but-different fighters developed by North American were given the name Fury and the letter identifier FJ, with subsequent numbers identifying models. FJ-3 Furies included the modified FJ-3D that operated as a director aircraft for the SSM-N-8 Regulus cruise missile and the closely related KDU-1 target drone. Post-1962, the Fury directors were designated DF-1Cs. FJ-3D2 drone directors were set up to handle F9F Cougar drones. After 1962, these directors were known as DF-1Ds.

A US Navy QF-86H drone with a safety pilot aboard negotiates the pattern above Point Mugu in the company of a PMTC DF-8 Crusader director aircraft in January 1978. *Frederick A Johnsen*

F8U Crusader variants

The Vought F8U Crusader was the US Navy's first supersonic fighter that served on board fleet carriers from 1957 through to 1976, and with other units undertaking various support missions after that. Redesignated F-8 in 1962, some F8U-1KU drones, later QF-8As, became targets. The F8U-1D, later DF-8A, was also a director for the Regulus missile as well as for QF-9 Cougar targets. Some of these were used to support operations in the Atlantic Fleet Missile Range, flying from Roosevelt Roads. More retired F-8As became DF-8F drone directors, and could be found at places like China Lake and Point Mugu into the late 1970s.

QT-33A

As the US Navy 'consumed' its QF-9 jet drones, remotely-piloted T-33s became one replacement option from the late 1960s until surplus foreign and USAF QF-86s and recently retired QF-4s were eventually made available.

By the end of 1971, the US Navy tallied twenty-three QT-33As in its inventory. Eighteen of these were at Point Mugu and China Lake, with the remaining five listed as being at Pensacola. Another batch of eighteen, designated QT-33AXs, consisted of jets held in storage at the MASDC at Davis-Monthan. By the end of July 1976, thirteen QT-33As were listed at Point Mugu and two at China Lake. By then, sixteen former ANG F-86Hs, now designated QF-86Hs, were also at Point Mugu and China Lake. The QT-33A inventory had dwindled to just three jets at Point Mugu by 31 July 1980. The common colour for US Navy QT-33As of this era was overall orange for visibility.

Versions of the QT-33A jet trainer drone served a number of US Navy test programmes. Three examples, along with a similar number of Firebee drones, were mustered on 21 November 1973 to present six aerial targets in a test of a Grumman F-14 Tomcat armed with six AIM-54 Phoenix AAMs. The fighter, assigned to the Pacific Missile Test Center, was flown from Point Mugu by Cdr John R 'Smoke' Wilson Jr, backed up by Radar Intercept Officer Lt Cdr Jack Hawver.

A bustling ramp at Point Mugu in January 1978 features US Navy drones including a QT-33 in the foreground as a former USAF/ANG QF-86H taxies for a manned sortie, passing a DF-8 Crusader director aircraft.
Frederick A Johnsen

| A Crusader performs an engine run on the ramp at Point Mugu surrounded by drones in January 1978. *Frederick A Johnsen*

The radar-guided, long-range Phoenix had an unusual intercept profile, rising high above and ahead of the launching F-14 and then using ballistic flight at the end of its rocket burn if required. Some variants of the Phoenix boasted a then-unrivalled range of more than 100 miles. Hawver and Wilson launched the six missiles over a span of thirty-eight seconds, and the F-14's sophisticated AWG-9 radar and associated fire control system allowed the fighter to direct all six AAMs simultaneously to six designated targets. As the missiles got to within ten miles of their target, each weapon relied on their individual onboard radars for final guidance.

That day over the Pacific Ocean, two of the QT-33A drones took direct hits, as did two of the Firebees. The third QT-33 escaped owing to a radar problem with the F-14, while the AIM-54 fired at the third Firebee missed. The ability to send aloft a gaggle of six drone target jets of two different types characterised the assets available to AAM testers in the US by the early 1970s.

At the Naval Weapons Center (formerly NOTS) at China Lake, technicians developed a cleverly simple method for disabling US Navy QT-33s and forcing them down if their flight became errant. The mechanism consisted of an explosive charge fitted to a replacement cap for the filler opening in the aircraft's left and right inboard wing fuel cells. Electronics in the aft cockpit of the QT-33A could set the explosive charges to arm or safe. A command to activate the devices would reach detonating cord attached to the explosives.[347]

True to the nature of China Lake's role in understanding the destructive properties of ordnance, the specialised explosive fuel cell caps were devised to focus the effects of the blast. As described in a US Navy report, 'Metal anvils at each end of the charge direct the explosive energy wavefront laterally within the wing to destroy the spar structure with a minimum of explosives'.[348]

As previously noted, testers faced issues with creating usable smoke trails for visual acquisition by airborne and ground observers of drones like the QT-33A in flight. A 1969–70 development by China Lake came up with two answers, as described in this report:

This QT-33 at Point Mugu in January 1978 had a functional front seat for piloted flights. The rear ejection seat was removed and additional gear placed in that area. *Frederick A Johnsen*

'One system uses JP-4 from the aircraft's fuel supply. Another, with a 35-gallon supply tank, uses a mixture of petroleum white mineral oil and JP-5. Both systems eject fluid through a nozzle into the engine exhaust area to produce a smoke trail. Piloted flight tests showed that the JP-4 system generates a usable smoke trail only at altitudes where the temperature is -20°C or colder (about 18,000ft and above). Ground and unmanned flight tests showed that the tank system, filled with five parts mineral oil and one part JP-5, generates usable smoke trails from ground level to at least 28,000ft MSL.'[349]

Camera pod action

With the increasing speeds of drones, and the missiles fired at them, cameras aboard the target aircraft were vital to record the approach of the weapons in order to verify their proximity. Some missile shots were deliberately offset in tracking to preserve the finite number of drones for multiple missions. Furthermore, with both SAM and AAM warheads in the real world proximity-fused, a close miss perfectly simulated the correct flightpath for such weapons. So understanding just how close a missile with a dummy warhead came to a drone could provide useful information about the weapon's ultimate lethality.

Iterations of drone scoring and measurement devices paced the evolution of drones as research and test targets. By 1957, the well-known motion picture camera manufacturer Bell & Howell had been issued with a contract by the US Navy to produce cigar-shaped missile scoring pods with occasional protrusions that gave onboard cameras a specific angle of view. Not quite six feet long, the pod was eleven inches in diameter and weighed ninety-five pounds. They were designed to be mounted to the wingtips of drones to give their cameras a view of the approaching missile. Each pod contained four high-speed 16mm motion picture cameras with 200ft film magazines to provide wide coverage.[350]

This pod replaced an earlier design that carried cameras with only 50ft film magazines. Testers considered 50ft of film in a high-speed camera sufficient for one missile pass. With the 200ft film capacity of each of the 16mm cameras, the new pod could conceivably record four missile shots against the same drone in one flight, thus saving time, money and risk in landing the drone after each firing, as was required with the earlier pod.

The cameras ran at an impressive rate of 200 frames per second. Normal speed for 16mm cameras was 24 frames per second, so the extra frames provided slow-motion capability. Exposure time was 1/600th of a second per frame.

The loss of the drone from a direct missile hit, intended or otherwise, did not mean loss of the film, for the camera pods were designed to release themselves from the drone aircraft by way of an explosive bolt. A 16ft parachute would lower the camera pod to the ground. If over water, the pod would float and emit dye to help searchers find the device.[351]

US Navy QF-86Hs

As the ANG replaced its F-86Hs, this fast and heavyweight variant of the Sabre family was adopted by the US Navy as a drone, flying from China Lake as well as Point Mugu from the mid-1970s. The F-86H promised subsonic manoeuvrability that was representative of some of the real-world airborne threats then facing the US military. Nearly thirty H-models were droned for the US Navy, these aircraft – some in natural aluminium finish and others retaining their recent tactical camouflage, with bright orange and white panel highlights applied to increase visibility.

A ground-based F-86H cockpit trainer was used by the drone operator for the entirety of the mission from take-off to landing thanks to the QF-86H being fitted with a situational awareness forward-looking television camera. The US Navy had earlier pioneered the mounting of a situational awareness forward-looking television camera in drone aircraft.[352]

As a weapons testing facility, China Lake was appropriately remote from population centres. However, it was also a considerable distance from the aviation industry of southern California. When the US Navy wanted F-86Hs to be droned, the assignment was tackled successfully by civilian and military personnel at China Lake. The project started with the development and droning of two QF-86Hs, plus the creation of a suitable ground control station. Presuming the success of that phase, the programme would move into conversion of a quantity of F-86Hs into drones for service use. F-86H serial 53-1294 was picked as the first jet for conversion, with the second being 52-2091.[353]

The QF-86H concept initially did not call for retaining man-rated status, since the Sabres would be modified and used until destruction at China Lake. Later in development when Point Mugu was added as a site for QF-86H operations, the drone system was set up to retain onboard piloting capacity – especially useful for ferrying and positioning drone aircraft.

Avionics removed from the fighter's nose bay provided space to instal droning and navigation equipment, as well as a forward-looking television camera for the benefit of the remote operator on the ground. The controller Airborne Interface Unit (AIU) was part of this installation. It had the ability to translate digital input signals into analogue outputs that electrically actuated the controls of the QF-86H. Hydraulics moved the horizontal tail surfaces and ailerons, and were involved with the steerable nosewheel and differential braking.

The QF-86 rudder and throttle were cable actuated, and required installation of electromagnetic rotary cable drums in the cable runs. These actions were all proportional or variable in nature. Another set of commands, called discrete control functions, were for on–off operations and were not variable or proportional. This included functions like speed brakes, flaps, external stores jettison, smoke system for visibility, landing gear and rudder trim.[354]

A flight safety electronics (FSE) system enabled the QF-86H to right itself from any attitude and climb to an orbiting altitude in case of a command radio failure, buying time for the ground controllers to re-establish authority over the aircraft, or conceivably to employ the destruct system to bring the QF-86H down while over an uninhabited area.

With a larger-than-normal and irregular orange panel on its vertical tail, QF-86H 0-31351 is readied for a flight at China Lake in January 1978. This QF-86H would be off the active books in a little over two years. *Frederick A Johnsen*

Orange and white visibility paint panels overlay an ageing camouflage scheme on this QF-86H taken on charge by the US Navy and seen at Point Mugu in January 1978. The QF-86's use of a forward-looking television camera enhanced situational awareness for its remote pilot, especially during take-off and landing. *Frederick A Johnsen*

China Lake gave the requirements for the FSE to Sperry Flight Systems for construction.

The destruction mechanism was an explosive charge placed in the fuel tank filler necks in each wing, borrowed from the installation earlier perfected for the US Navy's QT-33As and modified slightly for the QF-86H. A surplus H-model airframe was used for a ground test of the destruct system, which succeeded in cleaving the aircraft's right wing from the fuselage when detonated.

In order to receive command signals and transmit telemetry and other data, the QF-86Hs sprouted five antennas. The top of the vertical fin hosted a television transmitter antenna. A destruct system antenna resided under the wing centre section. For air-to-ground telemetry transmission, an antenna was mounted atop the fuselage, while one beneath the forward fuselage and another on the nose of the QF-86H were command signal antennas.[355]

An available trailer housed a procedures trainer cockpit for the F-86H, modified to serve as the ground control pilot's station. An MSQ-51 radar van was linked to this trailer, and the ground pilot flew the drone QF-86H from take-off to landing via a two-way data link. The ground control cockpit featured a normal F-86H instrument panel, plus special indicators for drone g-loading, longitudinal deceleration and angle of attack. The traditional F-86H's gunsight above the instrument panel was replaced by a television monitor that provided the ground control pilot with a forward view from the cockpit. A plotter, informed by the MSQ-51 radar, showed the location of the drone on the range.[356]

By 12 September 1972, the prototype QF-86H was ready for remote piloting test flights. A safety pilot aboard the Sabre was ready to take command if needed. Early flights were frustrated by a loss of command signal to the drone. One spurious signal caused the Sabre's landing gear to start extending, and then retract, at an airspeed faster than the allowed 220 knots. No damage occurred, and the safety pilot landed the QF-86H at China Lake. Subsequent modification to the AIU prevented extension of the gear above 210 knots, and would also set in motion automatic retraction of the gear if this speed was reached with the gear still down.

Not all of the US Navy's QF-86Hs were flown in camouflage paint, as this bare-metal example shows. It was photographed at China Lake in January 1978. *Frederick A Johnsen*

After wringing out and debugging the QF-86H system through the rest of 1972 and into the new year, on 30 March 1973, the first NOLO QF-86H mission was launched with aircraft 53-1294. The jet was preflighted and taxied by an onboard pilot who lined the drone up with the centreline of the runway at China Lake and then climbed out of the aircraft, closing the canopy on an empty cockpit.[357]

The remote pilot that day was civilian Harlan Reep, a former Naval Aviator with drone experience that included QT-33As and QF-9s. The US Navy sent another piloted F-86H aloft as a chase aircraft for the drone. Among contingencies covered by the testers, the loss of television signal from the drone, which would hamper the ground pilot, would be countered by having the chase aircraft accompany the QF-86H to an unpaved landing strip in the China Lake complex, where a safe recovery would be attempted.

No incidents happened on this first flight, with the landing gear remaining extended and speed only reaching 155 knots. Reep landed the drone from his console and taxied it to an unused runway area, where the explosive destruct system was disarmed before a pilot climbed aboard and taxied the drone to parking.

The development of the QF-86H was hailed as an economical and successful venture by the China Lake team. Records vary, but either 31 or 32 QF-86Hs, including the two prototypes, were created in a hangar at China Lake, with final delivery anticipated by the end of 1974 – the last QF-86H was not actually delivered until February 1976. Cost per jet was initially put at $80,000, rising to $130,000 by the time of the last delivery.[358]

In 1974, QF-86Hs were also deployed to Point Mugu, which necessitated a piloted flight from China Lake. Once at Point Mugu, a prohibition on drone flights from there led to the need to ferry the QF-86Hs out to San Nicolas Island with a pilot onboard. When flying a drone mission from there, a van beside the San Nicolas Island runway housed a pilot who made the take-off, before handing the QF-86H over to another pilot ensconced in a control building back at Point Mugu. The distances involved made the use of the QF-86H's television camera unworkable, so the pilot in the van handled flight chores close to the runway. Safety chase was sometimes provided by a piston-engined North American T-28 Trojan.

Versions of the Phoenix, Sparrow and Sidewinder AAMs engaged the QF-86Hs in California skies from 1973. Even with multiple flights planned for the H-model drones, on 11 October 1973 the prototype QF-86H, 53-1294, became the first example to be destroyed. On another mission, a Sidewinder successfully engaged a QF-86H that was in the process of generating an incredible 8.2g turn – well above the Sabre's design limit.[359]

By 1979, use of QF-86Hs as targets was waning, but a surviving example fulfilled a significant remotely-piloted task in the interest of safety on 3 November that year at China Lake. Rather than being shot at by missiles, the aircraft was tasked with flying behind the prototype Boeing 747 N7470 jetliner in tests conducted by the Federal Aviation Administration (FAA) and NASA to determine safe distances for small aircraft to follow to avoid potentially catastrophic wake turbulence upsets. Legendary NASA research pilot Fitzhugh L 'Fitz' Fulton joined Boeing's Paul Bennett in the cockpit of N7470 that day. Smoke generators on the wingtips of the airliner gave graphic visual proof of the turbulent vortices spiralling from the tips.

The test flights represented landing approaches, and the 747, with the QF-86H behind it, would be around 100ft above ground level, where a turbulence-induced upset could prove fatal for the Sabre – hence flying it unmanned was validated. Testers soon learned the expanding spirals of smoke from the wings of the 747 were laden with oil that

While at China Lake, Lt(jg) Rosemary Conatser (later Capt Rosemary Mariner), one of the first six female Naval Aviators, flew jets like this QF-86H (0-22094) emblazoned with her name beneath the cockpit. It was photographed in January 1978. *Frederick A Johnsen*

Vintage pierced-steel-planking forms the parking apron for this US Navy QF-86H at China Lake in January 1978. If the fuselage star insignia is mis-proportioned, it did not hinder this drone's flyability. *Frederick A Johnsen*

obscured the nose camera lens in the QF-86, making the use of a second Sabre as a piloted 'seeing-eye' for the drone operator necessary. Seven times the QF-86H landed four miles behind N7470, and still the fighter drone was tossed about from the large aircraft's turbulence. The QF-86 sorties contributed to the knowledge of vortex problems, and subsequent tests continued with other aircraft.[360]

As the use of QF-86Hs wound down, one was destroyed by an AIM-9L launched from a Bell AH-1 Cobra helicopter in June 1980. Two months later, on 6 August, a QF-86H showed signs of problems at 5000 ft, leading to its commanded destruction from the ground station. The wreckage crashed on a remote part of the China Lake complex. The last use of a QF-86H as a missile target came the following year.[361]

QT-38s and QF-86Fs

As the limited supply of about 30 QF-86Hs dwindled, the US Navy considered the possibility of obtaining a sizeable number of the Northrop T-38 Talon trainers due for retirement by the USAF. Eight QT-38A Talon drones were in fact flown by the US Navy at China Lake, with the first NOLO flight taking place in November 1975. However, a change in USAF plans meant its Talons would no longer be available, so a quantity acquisition of QT-38s was off the table. Now, the US Navy looked at the feasibility of droning older F-86Fs, possibly from foreign air forces.

The US Navy briefly flirted with the idea of droning T-38 trainers, but opted for F-86s when the USAF changed its mind about excessing a quantity of Talons in the 1970s. This QT-38A was seen at China Lake in January 1978. *Frederick A Johnsen*

Opposite: During the American bicentennial year 1976, many military aircraft were adorned with patriotic paint schemes in red, white and blue, as seen on this China Lake-based QT-38A, which did not bother with national insignia. *US Navy*

The bicentennial scheme QT-38A was still painted in its unique markings in January 1978 when the author photographed the jet at China Lake. *Frederick A Johnsen*

Two QT-38As sit on the China Lake ramp in January 1978 alongside the QF-86Hs they were supposed to replace. The aircraft nearest to the camera has evidence of plumbing for a smoke system between its twin exhaust cans. *Frederick A Johnsen*

The Japanese Air Self-Defense Force (JASDF) used large numbers of F-86Fs which had been built under license by Mitsubishi in Japan. As these Sabres were retired in the 1970s, the rules by which the JASDF had acquired the aircraft under the auspices of the US Military Assistance Program included an option for Japan to turn the jets over to US control. That fitted perfectly into the US Navy's post-QT-38 plans, and remaining funds from this stymied acquisition were now identified for use on the QF-86F effort.[362]

The JASDF Sabres were basically available for the cost of disassembly and shipping to the US. Four crated F-86Fs arrived in California in 1977, where the first reassembled jet tested its wings over the Mojave Desert on 30 June whilst still carrying Japanese military insignia. It and another of the first four ex-JASDF jets became pilot proficiency aircraft without being converted into drones, while the remaining two airframes served as the QF-86F drone prototypes.

A further fifty-five Japanese F-86F airframes were earmarked for shipment to the US, and more than 600 tons of spare parts were located in Spain. Other foreign sources of F-86F parts would be identified over the long service life of these drones. The number of Japanese Sabres available for US Navy droning swelled to 150 aircraft, including four RF-86Fs.

A QF-86 meets its end over the China Lake range on 29 October 1977, the drone being hit by an AIM-9L that had been fired by an F-14A Tomcat. The latter is visible in the final photograph in this sequence, the fighter backdropped by the smoke left behind by the flaming wreckage of the Sabre as it plummets to the ground. *US Navy*

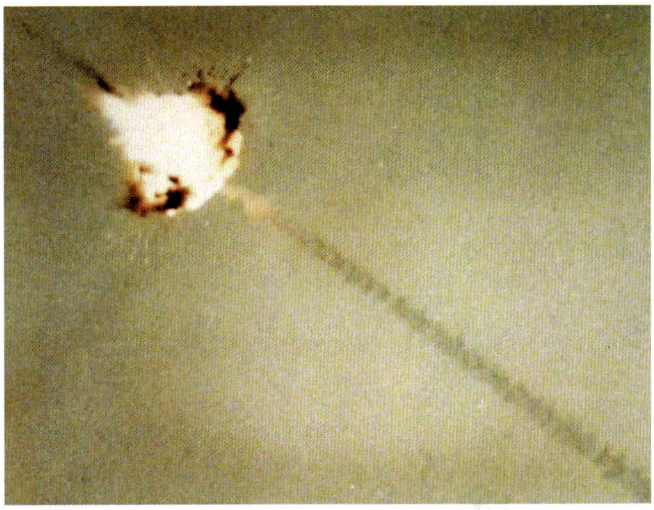

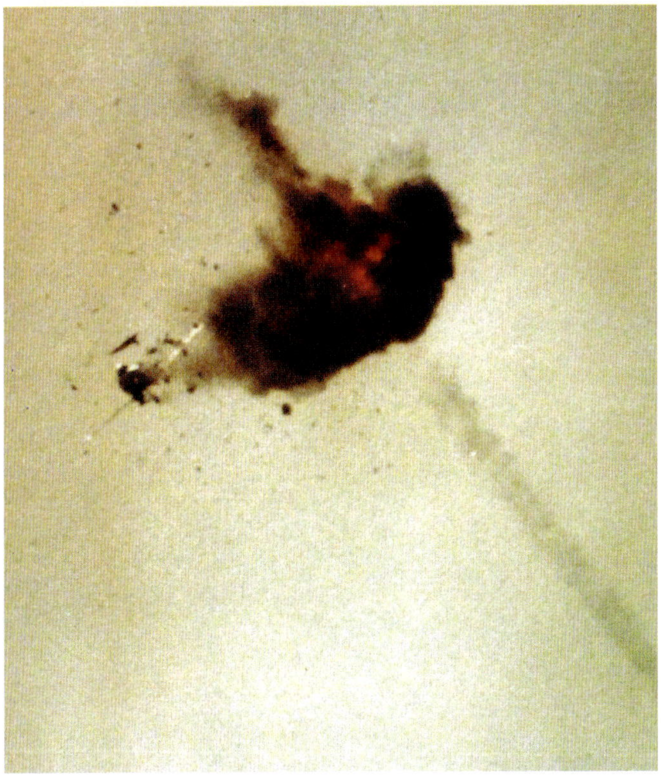

Additionally, a further fifteen F-model Sabres arrived from Taiwan for US Navy use, as well as some ex-South Korean Sabres. Around 140 of the jets supplied were earmarked for droning, with the remaining airframes yielding useful spare parts. The Japanese Sabres were generally noted to be in the best condition, not suffering as much from corrosion as some of the other nationalities' F-86Fs.[363]

The first thirteen F-86Fs converted to drone status were initially reassembled and verified for flight as manned fighters at China Lake by contractor Kentron, working with engine specialists in house at China Lake. The jets were then ferried to Palmdale, where, in Plant 42, Kentron completed the drone conversion process. The first approved QF-86F drone conversion was delivered to the US Navy in 1978, with full-up operations commencing the following year. The production rate for QF-86F conversions ran at about twelve jets per year until the line closed in 1991.

A single QF-86F was downed in 1980, two in 1981, twelve in 1982, nine in 1983 and seventeen in 1984. The majority of the US Navy's F-model Sabre drones played out their lives at China Lake. By late 1983, conversion of F-86Fs had been contracted to Northrop at a special site at Inyokern airport, close to China Lake. Six F-86Fs could be in work at a time, with airframes being trucked several miles from storage at China Lake to the Inyokern facility for conversion.[364]

Where the QF-86H ground operator sat in a converted F-86H cockpit simulator, the QF-86F programme used a generic built-up cockpit station that also served QT-38 and later QF-4B drone operations. More than one QF-86F could be flown at the same time by target control console operators after take-off, and this enabled the US Navy to present multiple targets to a McDonnell Douglas F/A-18 Hornet under evaluation on 22 July 1982, when the pilot handily downed both QF-86Fs with AIM-7 and AIM-9 missiles.

The experience gained by the US Navy with droning the F-86H was apparent, as the QF-86F operated similarly for take-off preparation, launch, mission and recovery. Again, in the F-model drones, a nose-mounted video camera gave the ground pilot a forward view that was especially useful in take-off and landing. The right-hand gun bay of the QF-86Fs carried an internal smoke tank, feeding smoke oil through a small external pipe down the right side of the fuselage to the engine exhaust area.[365]

When QF-86Fs were operated over the Pacific Missile Test Center's overwater range, they were ferried in manned flights to Point Mugu and then out to San Nicolas Island, where they could be remotely taken off. Instead of an onboard explosive to disable an errant QF-86F on an overwater sortie, the plan was to descend a malfunctioning drone into the ocean. Typically a manned F-86F acted as a chase aircraft for the QF-86F to observe any post-missile damage to the drone and, in some instances, to act as an IFF (Identify, Friend or Foe) transponder for identifying the two-ship F-86F and QF-86F flight as the aircraft passed through FAA airspace. This was especially true when QF-86Fs were used as targets at Roosevelt Roads.

Knowing the history of drones blocking a runway on landing, pilots of the chase F-86s were wise to keep enough fuel for a diversion from San Nicolas Island to Point Mugu. At Roosevelt Roads, one chase pilot remembered landing facing a drone stuck on the runway since no other option presented itself. Chase pilots could be useful eyes in the sky for the ground pilot of the drone on landing,

An F-14A Tomcat has successfully launched an AIM-54A at a QF-86 target, visible as an elliptical ball of flame at the far right of the image. The action took place over the Atlantic Fleet Weapons Training Center off Puerto Rico in the summer of 1984, with the Tomcat hailing from VF-143, then embarked in USS *Dwight D Eisenhower* (CVN-69). *NARA*

US Navy QF-86F drones frequently received a simple aluminium silver paint scheme, this proving to be an efficient way to remove foreign national markings from the Sabres received from countries like Japan. This aircraft was photographed at China Lake in January 1978. *Frederick A Johnsen*

especially if the sun was low enough on the horizon to render the televised view from the QF-86F ineffectual.[366]

Seldom written about, the use of Sabre drones at Roosevelt Roads was a bustling industry geared less towards testing and more focused on missile training for fleet fighter units, as well as some shipboard missile development after the depletion of QF-9 Cougars. If the drone sortie involved jets other than the chase aircraft, it was not uncommon to have the former armed in case an errant and damaged QF-86F needed to be shot down. The flight back to Roosevelt Roads from the range area often overflew many civilian ships, and the policy was to destroy a questionable QF-86F before it passed over such vessels.[367]

An irony of history is the first use of Sidewinder missiles (in AIM-9B form) in combat was from F-86Fs of the Republic of China Air Force on 24 September 1958 against communist Chinese MiG-17s. Then, decades later, the vastly improved AIM-9L version of the AAM would be tested against droned QF-86Fs over California. It is believed the last QF-86F to be despatched by a test Sidewinder occurred in 1994. The QF-86F was to be supplanted by QF-4 Phantom II jet drones, the latter providing supersonic targets that could fly night missions using a special camera tested on a QF-86F in 1989.

The QF-86F enjoyed a high reliability rate and was easy to maintain. The drone team at China Lake appreciated having civilian ground control pilots for the Sabres because there was a learning curve to become proficient at handling the remote droned F-86. Civilians could be on the job for an indefinite number of years, versus active duty pilots who would be rotated to another assignment more regularly.

A variety of paint and lettering schemes appeared on QF-86Fs during their service careers. Notable was the application of white paint on the upper nose surface to reflect desert heat away from the avionics contained inside. Several paint schemes came and went over the years of the programme, including a number of aircraft that featured an overall grey subdued finish.

This ex-JASDF QF-86F featured a silver and International Orange scheme that was seen on a handful of Sabre drones at Point Mugu. Photographed on 30 December 1991, the aircraft featured an impressive scoreboard that showed it had survived six missile shoots to date. *US Navy*

11 Reusable Drones

The B-47 Stratojet earns accolades for its pacesetting development and design, as well as its standout aesthetics. A key American nuclear bomber in operational service in a variety of roles between 1951 and into the 1960s, more than 2000 Stratojets were built by Boeing (and under license by Lockheed and Douglas). A small number became QB-47 drones to test advanced SAM systems. The rationale behind this was to programme flights in such a way that the expensive QB-47 could be spared to fly again. Droning of B-47s was accomplished by Lockheed's Plant 06 at Dobbins AFB in Marietta, Georgia, in collaboration with the Sperry Gyroscope Company and the USAF's Air Proving Ground Drone and Targets Test Branch.

A QB-47 Stratojet drone fitted with an arrestor hook for landing. *USAF*

QB-47E 53-4250 was one of twenty RB-47Es converted into expensive reusable drones by Lockheed's Marietta plant in 1959–60. Liberally marked with high-visibility Fluorescent Red Orange range markings, this aircraft survived its brief career as a drone at Eglin to be salvaged.

The B-47 was ideal for CIM-10 BOMARC SAM testing because its large size was representative of possible hostile bomber targets. The Stratojet's range of five-and-a-half hours was long enough to accommodate potential delays in BOMARC test launches, and it also gave the possibility of more than one launch per QB-47 sortie. The size of the B-47 also meant it could accommodate more sophisticated scoring and countermeasures equipment than smaller aircraft. Reconnaissance-optimised RB-47Es were preferred because they offered more opportunities for installation of the electronics needed for the drone programme. The QB-47s were man-rated for ferrying and for equipment checkout flights.[368]

A drone director DT-33 jet trainer could handle the QB-47 by way of a UHF AN/ARW-65 transmitter. Two 'air-beeper' pilots atop a special truck controlled the QB-47 for take-offs and landings, with one responsible for elevator inputs and the other for rudder control. After take-off, control of the QB-47 was transferred to the DT-33 flying overhead. The Shooting Star flew the QB-47 to a desired area where control could again be transferred to a ground handler. The ground pilot established the altitude, heading and speed required by BOMARC testers.

Seconds before the SAM intercepted the QB-47, the drone bomber's scoring cameras were turned on to record the weapon's intended near-miss. Twelve Bell & Howell 16mm motion picture cameras whirred at 200 frames a second to yield an effective slow-motion account of the BOMARC's arrival. Contained in pods under the wings of the QB-47, the cameras covered a spherical view around the bomber.[369]

USAF plans in 1960 called for two prototypes and twelve converted production QB-47s. As deliveries mounted that summer, in August a BOMARC inadvertently struck a QB-47, diminishing the fleet. Modifications to the bombers included a hook mounted to the rear set of bicycle mainwheels that engaged a special arresting cable spanning a runway at Eglin used for the QB-47 take-offs and landings.[370]

By 1962, QB-47s were flying in the Eglin Gulf of Mexico test range to challenge CIM-10B BOMARC SAMs in low-level flight. A microwave command guidance (MCG) system was employed with the drone Stratojets. The system could be used for high-altitude drones, low-level drones, drones beyond the horizon at extended range and all the way from take-off to landing.[371] Earlier flight tests of the system at Holloman had quantified its performance. MCG was a guidance system for commanding, tracking and receiving flight data from high-performance unmanned vehicles. The basic elements of MCG included the Flight Control Central AN/TPW-l, the Command Guidance-Interrogator Set AN/APW-23(XY-l), the Data Transponder Set AN/APW-22(XY-1) and test equipment.

With a ground controller, the QB-47 system had a 200-nautical-mile range as long as the drone remained above the radar horizon. The QB-47 drone could be controlled from a minimum altitude of about 500ft up to its maximum cruising altitude. A technical paper described the operations as follows:

> 'Flight data and command data are directly exchanged between the ground director and the data transponder in the unmanned vehicle. The position of the unmanned

High-visibility orange markings made QB-47 Stratojet drones at Eglin stand out. *USAF*

vehicle is displayed on the ground director plotting board in X–Y coordinates derived from radar tracking information obtained from the interrogation radar and computer in the ground director. Upon a verbal command from the primary control operator in the ground director, the airborne director can assume full command of the unmanned vehicle. In this case, identical control features are exercised by the airborne director and full flight information and position of the airborne director is relayed to the ground director.

'The positions of the unmanned vehicle and the airborne director are plotted on the ground director and airborne director plotting boards. The relay mode extends the control range of the ground director to approximately 400 nautical miles through use of the relay capability in the airborne director.

'Operation of the unmanned vehicle below the radar horizon is now possible since the airborne director can control the unmanned vehicle at elevation angles below the horizon as long as the ground director is within radar line-of-sight of the airborne director. Over-the-horizon control is presently being exercised at the EGTR [Eglin Gulf Test Range].

'The airborne director receives position and flight data from the unmanned vehicle and stores it in the relay transponder equipment. The ground director then interrogates the airborne director, thus deriving the position of the airborne director plus the stored flight data from the unmanned vehicle. The ground director is now capable of displaying flight data information plus the position of the unmanned vehicle and the airborne director. Commands from the ground director are relayed to the unmanned vehicle by the airborne director.'[372]

The QB-47's Sperry control system was also used on smaller drones like the QF-80, with the MCG equipment initially being validated on the QB-17. The more complicated Stratojet required additional commands to operate its systems. An explanatory paper on the Sperry MCG system posited a bright future:

'One significant factor is that with tracking capabilities of 12 to 15 degrees per second, MCG enables the system to track targets with speeds in excess of Mach 20 when at the range of 25 nautical miles. Therefore, MCG is definitely capable of tracking and controlling supersonic vehicles such as the F-101, F-105 and F-106 should such a requirement exist.'[373]

A typical lower altitude QB-47 mission undertaken to test the CIM-10B BOMARC capability usually went as follows:

'A checkout procedure is followed when qualifying a QB-47 for a controlled NULLO flight. On the day preceding the planned mission, the entire complement of QB-47 electronic equipment, including the airborne and ground director equipment, is ground tested and inspected. This is followed by a complete maintenance preflight check including fueling and necessary mechanical testing.

'At the conclusion of the preflight, the QB-47 is flown for a two-hour in-flight test checkout of all subsystems. During this in-flight check, the airborne director conducts routing airborne command control checks with the ground director and the QB-47 drone. At the completion of the in-flight check, the QB-47 is qualified or unqualified for NULLO status and returns to base for correction of any equipment discrepancies. If qualified, a complete post-flight maintenance check is made, and the QB-47 and airborne director are refueled. The ARW [UHF radio] guidance system controls the landing and takeoff of the test vehicle. Transfer of control to MCG is automatic when the ARW removes its carrier and an MCG signal is present.

'(Loss of signal control) shall cause the QB-47 to climb to radio line-of-sight altitude, up to 20,000 feet, in a left circle turn. If control is not regained, the drone will orbit in a left circle turn at a preset airspeed.

'On the actual day of the mission, a confidence type of ground check is performed to cover all subsystems. The airborne director then takes off and makes a final check with the drone and proceeds to check with the ground director. When the check is complete, the airborne director proceeds to its rendezvous orbit area and waits the delivery of the QB-47 by the ARW command guidance air director [in a T-33]. Upon arrival, verified command and flight data checks are made between the airborne director and the QB-47 prior to continuing further down range. During the checkout period a pace aircraft determines if extensive barometric pressure changes have occurred down range before proceeding.

'When all conditions are satisfied, the mission continues with the relay mode of operation established, and the pace aircraft returns to base. Control of the QB-47 is transferred to direct control by the ground director while the airborne director obtains a position fix to update its AN/APN-99 navigational equipment. The airborne director then climbs to its mission altitude, where transfer is again made to the relay mode of operation. The mission then continues through the predetermined pattern at the coordinates required as defined for the particular BOMARC mission. Upon completion of the mission, normal recovery procedures are initiated to return the QB-47 drone to the base'[374].

YF-12's missile strike

Just three Lockheed YF-12A interceptors were built, featuring top speeds as high as 2275mph. Although the aircraft ultimately failed to secure a production contract, the YF-12A did fire missiles to validate its armament system. Two examples were flown from Edwards to Eglin, where drone capacity was already established for operating QB-47s.

On 25 April 1966, Lockheed test pilot Jim Eastham fired an inert AIM-47A Falcon AAM (a long-range development of the AIM-4) at a QB-47. Eastham described the event as follows:

> 'We were to run at 75,000 feet at 3.2-Mach number in a head-on attack against the QB-47, which would be flying at under 1000 feet, and it would be approximately, I guess, at about 0.6-Mach number. And it was over water, which is the worst environment for a pulse-Doppler [radar] system, because over water it's like flying over a mirror. You get an image phenomena, and it was serious enough that the Boeing BOMARC missile was canceled because the system they had in there, they couldn't fix it. It would go out for a target and it would dive in the ocean under it. It was going after the image off this thing.'[375]

Eastham said the closing rate was Mach 3.8, and the YF-12's firing altitude of 75,000ft placed it about fourteen miles higher than the low-flying QB-47 approaching it. As he put the YF-12 on heading and on altitude, the QB-47, launched from Eglin, was about 200 miles distant. Eastham recalled the shot:

> 'My good right arm in the back cockpit, George Parsons, he locked onto this thing at 130 miles, and we were tracking in at this tremendous closing rate. We launched the missile at 53 miles from the target, and it actually impacted. We took off a part of the horizontal stabilizer on the B-47. Fortunately, it didn't knock it into the drink, and they were able to bring it back, repair it and use it again. When the missile impacted the target, we were looking down at it from [an angle of] 73 degrees.'[376]

Lockheed test pilot James D 'Jim' Eastham was involved in the YF-12A AIM-47A Falcon trials that saw an inert example of the AAM fired at a QB-47 flying over the Gulf of Mexico from Eglin. ***USAF***

Although the YF-12 programme was now at an end, the success of the AIM-47A in trials such as this one gave impetus to the AIM-54 Phoenix missile that achieved operational success with the F-14 Tomcat.

YF-12A 60-06936 and an AIM-47A sit side by side on the ramp at Edwards AFB in 1966. ***USAF***

DB-47 directors

Although DB-17 directors were created to escort QB-17 drones, the role of DB-47 Stratojet directors was markedly different, with the jet typically being paired with other remotely-piloted aircraft. The first director DB-47Bs (51-2160, 51-2162 and 51-2234) did ostensibly have the capability to be mother ships for QB-47s, but they are more often associated with weapons like the rocket-powered Bell GAM-63 RASCAL (RAdar SCanning Link) ground-launched stand-off missile. In fact, the sole YDB-47B director (51-2186) was structurally modified in 1953 to carry a Rascal that would be guided to its target by a controller in the YDB-47B.[377]

The B-47E was the ultimate Stratojet bomber, and four examples were converted into DB-47Es. A pair of YDB-47Es (51-5219 and 51-5220) were modified at Wichita in January 1954 for service tests with the RASCAL missile, which was attached to the right side of the fuselage behind the wing of the Stratojet. The remaining two DB-47Es were 53-2345 and 53-2346.[378]

At least two B-36 Peacemakers were modified as DB-36s, with these aircraft being intended to carry, launch and direct the flight of a RASCAL. Although some test sorties were flown, the USAF cancelled the GAM-63 and replaced it with the air-breathing North American AGM-28 Hound Dog air-launched cruise missile, two of which could be carried under the wings of a B-52.

DF-89 and DB-45 directors

Northrop's long-range SM-62 Snark ground-launched cruise missile developed for SAC in the 1950s prompted the creation of some unorthodox director aircraft for test purposes. A Northrop official history cites the use of director F-89 Scorpion and B-45 Tornado jets during the Snark programme. The N-25 precursor test vehicle to the Snark was flight tested before its automatic guidance equipment was developed. This meant a radio control receiver system had to be installed in the N-25, with appropriate transmitters in the B-45 director. The larger N-69D Snark that followed the N-25, and which was also used in guidance system tests for the production SM-62, could be recovered via skids, a drag chute and radio control provided by an F-89 Scorpion.[379]

The seminal descriptive work on USAF aircraft, *United States Military Aircraft Since 1909* (published by Putnam) by Gordon Swanborough and Peter M Bowers, lists DB-45A and DB-45C director variants employed in unnamed guided weapon development. DF-89A and DF-89B are also mentioned as directors in that volume.[380]

The world of director aircraft for a variety of smaller remotely-piloted vehicles included DC-130 Hercules transports capable of carrying up to four Firebees aloft for launching. Likewise, versions of the B-26 Invader bomber of the Second World War became DB-26 director aircraft for subscale drones like the Firebee.

By September 1968, QB-47E 53-4256 was a candidate for the MASDC at Davis-Monthan. Three black hash marks on the side of the forward fuselage are YF-12A silhouettes, which indicate some of the drone target sorties this Stratojet flew. The perishable nature of Day-Glo orange paint is evident near the base of the vertical fin, where the upper fuselage paint is fading. *Robert A Burgess via Gerald Balzer collection*

12 Drones and More Drones

SB2C Helldiver drone

In the first half of the 1950s the National Advisory Committee for Aeronautics (NACA) investigated the potential for using remote control of high-performance aircraft during flight testing. Benefits included the conduct of risky flight test manoeuvres without endangering a pilot, as well as the potential for duplicating precise manoeuvres with a droned aircraft, yielding more repeatable and informative data.

The drone test aircraft chosen by the NACA was Curtiss SB2C-5 Helldiver BuNo 83135 flown from the Ames Research Center at Moffett Field, California. Its mother ship for the research flights was F6F-5 Hellcat BuNo 79669.[381]

The Helldiver's take-offs and landings were made via a ground station. A check pilot was aboard the SB2C-5 for safety, but according to the NACA report on the project, 'the check pilot did not control the airplane during the remote-control tests'. Landing gear operation, flaps and brakes remained the responsibility of the check pilot in the SB2C 'only at the command of the remote-control pilot' the report explained. It must have taken a cool-headed check pilot to taxi the SB2C to the end of the runway and then relinquish take-off control to the remote pilot in the station near the runway threshold. The NACA report explained the process:

> 'When ready for take-off, the check pilot released the brakes and transferred control to the ground control station. The ground control pilot applied power gradually and controlled the elevator to effect a take-off. Directional control was maintained automatically by the directional rate gyros through the rudder and was excellent for these propeller-driven airplanes.'

The SB2C's radio control equipment was proven to be able to allow remote pilots to make take-offs and landings in crosswinds up to at least thirty-five knots at thirty degrees. Remote control take-offs proved generally easier than landings, with the latter having a 'learning curve', as the report noted:

> 'Drone landings were remotely controlled from a ground control station located some 50 feet to one side of the runway and approximately opposite the point where the initial touchdown was to be made. The drone,

SB2C-5 BuNo 83135 became NACA-147 after the US Navy transferred it to the Ames Research Center at Moffett Field in the late 1940s. Fitted with a windscreen and canopy from an F8F Bearcat mid-fuselage, the aircraft was initially involved in gunsight research. However, in the early 1950s, the Helldiver was modified into a drone aircraft as the NACA investigated the potential for using remote control of high-performance aircraft during flight testing. A check pilot remained aboard the SB2C-5 at all times during the evaluation. *NASA*

under the command of the control plane, was aligned with the runway with its flaps and gear down and at a throttle setting that was held fixed until the final cut. Control was turned over to the ground control station when the drone was approximately two miles off the end of the runway. The drone airspeed was controlled by changing its attitude. When the drone was over the runway in the proper position for landing the power was cut and a landing accomplished. A wave-off could be controlled by the ground control station if conditions warranted such action. For landing runs after touchdown, brakes were controlled by the check pilot in the SB2C-5 drone.

'Considerably more training was required for an experienced test pilot to become proficient at controlling the drone in landings than was required for take-offs. Maintenance of precision directional control, sufficient to effect a landing on a runway, was most critical, particularly when landings were made under cross-wind conditions.

'Thirty-six landings were made during the training period. Of the first nine landings, four touchdowns were accomplished, none of which were particularly satisfactory; two wave-offs were made under remote control; and the check pilot took over control three times prior to touching down. On the last series of nine landings, the check pilot took over control prior to touchdown only once. Of the other eight landings in this series, five were excellent and three were not satisfactory, although loss of the drone in remote operation would probably not have occurred.

'Of the entire 36 training landings, 22 touchdowns and 14 wave-offs were made. Of the 22 touchdowns only 5, made under adverse cross-wind conditions, were poor enough to have possibly caused damage to a NOLO drone.'[382]

Dive tests were conducted from an altitude of 11,000ft at 120 knots. When the SB2C reached about 200 knots, a pull out was initiated. The diving and recovery manoeuvres were made by the pilot in the F6F control aircraft. The SB2C's onboard check pilot was required to set dive and recovery intervalometers only.

F7F-3 Tigercat drone

NACA's research with a droned SB2C Helldiver benefitted from testing that the US Navy had undertaken with F7F-3 Tigercat BuNo 80531 in NOLO flight configuration. The aircraft had performed some risky structural dive tests with no pilot onboard in a programme using radio control. A series of three dives each culminated in a recovery commenced by a pressure switch that activated automatically at a preset altitude. The Tigercat's dive angle was fixed at 30 degrees nose down.[383]

USAF A-24 droned

After the Second World War, the USAF flew one Douglas A-24 dive-bomber as the sole QF-24A drone, escorted by a DF-24B mother ship. The nomenclature for the aircraft is somewhat convoluted. When the USAF switched the A-for-Attack designation to B-for-Bomber in 1948, a few remaining B-24 Liberators in service meant the A-24 could not become the B-24, so it was given an F-for-Fighter prefix as the F-24. The basic A-24 was the USAAF's Second World War equivalent of the SBD Dauntless dive-bomber. Sources are in conflict as to whether the A-24 was officially called the Banshee, a name sometimes associated with the aircraft; one 1951 USAF document calls it a Dauntless, however.

The QF-24A drone tested a control system using television and remote pilot controls said to be smoother than the classic 'air-beeper' method. Development and tests of the QF-24 were made at Grand Rapids, Michigan, where William P Lear worked on the design with the USAF.

The QF-24A originally carried the USAAF serial number 42-6783, but during post-war remanufacturing it was renumbered 48-044. The director DF-24B had almost certainly been acquired from US Navy stocks in 1948, the aircraft having been built as an SBD-6 Dauntless.[384] This director Dauntless ultimately carried USAF serial number 48-045.[385] Early photographs indicate the serial number 254664 was painted on the tail of the mother ship DF-24B. This might contain a US Navy BuNo (54664), with another digit (2) preceding this.

The USAF's droned Douglas A-24 dive-bomber became the sole QF-24A when nomenclature for the A-24 was revised to F-24 in 1948. In this photograph, a belly housing on the centreline carried a television camera to give the drone pilot a view of the orientation of the aircraft. The pilot seen here with the QF-24A is Capt Jim Butler, who capped Pacific fighter experience in the Second World War with a long post-war career in USAF flight testing. *Gerald Balzer collection*

Banshee B-29

In the post-war 1940s, the USAF charted a course that fostered its nascent nuclear weapons delivery capability. Both it and the US Navy looked at ways to offer strategic value. With the B-36 yet to enter service and other strategic bombers in development, the USAF hit upon a seemingly inexpensive way to extend its bombardment reach toward an increasingly hostile Soviet Union. For the moment, only the B-29 Superfortress could carry an atomic bomb. The USAF had several thousand B-29s available.

Using the project name *Banshee* (MX-767), in January 1948 the USAF summarised the potential to use radio-controlled drone B-29s to carry a nominal 10,000lb bomb load a maximum range of 3472 miles. At that time, the USAF envisioned placing a flight crew aboard the *Banshee* bomber to execute take-off before bailing out once the B-29 was under control of a director aircraft.[386] The USAF described the concept as follows:

> 'The "Banshee" project is the development of a long range remote control system for B-29 missile aircraft utilizing airborne SHORAN [SHOrt RAnge Navigation] for precision control during the bombing run. AN/ARW-1 and AN/ARW-18 augmented by AN/APW-5 and -6 will be used to accomplish flight of the missile to the target area, where a SHORAN adaptation will assume control and deliver it to the target.'[387]

SHORAN used radar and triangulation from two stations to designate a pinpoint on the map for aircraft arrival and delivery of its bomb load. Planners figured the *Banshee* B-29 missiles could be under SHORAN control for a maximum of 152 nautical miles, and under remote control from a director mother ship over a distance not exceeding ninety nautical miles. The proposed mission profile for Banshee said:

> 'Takeoff will be accomplished manually by skeleton crew [later discussions of Banshee contemplated the possibility that remote-control take-offs of MB-29s could be perfected]. When the missiles become airborne, control will be switched to an already airborne mother aircraft and crew will bail out. Two additional mothers equipped with airborne SHORAN will assume control when the missile is guided to within approximately 152 nautical miles of the target and will guide the missile to bomb release point. Missile is conventional B-29 aircraft stripped of all unessential equipment and having installed the necessary remote control equipment. One quarter mile accuracy is desired.'[388]

The Engineering Division of Air Materiel Command conceived the theory of operations and equipment required for *Banshee*. Design, fabrication and installation of *Banshee* hardware was undertaken by General Electric (GE) and RCA. *Banshee* suffered a great loss on 6 October 1948 when an MB-29 crashed near Waycross, Georgia, whilst on a functional test flight of its RCA equipment out of Robins AFB, Georgia. Most of the test crew died.

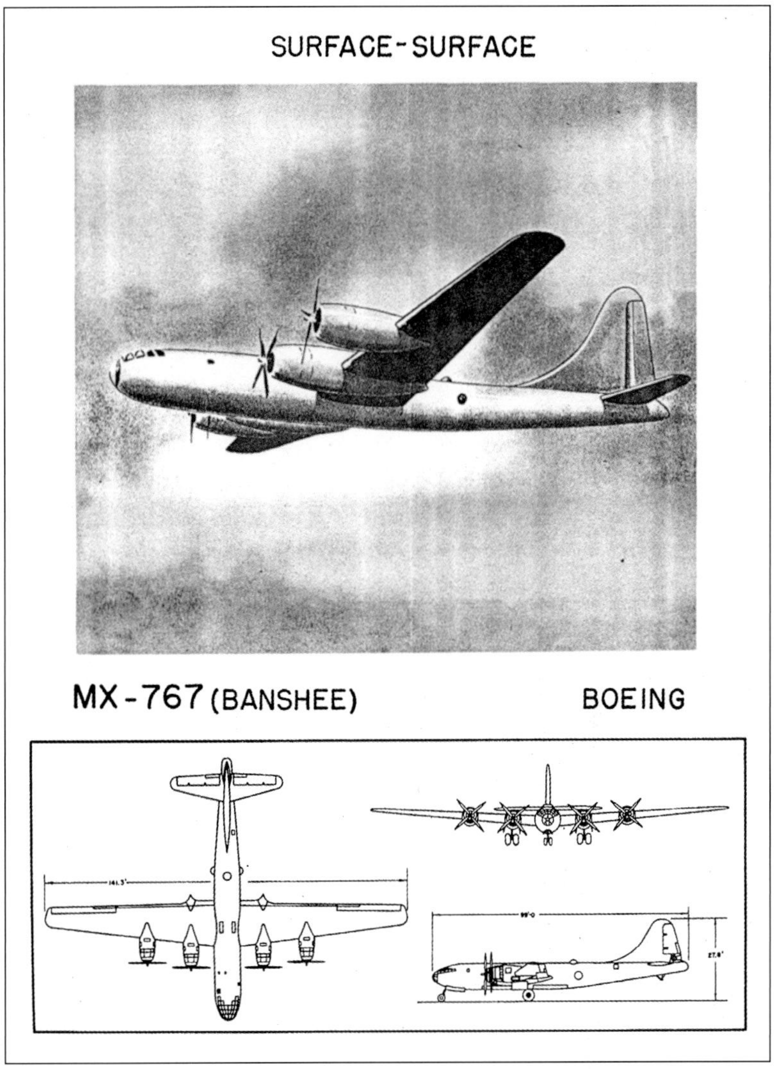

Project MX-767 (as illustrated by this page from the USAF's TSENG Report No 3, dated 1 January 1948) contemplated flying unmanned B-29 drones under the project name *Banshee*, achieving long-range accuracy with the help of SHORAN for precise bombing. The TSENG document listed *Banshee* under the category of 'Surface-to-Surface'. When *Banshee* was conceived, planners still envisioned having the large bombers take off under the control of a skeleton crew who would then bail out. After some initial post-war testing, especially involving modified DB-29 director aircraft, *Banshee* faded from importance as longer range manned bombers, and the potential for purpose-built missiles, took hold. *USAF*

That same month, contract issues between GE and Air Materiel Command delayed testing on a *Banshee* Superfortress at the company's Schenectady base in New York state, so USAF pilots returned the aircraft to Eglin awaiting a resolution to the dispute. SHORAN DB-29 292 was converted at Schenectady in November and then returned to Eglin to allow more training flights to take place in Florida.

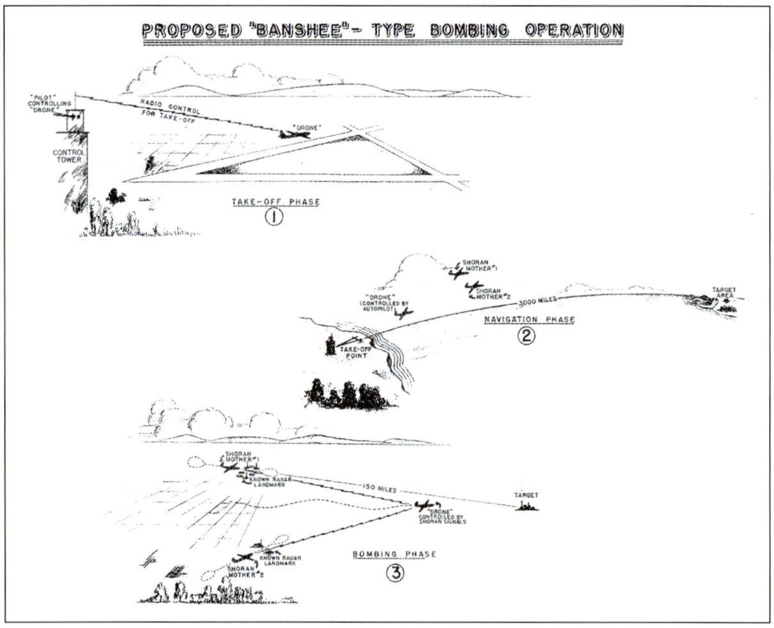

Artwork from a USAF report depicting a notional *Banshee* mission, with two mother ship directors and a single drone (or missile) aircraft. *AFHRA*

On 19 November the MB-29 identified as 'Missile 860' (45-21860) made a 4024-nautical mile crewed flight from NAS Barbers Point, Hawaii, to Selfridge AFB, Michigan. The flight was a long-range test of *Banshee*'s E-4 autopilot. The latter experienced a nearly 100-mile error by the time the MB-29 reached Selfridge – something that may have been attributable to adverse winds and extremely low pressure during part of the flight.[389]

Following its departure from Hawaii, the MB-29 flew at 9000ft for the first six hours of the flight in part as a cruise-control efficiency measure since the aircraft had taken off with a heavy gross weight of 127,000lb. A post-flight evaluation said weather forecasts for winds aloft were not accurate enough to allow for precision navigation with the E-4 autopilot on a 2000-mile mission – the error was worse for a 4000-mile flight. The after action report noted, 'Unless Weather Service can make better forecasts for these flights, accuracy cannot be expected'. The 19 November flight validated the need for cruise-control at a low altitude for several hours after take-off to ensure sufficient fuel remained for the entire sortie.[390]

B-29s were earmarked for use as *Banshee* drones and mother ship director aircraft. In December 1948 the USAF listed the following seven Superfortresses participating in the *Banshee* project:

DB-29	44-62223	radio control mother
DB-29	45-21870	radio control mother
DB-29	44-62291	SHORAN mother
DB-29	44-62292	SHORAN mother
DB-29	44-62300	SHORAN mother
MB-29	45-21852	missile
MB-29	45-21860	missile[391]

The droned *Banshee* B-29s were given the prefix letter 'M' for missile, as in MB-29, while the mother ship director aircraft were DB-29s.

A SHORAN-equipped mother ship B-29 for *Banshee* was delivered to Eglin on 21 January 1949, and some test flying was done with this aircraft the following month. On 7 April the first combined *Banshee* mission was launched. The final *Banshee*-modified B-29 was delivered to Eglin on 17 May. On 14 June the first bombs were dropped during a *Banshee* mission.[392]

A *Banshee* crew stands in front of DB-29 45-21870 as they discuss the results of a mission in 1948. *AFHRA*

Eglin in the first half of 1949 was heavily involved in drone activities. To the left in this photograph is a QB-17G drone still in its 'Hollywood paint', including the painted-on nickname *HIGH FLIER* on the nose, following its stint as a wartime Flying Fortress in the film *Twelve O'Clock High*. The pair of DB-29 Superfortress director aircraft to the right were part of the *Banshee* project. 45-21870, furthest from the camera, was a radio control mother ship, while 44-62291 was a SHORAN mother ship. *USAF/AFHRA*

USAF historical reporting from 1949 said the objective of *Banshee* was 'to fly an MB-29 2,000 or more miles remotely and drop a bomb on a target by remote control utilizing two airborne Shoran stations'.

Before flights began, the complex electronics intended for *Banshee* were studied and tested in bench-set and mock-up phases that helped reduce future surprises and failures. As *Banshee* heralded a more electronics-centred future for the USAF, a special electrostatically shielded room for the project was constructed to facilitate tuning and calibration of sensitive electronic equipment. Even though *Banshee* ultimately did not yield operational status, its research efforts helped set a tone for the future. The intended range for *Banshee* tests flown from Eglin was to be over south Florida. By the end of June 1949, Eglin considered *Banshee* to be nearing completion in development.[393]

The results of *Banshee* were mixed. Reliability was uneven, but valuable insight into the problems and solutions of long-range drone operations was gleaned. There is no indication that any *Banshee* MB-29 flights were made without a safety crew onboard.

Contemporary documentation and discussion relating to *Banshee* shows a hint of ambivalence about the project's final delivery of bombs on target. A January 1948 description talks about bomb release over the target. A March 1947 planning letter describing a desired *Banshee* demonstration flight said 'The airplane will not be dived into the target, but will drop a conventional bomb on the target'. Such a distinct statement suggests some in the service thought diving the *Banshee* B-29 into the target was not an option, possibly because of the lack of success with earlier *Aphrodite* operations with war-weary B-17s in Europe. What remains unclear is how much consideration, if any, was ever given to making *Banshee* MB-29s devices that would impact their targets.[394]

An instructional letter dated 3 October 1949 may shed light on the ultimate intent of *Banshee* bomb delivery when it addresses 'final or terminal guidance of guided missiles', stating 'No evaluation can be made since this is an automatic bombing system and not a terminal guidance system'.[395]

The Air Proving Ground at Eglin published a termination report on *Banshee* in July 1950, analysing several aspects of the effort. Its authors were blunt in their assessment that the programme never had enough qualified technicians to enable work to proceed in a timely manner. It was a brave new post-war world where electronics were increasingly important. The equipment involved in the navigation and droning of B-29 Superfortresses was tasked with remaining operable for a duration 'that far exceeded designed operating time', leading to ongoing maintenance and scheduling difficulties. The report observed:

> 'Because of the experimental nature of the equipment and its excessive operating time, much failure and breakdown of the equipment occurred. This condition was aggravated by the lack of a sufficient number of bench spares. Mission schedules were therefore not dependable.'[396]

The Banshee termination report was succinct in discussing trained personnel issues:

> 'The availability of skilled technical personnel presented a continuous problem throughout the project. Due to the complexity and the amount of equipment, it was established that a minimum of 90 highly skilled

electronics personnel (including AFCE [Automatic Flight Control Equipment] and radio control mechanics) would be required for adequate maintenance. A maximum of 40 airmen were available at any one time with skills varying from high to apprenticeship.'[397]

In response to queries about a *Banshee* demonstration mission to use the best long-range guidance system, the termination report was again blunt in its assessment that such a mission 'could not possibly be arranged before 1 July 1950 at the present rate of progress. It will be almost impossible to stage a successful demonstration due to the unreliability of the equipment as evidenced by the number of unsuccessful missions already attempted'.[398]

The *Banshee* end report also said the flight plan necessary for the MB-29 and DB-29s would make participants very vulnerable to all types of enemy anti-aircraft activity and jamming. An interesting side note was the brief discussion, during the work on *Banshee*, that droned B-29s or maybe B-50s might serve as ECM aircraft and decoys for a manned bomber formation, with the manned formation controlling the drones.

In the end, it appears from paperwork left behind that Banshee was beset with problems, both technical and personnel-related, at a time when other projects at Eglin also demanded increasing numbers of electronics specialists. The termination report does not shed any tears over the end of *Banshee*, but looks ahead to other USAF missile programs on the horizon like Snark and Matador.[399]

Drone AJ Savage

The post-Second World War scramble by the American service branches to find viable nuclear delivery roles included a suggested one-way droning of the North American AJ Savage carrier-based bomber. Even before the US Navy placed its first order for AJ-1s, US Navy drone pioneer and advocate Capt Delmar S Fahrney proposed droning AJ-1s for intentional one-way missions covering 1400 miles – much longer than a round-trip in a piloted AJ.

The Savage was a high-wing carrier-based nuclear-capable bomber powered by a pair of wing-mounted Pratt & Whitney R-2800 Double Wasp piston engines and an Allison J33 jet fitted in the tail. Other engineers at the US Navy's BuAer expanded on the idea, and in 1947 it went into research and development as Project *Taurus*. The plan was to guide the AJ-1 drones from ships or other aircraft. Because a flyable AJ-1 was not yet available, some research was conducted with an F6F-3K Hellcat drone standing in for the Savage. *Taurus* was cancelled in 1948 by an admiral who was determined that missiles would not replace pilots in war.[400]

QF-104A Starfighter

The quest for weapons that could down high-speed, high-altitude, high-performance aircraft from adversarial countries demanded realistic flying targets to test the missiles expected to destroy them. In the 1960s, the USAF had more than twenty Lockheed F-104A Starfighters converted to QF-104A drone configuration. Approval for modifying the interceptors into drones came from the USAF in February 1960.

The F-104A had a top speed of about Mach 2 and a service ceiling of nearly 65,000ft. This made the Starfighter a worthy target as a high-speed, high-altitude surrogate to be thwarted by BOMARC SAMs and several AAMs then in development.[401] The Starfighter had come full circle, as earlier F-104s had despatched aircraft including the QF-80 in test work. The QF-104s took up residence at Duke Auxiliary Field No 3, its historic use by pilotless aircraft being underscored by the name of one of the base's roads – Drone Street.

Radio and radar guidance systems were installed in the QF-104As, along with drone stabilisation and control equipment (DSCE). Scoring cameras were fitted in both the modified left tip tank and the nose of the QF-104A. All nose radome radar fire control gear was taken out, as was all optical gunsight equipment. The M61A1 Vulcan 20mm cannon and its support gear was also removed.[402]

Additions to make the Starfighter a viable drone included the following: AN/ARN-31 glide slope antenna and receiver; AN/AKT-7 telemetering system and antenna; AN/ARW-56 guidance equipment and antennas; AN/APW-20 radar guidance equipment and antennas; DSCE-104 drone stabilisation and control equipment including air data computer, throttle servo motors and mounts, aileron stabiliser and radar servo motors and brackets, accelerometers, amplifiers, power converters, Mach and airspeed reference controls and vertical gyro reference; X- and L-band radar augmentation equipment and antennas; PARAMI miss distance indicator equipment and antennas; optical camera scoring system; anti-skid power brake equipment; 200-amp transformer-rectifiers; 2500-VA inverter; 22-AH battery; extra fuel storage in the gun bay and case; and the all-important range safety destruct system.[403]

The batch of A-model Starfighter drones included seven YF-104As that had completed their test and research careers at places like Edwards. Other production F-104As rounded out the drone batch, converted over a number of years. QF-104A drone modifications were variously handled at Lockheed Burbank, Lockheed Palmdale and McClellan AFB. Some, like 55-2969, had previously served as test aircraft for GE, maker of the J79 engine fitted in the F-104. With the A-models being the first F-104s delivered to the USAF, these older Starfighters were the obvious candidates for droning.[404]

Looking immaculate in its recently applied high-visibility drone scheme, this QF-104 poses on the Eglin runway with a mobile control van complete with director pilots at their respective stations. *USAF*

QF-104s served at Eglin originally with the 3205th Drone Group. Some were also flown from Holloman over the White Sands range complex, and also in support of US Navy missile tests at Point Mugu. A QF-104 mission typically involved a remote pilot at a truck near the runway for take-off, after which an overhead DT-33 jet took over drone direction duties until landing, when the ground pilot again flew the unmanned Starfighter in for a recovery on the runway.

Veteran Starfighter pilots became QF-104 drone pilots at Eglin. They took pride in being able to recover damaged jets that could be repaired to fly another day. As with so many drone target programmes, the rationale was to husband the limited drone resources as long as feasible, programming near-misses to allow missile tracking system validation while keeping the drone safe. But ultimately, whether as a result of a deliberate proof-of-concept shot or an unplanned ballistic encounter with an inbound anti-aircraft missile, most of the QF-104As were downed, along with others that succumbed to operational losses like radio or control system failures.

One QF-104 that was landed with serious structural issues was spared a final shootdown when the Starfighter drone programme concluded in 1972, and it survives in Tyler, Texas, displayed in the markings of a manned operational F-104. The last QF-104 shootdown came on 3 July 1972, when an AIM-9J despatched 56-737 as it was flying at 10,000ft and 0.95 Mach.[405] Records maintained by the International F-104 Society document the demise of many of the QF-104s. BOMARC SAMs accounted for at least three, including the first example to be downed, 55-2963, on 1 February 1962 during the aircraft's one and only drone sortie.

QF-104A 56-734 was another BOMARC casualty after surviving barrier engagement landings and the fracturing of its nose gear. On 1 August 1963, this QF-104 rained down as wreckage from the BOMARC interception. QF-104 56-746 was on its first drone flight when another BOMARC ended its career on 17 March 1964.

AIM-4 Falcon AAMs downed a handful of QF-104As including 55-2965 on its fifth drone mission on 1 March 1967. 55-2968 enjoyed longevity, logging 25 drone sorties between 1964 and 26 January 1971, including a 1968 strike from an AIM-9 that only inflicted repairable damage. On its last flight in 1971, the aircraft was destroyed by an AIM-4 fired from a USAF F-4E.

QF-104A 56-739, also an early prototype of the series, was felled by a GAR-2B missile (a forerunner of the AIM-4) on 8 October 1963. QF-104A 56-836 was on its second drone flight when it too had been downed by a GAR-2B five days earlier. Drone 56-747 survived an AIM-4 encounter that included impact in the engine nozzle area on 22 March 1967. The control pilot had difficulty with the damaged Starfighter and tried to activate the destruct package, which failed. Dropping from 30,000ft down to 8000ft, the drone was recovered under control for a safe landing, albeit with damaged landing gear. It flew eight more missions until 13 July 1971, when an XAIM-4H under test (this improved variant never went into production) took the Starfighter from the roster.

Even with the drone's bright red paint, the USAF deemed it necessary to add the letter 'Q' to the buzz number of this QF-104 Starfighter at Eglin. *USAF*

AIM-7 Sparrow AAMs also destroyed QF-104s including 55-2971, bagged on 27 October 1966 on its 11th drone flight. QF-104 56-735 succumbed to a Sparrow launched from a US Navy F-4B on 17 June 1965.

Starfighter 55-2966 was an operational write-off on 14 June 14 1967 following the loss of pitch controllability. A manned F-104 stayed with the errant QF-104 while the slower DT-33 director aircraft caught up to it. Unable to achieve pitch control, the DT-33 director pilot attempted to blow up the Starfighter drone, but its destruct package failed to activate. The director was able to get the erratic QF-104 flying in an orbit over the Gulf of Mexico until the drone's fuel was deliberately exhausted and the Starfighter flamed out and crashed into the water.

QF-104A 55-2968 lasted from April to 14 September 1962, when, on its second drone flight, the jet plunged into the Gulf of Mexico. An unspecified technical problem was the likely culprit.

Prototype XQF-104A 56-730, modified by Lockheed in 1960, made 14 drone flights and suffered calamities including the loss of its canopy and having landing gear doors fail to retract, before it was intentionally terminated by activating its destruct package on 26 October 1967 following a loss of pitch control while flying at a blistering 1.4 Mach at 30,000ft. After climbing as high as 55,000ft and diving repeatedly, the destruct switch ended the flight.

QF-104A Starfighter 56-739 served as a test XQF-104A, being modified by Lockheed into a drone at its Burbank plant in 1959–61. The aircraft was destroyed by a GAR-2B Falcon AAM on 8 October 1963.

Probably a Day-Glo orange QF-104 bleached nearly white in the Florida sun, this jet (56-735) was felled by a Sparrow missile launched by a US Navy F-4b on 17 June 1965. *NMUSAF*

QF-104 56-741 performed 22 drone flights between 1961 and 1972, including high-speed, high-g, high-altitude runs. On 16 May 1972, control was lost on long final approach, and the Starfighter crashed two miles short of its intended runway.

QF-104A 56-743, at one time a North American X-15 chase aircraft at Edwards, arrived at Eglin in November 1967. On its second drone flight, the Starfighter was at 5000ft over the Gulf of Mexico when it plunged into the sea while rolling out of a 3g turn on 25 September 1968. 56-745 was the first QF-104A lost by the drone organisation at Eglin. On its third drone flight on 16 January 1962, the aircraft experienced an elevator malfunction on take-off, crashing to its destruction. Starfighter 56-796 sheared its nose gear on landing after its first drone mission, rolling over on its back on the ground and bursting into flames.

The Eglin QF-104As were given bright Day-Glo orange paint for some of their careers. That part of Florida logs an average of 230 sunny, if humid, days each year – the type of days that slow down human activity and can make metal airframes too hot to touch. The fragile high-visibility orange paint on the QF-104s took on a weathered look as the Starfighter drones dodged missiles until their number was up. To help drone director pilots see the high-flying QF-104s when the Day-Glo orange paint was not enough, a smoke generator system was installed. It consisted of a pipe that allowed for the release of controlled amounts of JP-4 jet fuel from the drone's tanks into the exhaust, where it generated white smoke.[406]

In 1963 the Sperry company, working for the USAF's Flight Test Center, found it useful to earmark a QF-104 to be a surrogate for the Boeing X-20 Dyna-Soar space vehicle that was then in design. It was planned that the aircraft would test the X-20's Remote Control Recovery System (RCRS). A synopsis of the Sperry plan stated 'The flight test program is designed to check out the RCRS, simulate X-20 recovery, and provide controller familiarization'. The synopsis noted the test bed QF-104 'system configuration consists of an airborne radar transponder, flight control coupler, and airspeed sensitive unit installed in the vehicle to be controlled, and two ground control stations.'[407] But Dyna-Soar was cancelled by the DoD on 10 December 1963.

Boeing 720 drone

In July 1980, plans were made by the FAA to create a drone using a four-engined Boeing 720 airliner for the Full-Scale Transport Controlled Impact Demonstration (CID). The FAA stated:

> 'The FAA's aircraft safety program, as proposed to Congress in mid-1980, identified a need for a large transport crash test which would demonstrate and validate technology that can improve transport aircraft crash survivability through: (1) reduced post-crash fire hazard; and (2) improved crash impact protection.'

This was to be the first time a four-engined jet airliner would fly as a drone. The ultimate flight of the programme was to result in the deliberate crash-landing of the drone airliner in front of steel obstacles that could rupture fuel tanks to see if an anti-misting formula for its jet fuel, called AMK, could suppress fire. The test was a joint NASA and FAA project. It was conducted at Edwards AFB, where the broad expanse of Rogers Dry Lake provided the perfect setting for the controlled crash-landing.

This manned QF-104 equipped with drop tanks was photographed during a target simulation flight. *USAF*

This spectacular crash-landing on Rogers Dry Lake on 1 December 1984 was a deliberate drone flight to serve NASA and FAA research purposes. The aircraft involved was a former FAA Boeing 720 airliner. *NASA*

As with military target drones, the 720 was fitted with a destruct system.[408] The latter was described in the following NASA report:

> 'The profile for the final remotely controlled crash flight was carefully considered to minimize danger to ground population should the aircraft primary system fail and control of the aircraft be lost. The flight termination system was an independent aircraft radio uplink at 421 MHz to command an intentional crash of the CID aircraft should this occur. The termination system contained several safety features to prevent inadvertent activation such as an interlocking arming sequence and dual-coded command tones. The termination command would have energized appropriate relays to complete sequences such as shutting the engine fuel off, retarding throttles, lowering landing gear, and commanding a pitch-down right turn to the control system.'[409]

The FAA's original intent was a demonstration of the actions of the AMK jet fuel in an intentional crash-landing. As the test plan developed, it became apparent this would also be an opportunity to study things like cabin fire safety, restraint and crashworthiness. At that point, the FAA invited NASA to join the project to support the flight operations and crashworthiness aspects. The overall outcome of the test was to inform the FAA 'for criteria for consideration of rulemaking action'.[410]

A spectacular fireball erupted when the wing of the drone Boeing 720 jetliner was pierced by steel obstacles during the crash test at Edwards AFB. *NASA*

The 720 to be droned was considered a good representation of airliner construction methods then employed by US and foreign airframe manufacturers. The 720 was fitted with a remote flight control system that allowed a pilot on the ground to direct the actions of the aircraft in flight. NASA research pilot 'Fitz' Fulton, who had an impressive record of large-aircraft testing, was selected to fly the 720 drone.[411]

Visible to Fulton at his ground control station were video images from either of two nose-mounted, forward-facing video cameras 'to aid in flying the aircraft and in final guidance to the crash site', according to a NASA post-mission report. The primary camera provided colour video, while the feed from a back-up camera was in black-and-white. The nose-mounted cameras were also said to be sufficient to enable Fulton to make a landing on Rogers Dry Lake if the impact test had to be aborted. The remote cockpit used by Fulton for the CID effort made no attempt to simulate a 720 cockpit. Rather, it featured significant instrument presentations and a video monitor to enable him to fly the drone. A control column instead of a control yoke was used in the remote cockpit.[412]

Drone systems were tested by the end of February 1984 and a manned flight of the 720 was made on 7 March. Other manned flights were scheduled for April, May and June, with the climactic drone crash demonstration set for July. Problems with some of the aircraft and test systems delayed the programme, however, with the actual crash demonstration not taking place until 1 December 1984.

The FAA had acquired the 720 (for $4.2 million) in May 1961 for training its jet operations inspectors. Carrying FAA registration N23, it had logged more than 20,000 flight hours and 54,000 take-offs and landings, and by 1984 was considered at the end of its useful life. For the crash test, the 720 was instrumented with accelerometers and strain gauges and fitted with cameras to record the demonstration. Fourteen manned flights with safety pilots allowed for remotely-piloted checkouts, including nine remotely-piloted vehicle take-offs and thirteen landings.[413]

On the dry lakebed, a mat of crushed rock some four to six inches deep and 300ft wide by 1200 ft long was arranged. Landing approach lights were placed in a way that would make their 300-watt lamps a realistic fuel ignition source. Eight wing opener blades were placed at the impact site to intentionally rupture the fuel tanks of the 720.

NASA research pilot Fitzhugh L 'Fitz' Fulton used this cockpit simulator with a television monitor to fly the Boeing 720 CID in a deliberate wheels-up crash landing into obstacles placed on Rogers Dry Lake at Edwards AFB. The crash was documented with sensors and cameras that revealed fire propagation characteristics. *NASA*

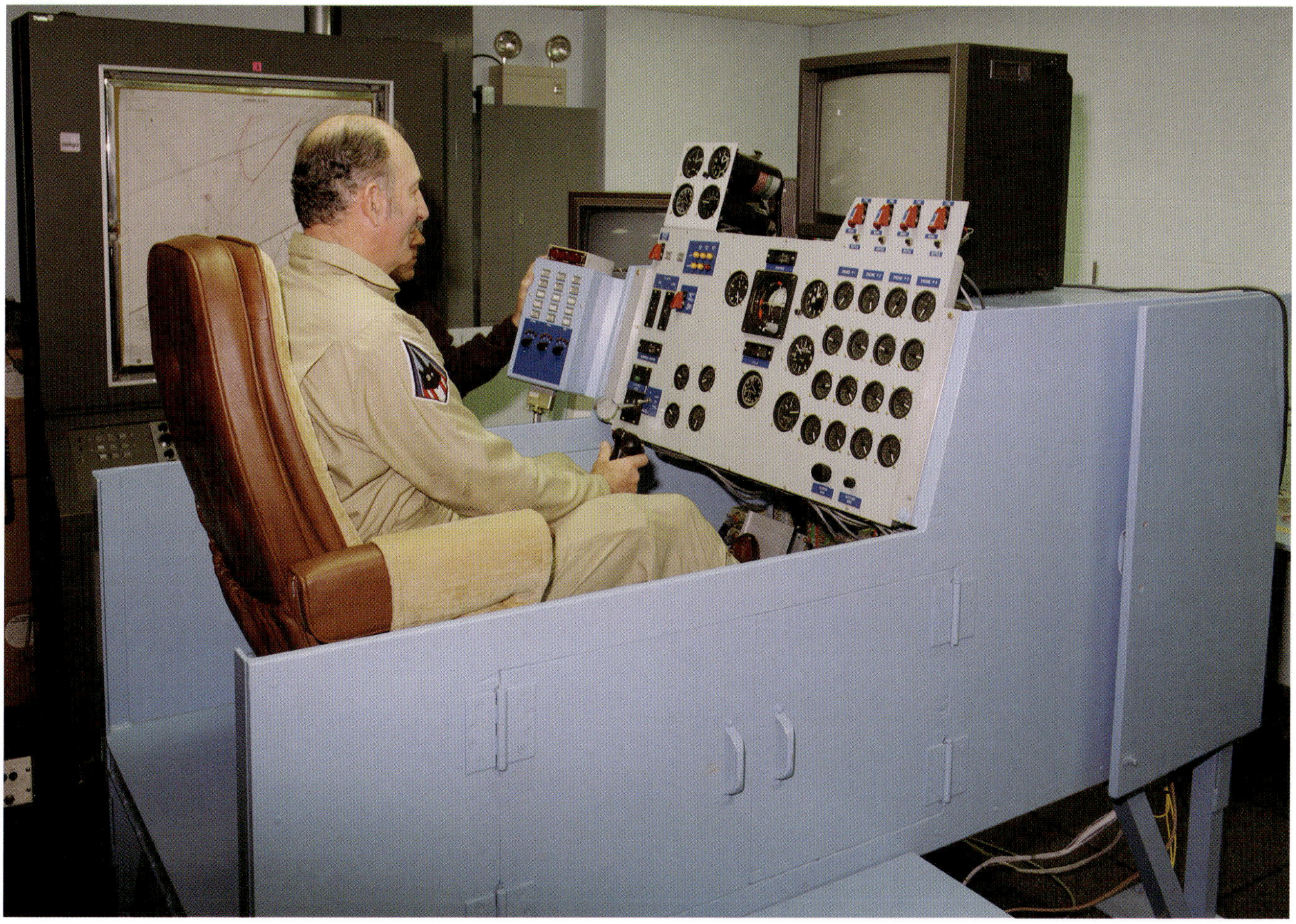

For the final drone flight, the airliner was to take off from Rogers Dry Lake and climb to an altitude of 2300ft, circling the lakebed and intercepting a simulated instrument landing system signal beam. With flaps at thirty degrees and landing gear retracted, the 720 was to contact the impact area in a nose-up attitude. The wings would quickly be ruptured by the wing openers on the ground, releasing a stream of AMK jet fuel to create the potential for a post-crash fire. The 720 would then continue on the prepared gravel surface, striking frangible approach lights. Testers acknowledged the ability to place the drone on the ground at the desired impact point had a longitudinal accuracy of +75ft (landing long) and -125ft (landing short), with ground effect a factor as the airliner flew near the lakebed surface.[414]

On the actual drone flight – the 720's only truly remotely-piloted flight – duration was eight minutes and fifty-four seconds from brake release to impact. Descent appeared normal to about 500ft, at which time the 720 began drifting to the right. At 260ft above ground level, remote pilot workload increased as he attempted to align the airliner with the centreline of the impact runway area. At impact, the drone was fairly aligned with the runway, but offset to the right.

With some bank induced by manoeuvring to get back into position, the left outboard engine on its underslung pylon beneath the wing made first contact about 410ft short of intended impact. Sink rate was 18.5ft per second. The left inboard engine next contacted the surface, followed by the fuselage. The large drone was to the right of the runway centreline. The right inboard engine contacted one of the wing opener blades, which sliced the powerplant and halted its rotation, with fire ignition happening a tenth of a second later on the inboard side of the engine. The initial fire was aggravated by lubricating oil and hydraulic fluid, and fed by the AMK jet fuel. The 720 drone had not impacted the blades precisely as intended, and the action of destroying an engine and rupturing the lower fuselage created a scenario in which the anti-misting fuel was unable to suppress ignition.[415]

NASA and the FAA pondered the data and the evidence contained in the damaged and burned 720 and gleaned useful information about airliner fuselage structural integrity, materials flammability and other crash details best obtained from such a well-monitored and instrumented intentional crash-landing. The cutter striking an engine showed, without a doubt, that the anti-misting fuel was not a panacea to ward of all crash fuel fires.

Beechcraft QU-22 *Pave Eagle*

The USAF devised a drone version of the Beechcraft Bonanza civil utility aircraft but flew it manned over South East Asia during Operation *Igloo White*, gathering intelligence of enemy movements along the Ho Chi Minh Trail. The first six test airframes were derived from the Beech Model 33 Debonair, a conventional-tail model similar in other ways to the classic V-tail Bonanza. These were designated YQU-22As and combat-tested in South East Asia in 1968.

A follow-on production run of twenty-seven QU-22Bs started with a Beechcraft Model 36 conventional-tail variant of the Bonanza. Leveraging Beechcraft's interchangeability from several of its design offerings, the QU-22B had beefier wing sections from the company's twin-engined Model 55 Baron aircraft to allow the intended drone to carry more fuel for longer flight. The QU-22B was man-rated, and although the USAF designated the aircraft a Q-lettered drone, it was always operated by a pilot in the cockpit.

A hump atop the cowling accommodated a larger generator and extra air flow venting, and is a hallmark

A 'Frankenbeech' in some ways, the Beechcraft QU-22 was designed for drone operations, making use of a mix of Bonanza and Baron components, and flown as a piloted reconnaissance platform over South East Asia. This example was placed on display in the National Museum of the United States Air Force. *NMUSAF*

of the QU-22. The aircraft had an unmanned drone altitude of 30,000ft and a manned altitude listed as 'below 25,000ft'. The QU-22B entered service as a piloted aircraft with a detachment of the 553rd Reconnaissance Wing at Korat Royal Thai Air Force Base. The aircraft served as an airborne relay for acoustic and vibration signals from *Igloo White* sensors airdropped along the Ho Chi Minh Trail. The loitering QU-22Bs relayed this information to Nakhon Phanom, where its analysis could lead to targeting decisions. QU-22Bs operated from 1970–72, when they were removed from service following the loss of some of the aircraft.[416]

The QB-17 that shot itself down

In the late 1940s and into the 1950s, American military forces wanted to know the effects of incendiary ammunition on fuel in aircraft tanks. The US Navy experimented with expendable F6F drones (see Chapter 4), while the USAF fitted a QB-17G with 0.50-calibre machine guns fixed to fire into the aircraft's outermost wing fuel tanks, nicknamed Tokyo tanks, for high-altitude tests in April–May 1950. The tanks were set up as inboard and outboard sets.

One goal of the tests was to determine whether purging the ambient air from the fuel tanks with exhaust gases as an inerting agent would inhibit fuel combustion at 35,000ft. The QB-17 was duly fitted with an exhaust gas purging system. The Tokyo tanks were only filled to ten per cent capacity with JP-3 jet fuel on one sortie and 100/130 octane aviation gasoline on the next, which gave a large volume within the tanks for gaseous content, whether ambient air or the exhaust gases meant to replace the air.[417]

During preliminary planning for the mission in 1949, USAF drone experts requested a twin-engined F-82 Twin Mustang for use as the chase aircraft so that the fighter could shoot down the QB-17 should it lose radio controllability and pose a hazard. The rationale for using the piston-powered F-82 was because jet fighter pilots were reluctant to take their single-engined aircraft forty to fifty miles out to sea, where this test was to take place for safety reasons.

The drone operators initially said they did not want to bring the QB-17 back to land if it was not downed in the test because it would probably have sustained unknown damage. Furthermore, the bomber's controls were optimised for flight at around 35,000ft, and this introduced risk when landing at Eglin near sea level.[418] By the time the test was flown in 1950, the chase aircraft were jets after all – two F-80s and a pair of F-84s – and the aversion to landing the QB-17 had dissipated, for the bomber was safely recovered after high-altitude flight.[419]

The testers reviewed the available QB-17 drone records and selected aircraft 44-83610 as being capable of climbing to the extreme altitude required. On 3 August 1949 the aircraft was transferred to Wright-Patterson for configuring.

An M2 0.50-calibre machine gun was mounted in each waist window, able to be boresighted for hitting the Tokyo tanks and locked into place. GE pneumatic automatic gun chargers were connected to high-pressure oxygen tanks, and the chargers were added to the QB-17's radio control system. This enabled the 'air-beeper' pilot in the accompanying DB-17 to charge and fire either gun, expending one round at a time. The method for achieving single-round operation of the machine guns was accomplished by linking one live round spaced with three dummy rounds and then back to one live round in the belted ammunition fed to the guns.

The B-17 that shot itself down was photographed on the runway before a take-off. The remnant of the letter 'A' on the vertical fin may be an artifact indicating this was one of the bombers painted for use in the filming of *Twelve O'Clock High* in 1949. *USAF*

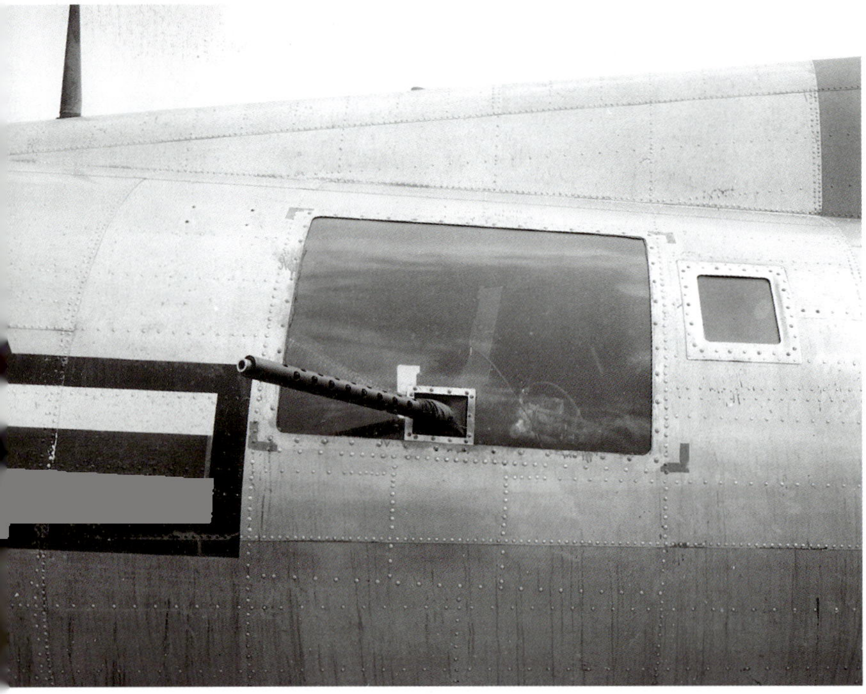

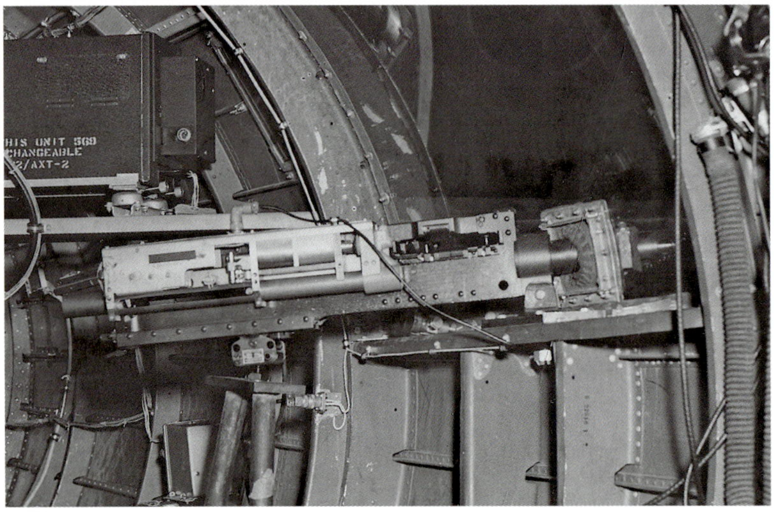

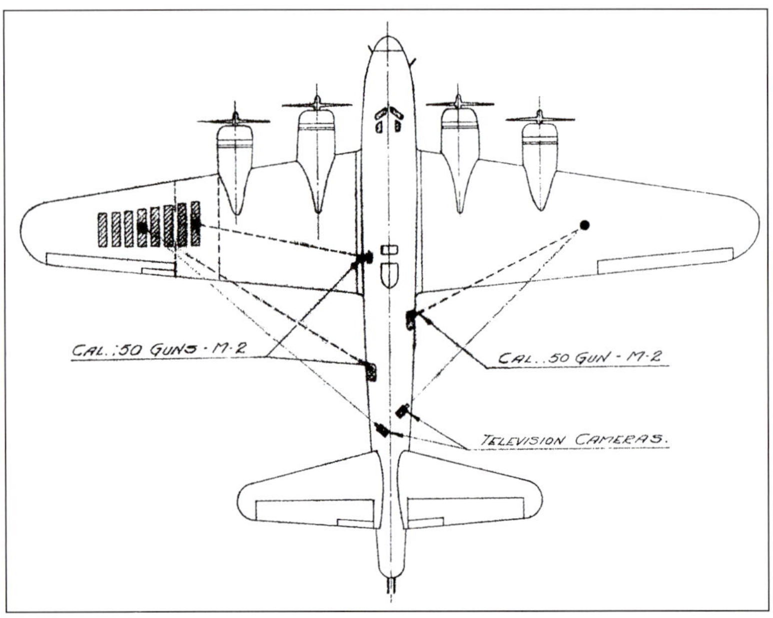

In addition to installing remote control equipment, the team at Wright-Patterson placed television cameras near both waist windows in an effort to give observers in other aircraft and on the ground a real-time view, as well as a record, of the 0.50-calibre incendiary rounds fired into the drone's wings. The 'air-beeper' pilot controlled activation of the television cameras in the QB-17.

The inert exhaust gas was captured from the QB-17's No 1 engine and cooled before being ducted into the five outer Tokyo tank cells in the left wing, as well as in the open spaces inside the surrounding wing cavity. A taped and caulked plywood bulkhead isolated this purged cavity from the remainder of the left wing.

Work on the mother and drone was finished at Wright-Patterson, enabling the two Flying Fortresses to be returned to Eglin on 29 March 1950. The aircraft were part of the 2nd Guided Missiles Squadron of the 550th Guided Missiles Wing.[420]

Using a light load of JP-3 jet fuel in the Tokyo tanks, the first test of the system at Eglin launched on 27 April 1950. It resulted in ammunition impacting the wing upper rear spar cap instead of readily entering the Tokyo tanks. The QB-17 was returned to base and results were not considered. The damaged outer wing panel was removed from the QB-17 and its special purging system was installed in a spare B-17 wing panel that was mated to the drone.[421]

On 24 May 1950, the second test flight, at a pressure altitude of 35,400ft, had the Tokyo tanks purged with exhaust gases. This time 100/130 aviation gasoline was used in the test tanks instead of JP-3. A third 0.50-calibre weapon was mounted in the QB-17's radio room to fire into the purged fuel cells of the left wing. Two 0.50-calibre M23 incendiary rounds were expended ninety seconds apart from the left waist window into the left wing's outboard Tokyo tanks. The rounds were observed to function, but the onboard television cameras and following fighter aircraft did not detect any subsequent fire or smoke from the tank where the rounds penetrated.

Top: This 0.50-calibre machine gun is one of two that shot at its own bomber for a fuel fire test. It was fixed in a special mount using the left waist window. Single rounds were fired from this gun into the wing fuel tank of 44-83610 at altitude. *USAF*

Middle: The B-17 that shot itself down had this M2 0.50-calibre machine gun specially mounted in its left waist window, the weapon being able to fire individual rounds aimed at its own wing tank. *USAF*

Left: This basic diagram showed placement of fixed 0.50-calibre machine guns to shoot at the wing tanks of the QB-17 for a high-altitude flame suppression test. *USAF*

44-83610 begins its round-out for landing at Eglin Auxiliary Field No 2 in May 1950, shortly before its final flight. The faintly visible small ring in the upper part of the Plexiglas nose is likely a leftover from a dummy gun mount used during the filming of *Twelve O'Clock High*, when several Eglin Fortresses were retrofitted for the motion picture. *USAF*

After final checkout, the safety crew leaves the QB-17 at the end of the runway at the Eglin complex for remote take-off in May 1950. *USAF*

Three minutes later, a single round was fired from a machine gun in the QB-17's radio room, aimed at the left wing inboard Tokyo tanks. A four by six-inch hole torn in the tank by the bullet issued a stream of unburned fuel. This was followed in 30 seconds by a fourth 0.50-calibre round into the left inboard cell.[422]

Peering through binoculars, this ground control pilot's task is rudder control for the QB-17 before an airborne pilot takes over. *USAF*

For five minutes, the drone B-17 flew on in the rarified air high over the Eglin test ranges, seemingly unhurt by the self-inflicted 0.50-calibre incendiary hits. To the surprise of the testers, after that time had elapsed, the left outer wing panel broke up and away from the aircraft, revealing fire blazing in the remaining portion of the wing attached to the QB-17. Now fatally out of balance, the drone fell into a tight spin, dropping about a mile before it was destroyed by a violent explosion. An accompanying B-29 photo aircraft carried a motion-picture camera fitted with a telephoto lens, and subsequent review of the camera's film detected fire in the wing before the break-up.[423]

The USAF pondered this test, and considered the possibility that an initial round ruptured the tank but did not cause ignition. This hole may have allowed the purging exhaust gases to be replaced with ambient air that was able to sustain combustion of 100/130 aviation gasoline from a subsequent incendiary bullet. Testers acknowledged a full-fledged investigation into the efficacy of incendiary ammunition against aircraft fuel tanks at high altitude would require more money, and more QB-17s, than were available for such a task, so the Flying Fortress that shot itself down remained an isolated incident in Cold War test annals. As an aside, the drone director mother ship used in this Eglin test was DB-17G 44-85738, an Operation *Crossroads* veteran that was later selected for static display in Tulare, California.

Airacobra Drones

The US Navy had a small quantity of Bell P-39 Airacobra tricycle-gear fighters that it had acquired for droning. As Bell F2L-1Ks, seven Airacobra targets were assigned BuNos 91102 through 91103 and 122447 through 122451. A single XTDL-1 (ex-USAAF P-39Q 42-20807) was also tested.[424]

An airborne control pilot aboard a director B-17 approaches Eglin Auxiliary Field No 2 to pick up a QB-17 that is taking off in 1950. *USAF*

QL-17 Navion vortex chaser

When the US Army and USAF collaborated to study the effects of jet wingtip vortices on smaller aircraft in 1956, the former contributed a droned North American L-17 Navion designated QL-17.

The rationale was succinct – testers believed small aircraft at low altitude near an airport could be fatally upended by the powerful wingtip vortices of high-performance jets, and valid testing of this could not risk an onboard pilot. Additionally, some small aircraft had been destroyed in flight in proximity to larger aircraft under circumstances that led testers to wonder about the severity of vortices. The tests included flying the Navion drone across and behind the flightpath of an F-100 from a ninety-degree angle, then at forty-five degrees and, finally, keeping it in a straight line while the jet overtook the aircraft from behind and below, before rising in front of the QL-17 to present its vortices in trail. For variety, a B-47 Stratojet bomber was also flown as a vortex-generating aircraft.[425] Testers found the vortices were most turbulent when the jet was in take-off configuration. This had implications for aircraft spacing on take-off.

USAF test pilot Capt Roscoe Tanner flew the turbulence-generating F-100 at 200 knots, with wheels and flaps extended. The Super Sabre did double duty, serving also as an ultimate range safety aircraft, with its 20mm cannons armed in case the QL-17 'went rogue' from its controllers and threatened mayhem. Normally, the QL-17's flight termination system was a device to programme it to dive into the ground if contact with the drone director pilot was lost. Special smoke tanks mounted to the F-100 enabled Capt Tanner to provide a visual cue for intercepts by the QL-17. A Hiller H-23 helicopter loitering about 1000ft away provided airborne observation of the drone-and-jet flight intercepts. Flights typically were made in the morning when calm air was likely. Set for 1000ft, the vortex incursions gave the remotely-piloted QL-17 enough altitude to recover from any steep banking upsets.[427]

The US Army and USAF study verified the hazards of wake vortices on small aircraft, but acknowledged more detailed study by other aviation organisations was needed.[428]

The US Army Aviation Board at Fort Rucker, Alabama, contracted Temco Aircraft to convert L-17 Navion 71344 into a QL-17 in 1956 so that it could undertake hazardous flights into wake turbulence produced by a USAF B-47 Stratojet and a F-100 Super Sabre flying from nearby Eglin. Aside from its standard Olive Drab camouflage and *US ARMY* titling, the aircraft had its upper wing surfaces painted yellow to improve visibility for the drone pilot flying in a US Army L-23 Seminole.

The Navion was converted to QL-17 drone configuration by Temco Aircraft of Grand Prairie, Texas. Temco had previous experience with Navions, working on twin-engined conversions of the design. As part of the conversion process, the QL-17 was fitted with a 12-channel oscillograph to record changes in acceleration in roll, pitch and yaw. Airspeed and altitude were also tracked.

The QL-17 was taken off and landed by a ground-based drone pilot. Once aloft, a US Army Beech L-23 Seminole twin-engined aircraft with a second drone pilot took over control of the Navion. The drone operator in the L-23 could turn the QL-17's oscillograph on and off as needed for data capture.[426]

Kaman drone helicopters

Charles Kaman perfected a series of 'eggbeater' helicopters – machines with two main rotors overlapping in their arcs – that found both civil and military customers. Inspiration came from German expatriate Anton Flettner, who had pioneered the concept before becoming a designer for Kaman. Said to be easy to fly, perhaps it was a natural that a Kaman 'eggbeater' would be droned in the 1950s. Designated HTK-1K by the US Navy, with the first K standing for manufacturer Kaman and the second identifying it as a drone, the helicopter made its first flight on 31 May 1953.

Kaman engineers and pilots flew the drone, sometimes with a safety pilot on board, from the company's Bloomfield, Connecticut, plant at the behest of the Office of Naval Research. Remote pilots had demonstrated the ability to take off, land and fly forward and backward in more than 100 hours of flight tests by the spring of 1955. To accommodate remote piloting, Kaman engineers devised a special autopilot for the HTK-1K.[429]

Around 1956 the US Army joined the US Navy in testing an HTK-1K for use in high-risk scenarios. When fitted with a television camera, the droned Kaman could perform battlefield surveillance. It was envisioned that the remotely-piloted HTK-1K could be used for laying battlefield communication wire, for making smokescreens and laying a line of explosive charges that could clear paths for friendly forces crossing minefields. Resupply was another possible mission. The drone could be controlled from a ground station, or from another helicopter. Testers said the drone could be manipulated by someone who did not have flight training experience.[430]

Kaman's early mastery of externally-controlled helicopter technology included a halter device with which non-pilot ground operators could quickly gain proficiency in moving the HTK-1K. The halter was connected to the Kaman drone's control system so that its movement in any direction would prompt the low-hovering HTK to head in that direction. Using the halter, a person on the ground could cause the HTK drone to take off, land and hover. The halter operator could also 'walk' the special HTK to a different location on the ramp.[431]

The Kaman halter was tested as a means to manoeuvre the HTK-1K over a pre-positioned cargo sling, which was then attached to the helicopter's cargo hook by a groundcrewman. At that point, the ground halter operator turned control of the Kaman drone over to a pilot in a ground control station, with the ground control station operator flying the helicopter to its destination, where another groundcrewman with a halter resumed local control of the helicopter, walking the loaded Kaman to the spot where the cargo sling was released. At that point, the halter operator had the option of returning control of the drone to a ground control station, so the helicopter could be flown cross-country to another location, or he could walk the helicopter to parking and land it.[432]

Suggesting an early form of autonomous flight, a story in *Naval Aviation News* said, in addition to being controlled real-time by human operators, 'the robot can be flown on a memory course fed into either airborne or ground control stations'.[433]

Another innovation followed the halter for the HTK-1K drone helicopter when Kaman announced it had flown a drone powered by an electric motor. A light high-voltage AC electric motor was kept continuously supplied with current by a cable connected to a 250-kilowatt generator on the ground. The electrified drone was said to be useful for keeping a helicopter airborne over a specific location for extended periods of time.[434]

A wide open cockpit reveals no occupants as the drone HTK-1 demonstrates its capabilities. *Gerald Balzer collection*

US Marine Corps personnel of Combat Logistics Battalion 5 familiarise themselves with the downward thrust of a Kaman K1200 K-MAX unmanned helicopter during initial testing in Helmand Province, Afghanistan, on 22 May 2012. VMU-2 pioneered the first unmanned, mid-flight external cargo hook-ups, and delivered approximately 6000lb of gear in the K1200 K-MAX's first day of testing. *US Marine Corps*

In the 1960s, two droned Kaman QH-43G Huskie utility helicopters deployed aboard the US Navy command ship USS *Wright* (CC-2) to test a very low frequency communications system with submarines at sea.[435]

Kaman continued its legacy of droning helicopters with the Titan unmanned derivative of the narrow piscine K1200 K-MAX helicopter. The latter had gained fame for lifting 6000lb more than its empty weight, although operational payloads may be closer to 4500lb. The company marketed the drone Titan for use in missions considered too risky for piloted aircraft.

From December 2011, the US Marine Corps evaluated two unmanned K1200 K-MAX helicopters in Afghanistan, where they were operated by Marine Unmanned Aerial Vehicle Squadron (VMU) 2. On 22 May 2012, the US Marine Corps made the first 'hot hook-up', with the K1200 K-MAX being remotely-piloted and hovering while a sling load was attached for delivery to Marines in the field in Afghanistan's Helmand Province. The hovering 'hot hook-up' saves time over conventional landing and taking off, and can be especially beneficial in a combat scenario.[436]

Boeing Little Bird

If Kaman is a pioneer in the use of drone helicopters converted from piloted vehicles, they are not alone in this field. Boeing developed its Little Bird drone from a McDonnell Douglas MD 530F, itself an outgrowth of the Hughes 500. Little Bird (designated ULB) first flew autonomously on 16 October 2004 (with a safety pilot aboard). On 30 June 2006, ULB flew a pre-programmed unmanned sortie around the US Army's Yuma Proving Ground in Arizona. Earlier tests included firing AGM-114 Hellfire air-to-ground missiles from the airborne ULB, with the flight conducted by a pilot strapped into the cockpit of a Boeing AH-64D Apache Longbow helicopter parked several miles away.[437]

Little Bird led to the more capable A/MH-6X helicopter that is considered optionally piloted, enabling a variety of mission scenarios. After remotely flying both the H-6U and the K1200 K-MAX, US Marine Corps evaluators said they made successful autonomous landings with both rotorcraft in April 2014. The K1200 K-MAX and A/MH-6X were equipped with the Autonomous Aerial Cargo/Utility System. The latter employs advanced algorithms with light detection and ranging and electro-optical/infrared sensors to enable a person using a tablet to choose a point to land the helicopter at an unprepared landing location. Autonomous landing without the requirement for remote control diminishes operator workload.[438]

The development of optionally piloted helicopters opens up a world of mission-tailored opportunities for aircraft, with sensor packages becoming smaller and ever more capable.

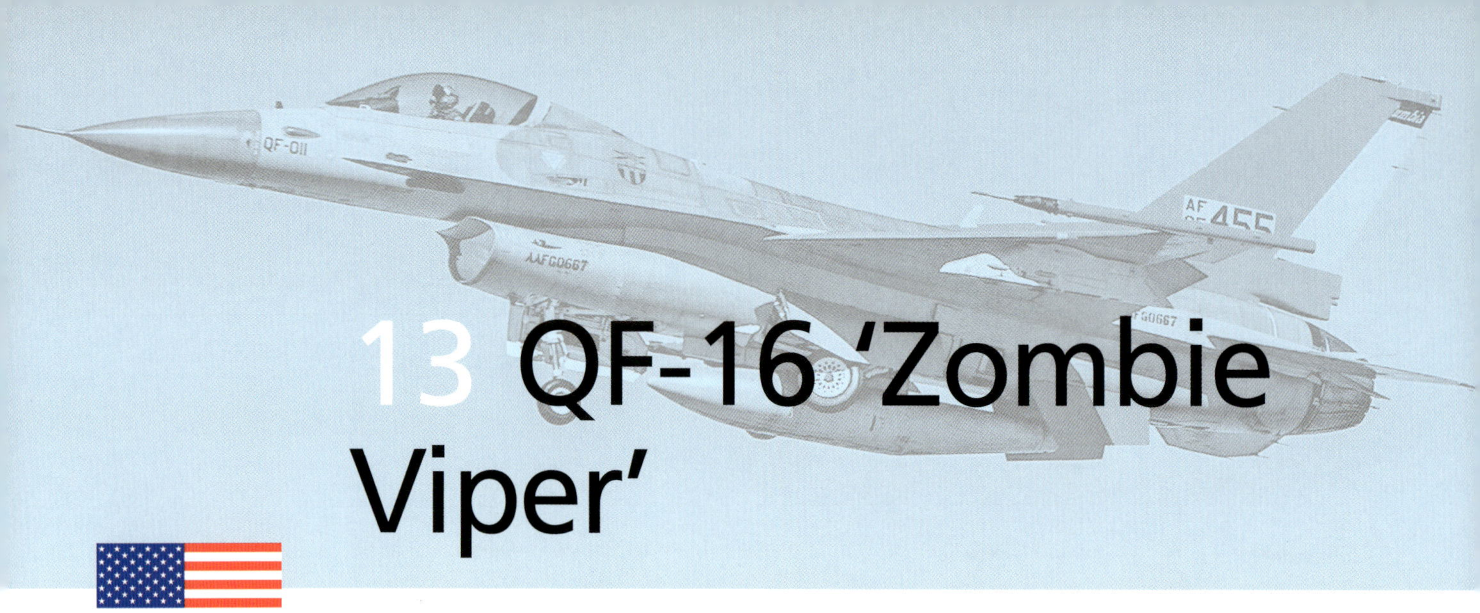

13 QF-16 'Zombie Viper'

The current FSAT drone is the Lockheed Martin (formerly General Dynamics) QF-16 Fighting Falcon, sometimes nicknamed the 'Zombie Viper'. As QF-4 Phantom II assets diminished, and as global threats increased in sophistication, the rationale for adapting a jet drone with the capabilities of a fourth-generation fighter were compelling. A 2005 DoD report made a case for adopting the F-16 as the stock of Phantom II drones decreased through attrition. Prepared by the Defense Science Board Task Force on Aerial Targets, the report stated that the F-16 was the best follow-on FSAT because of a plentiful supply of older Fighting Falcon variants.[439] Legacy F/A-18 Hornets were also contemplated for this droning project, but the F-16 was selected due to the sheer number available for conversion.

An F-16B explodes, sending debris and shrapnel into the air on the range at Eglin on 19 August 2010. The explosion was a static test of the flight termination system (FTS) to be used in the QF-16, a supersonic FSAT drone. The purpose of the test was to demonstrate that the FTS design would be sufficient to immediately terminate the flight of a QF-16, as well as to determine a range safety debris footprint. *USAF*

The task force revisited the tempting, but sometimes impractical, notion of having QF-16s be drones only, and not man-rated:

> 'The Task Force recommends our future full-scale target effort should strive to eliminate the need for a man-rated aircraft because it is a major driver of vehicle cost. The F-16 option would allow removal of the wings for ground transportation.'

Yet, as finally executed, man-rated QF-16s prevailed for all of the reasons previous FSATs, other than the PQM-102, retained the capability of flight with a pilot onboard. The report acknowledged the use of F-16s would be a transitory measure until some manner of Fifth Generation FSAT could be procured:

> 'Accordingly, the Task Force also recommends a concept development effort for a full-scale target to emulate advanced aircraft threats exploiting low-observables.'[440]

The report doubled down on its advocacy of keeping QF-16s cheaper by not having them man-rated:

> 'A key consideration in this decision is the need to have the drone man-rated. This is an important cost issue, with the man-rating capability costing roughly one-third of the $2 million cost of the drone. There may be substantial arguments for the man-rating, but the Task Force did not hear them. Man-rating makes it easy to ferry the drone aircraft to the range where it is to be used, but our impression is that there are few such ranges and the aircraft could readily be ground-transported there. Ground transportability would require removable wings. The F-16 has removable wings, the F-4 does not. Any analysis of full-scale target choices must consider the man-rating issue as an important cost element.'[441]

Those who did not support the drone-only idea said the PQM-102 required substantially more preflight

QF-16 FTS engineer Beth Bartlett surveys the successful intended damage after the explosion of the F-16B at Eglin on 19 August 2010. *USAF*

hours, hence costs, than did its man-rated counterparts. Losses, they argued, would be expected to be higher for a non-man-rated drone that could not be test-flown by an onboard pilot who could correct some problems and save the aircraft in some situations where a remotely-piloted machine would crash.

The F-16, a product of the fly-by-wire computer control revolution, was easier to augment for remote flying than previous mechanically-manoeuvred aircraft. The conversion of F-16s into drones started with aircraft from production blocks 15, 25 and 30. The initial contract called for 225 F-16 conversions. Block 15 aircraft are F-16As, while Block 25 and 30 aircraft are F-16Cs. Boeing secured the contract to be the creator and modifier of QF-16 drones, with the company installing its own Drone-Peculiar Equipment package in the aircraft at its Cecil Field, Florida, facility. The package includes features for everything from remote control of the aircraft to incoming missile trajectory scoring and flight termination. The QF-16 is classed as a Mach 2 aircraft with a ceiling of 50,000ft, and it can use chaff and flares and electronic jammers for missile attack avoidance.

With an eerily empty cockpit, a QF-16 FSAT from the 82nd ATRS flies over the Gulf of Mexico during its first unmanned flight from Tyndall on 19 September 2013. *USAF*

The low-angle sun behind a QF-16 at Holloman casts long shadows past a special crew stand which screens the large jet inlet and accommodates a pilot or maintainer who start the drone and then safely depart while it is running. (*USAF*)

On 19 September 2013, a QF-16A of the Tyndall-based 82nd Aerial Targets Squadron (ATRS) accomplished the type's first NULLO flight. As with previous drones, a pilot performed the preflight checks on the QF-16 before climbing out and latching the jet's canopy from the outside. Control of the drone was taken over by ground pilot Thomas Mudge of the 82nd, seated in a building elsewhere on base. A USAF article on this flight noted 'the QF-16 took off at 3 p.m. for an hour-long mission profile including take off, conducting a series of simulated maneuvers and reaching supersonic speeds before returning to base and landing'.[442]

On 23 September 2016, the USAF announced initial operational capability for the QF-16, which was put into service at Holloman and Tyndall. Both bases have long histories with drones and major infrastructure for drone operations over unpopulated desert or sea ranges.[443]

Development of the QF-16 FSAT flight programme had commenced with the first manned QF-16 flight on 5 May 2012. Boeing's chief test pilot for the program, Steve Rainey, flew the functional check flight that day. Rainey had amassed valuable experience and credentials as an operational F-4 pilot, a test pilot on several projects and the first USAF pilot to fly the Lockheed Martin F-22 Raptor. The USAF's previous drone, the QF-4, had used the classic two-pilot system for landing the drone, splitting duties for pitch, yaw and power settings, and developers initially proposed this for the QF-16. Rainey successfully resisted that idea, preferring to use Autoland to bring the QF-16 back for a safe landing. 'The F-16 control inputs are too sensitive to use the same concept that was used for QF-4 landings', he noted.[444]

To enhance the QF-16's capabilities, Boeing designed a unique auto throttle.[445] This system could control thrust and speed for all aspects of a drone mission from take-off to landing. Boeing had substantial previous experience in creating auto throttle systems for its aircraft.

Before testing the QF-16 drone system in flight, taxi tests were made with Rainey in the cockpit. Progressing from slow taxiing to high speeds on the runway, a remote pilot worked the system to make sure it could steer and stop the aircraft. In subsequent flights, Rainey took off and passed control of the QF-16 to a pilot on the ground.

Seated in the cockpit, Rainey had a quick release mechanism called a paddle switch to let him take control of the jet in an emergency. A typical feature in operational F-16s to enable the pilot to resume control of the aircraft in a number of situations, the paddle switch was especially handy during QF-16 testing. It allowed the pilot to quickly disconnect the drone-peculiar equipment.

Rainey found the F-16's computerised flight controls, now directed by the Boeing drone system, did not provide feedback in the cockpit. In previous drones, when the ground pilot input a control movement, the control column or rudder pedals physically moved. But in the QF-16, control inputs were electric signals to the controls, and the control column and rudder pedals remained motionless. 'You don't have any feedback because you don't see the stick moving', Rainey explained. It quickly became important for the ground control pilot to announce his intended control inputs, thus avoiding Rainey being unaware of an impending sudden high-g manoeuvre, for instance.[446]

The ground pilot procedure for landing called for lining up the QF-16 with the runway and engaging Autoland. To test this, Rainey flew in the QF-16 as it approached the runway, with the ground control pilot having activated Autoland. The latter was overseen by the Gulf Range Drone Control System, which attempted to fly the jet using an eleven- to thirteen-degree angle of attack (AOA) approach, which was correct for the F-16. However, its attempt to tightly control AOA resulted in abrupt throttle inputs that consequently caused pitch movements. The pitch and throttle inputs that were made to attempt tight control over AOA in turn meant poor glide path control. Rainey recalled:

> 'It was just obvious that there was more work to do to get the approach and landing to work. I told them to fly it like an F-16 pilot flies it and drew it in three phases on a white board. Probably the most important input I made here was referencing the airspeed versus weight chart in the flight manual. I gave it to them and asked them to fly airspeed based on weight rather than chase (the) AOA.'

Ultimately, the QF-16 programme and the range control system were made compatible, but not before a hair-raising landing adventure.[447]

After several changes that corrected glide path control, the team decided it was time to attempt the first full Autoland test. This would involve three approaches at the end of a normal test mission. The first approach was planned to use Autoland to a touchdown if Rainey assessed it was safe. He would then take control of the aircraft for a go around to set up for a second approach. The second approach was also planned as an Autoland to a touchdown, with a pilot-commanded go around after touchdown. These first two approaches were designed to allow the team to evaluate performance, and if the latter was good, the plan was to get the QF-16 to complete the first ever auto landing to a full stop on the runway.

The first touchdown was relatively uneventful. The second was not as good, but still acceptable. For the third, and final, approach and landing, everything was looking normal. However, at approximately 70ft in the air (too high), the auto throttle suddenly slammed to idle and the nose simultaneously pitched up to 15 degrees, resulting in the sounding of the AOA warning horn. Rainey immediately 'paddled off' the Autoland system, taking control. He selected full afterburner and attempted to keep the pitch attitude from dropping rapidly nose low into the runway. Rainey anticipated a very hard landing and instinctively put his left hand on the ejection handle.

The QF-16 hit the runway hard and bounced for a second landing, before responding to Rainey's commands for a go-around. He requested a tower flyby to check the aircraft, and the tower reported no apparent damage. Still anticipating the worst – speed brakes scraped, afterburner 'turkey feathers' scraped or gone, ventral fins scraped – he flew a manual approach for a full stop landing, and he was fully prepared to eject if required. The landing was smooth, and after exiting the jet for a post-flight inspection, no damage at all was observed, much to his surprise. 'They literally had to help me out of the cockpit I was shaking so bad', Rainey latter recalled.[448]

With its empty cockpit highlighted by the setting sun, a QF-16 of the 82nd ATRS takes off from an auxiliary runway at Tyndall on 29 September 2016. ***USAF***

Lt Col Ronald King, CO of the 82nd ATRS's Det 1 at Holloman, retracts the undercarriage of a QF-16 on 10 February 2017 at the start of the unit's first flight from the New Mexico base since its transition from the QF-4 to the QF-16. *USAF*

Control law corrections to the flare for landing were made, and on 12 October 2012, the first successful complete QF-16 auto landing through to a full stop was accomplished with Rainey aboard. No QF-16s have been lost during an auto landing to date. 'An obvious first, and ultimately a success unlike any other on full scale drone programs to date', Rainey said.[449]

When setting up the optionally piloted QF-16 for a drone NULLO mission, two tasks that needed to be carried out were the removal of the F-16's Emergency Power Unit and substitution of the Flight Termination System. The former used highly toxic hydrazine, and its presence in a crashed drone could cause safety problems. As with other drones, it was typical for a NULLO QF-16 to survive more than one sortie before succumbing to a shootdown.

In traditional manned F-16 operations, pilots are not entering or exiting the aircraft while the engine is running, when it can create dangerous suction at the large inlet. For the drone programme, designers created a bridge stand that allowed the pilot or crew chief to enter the cockpit, start the engine, hand off control of the drone to the control room, safely close the canopy and depart the aircraft without getting too close to the inlet.

The converted QF-16A drones can accumulate, ideally, 175 hours of flying time before being destroyed – the QF-16Cs can log about 275 flying hours. With the A-model drones, their flying hours are lower because they are older, have a single generator and can be more challenging to maintain. When major inspections loom, the QF-16 goes to 'Death Row' – a prophetically dooming status for the drone. At this point, after several conversions, the aircraft is flown exclusively unmanned. With some 20 hours left on the airframe before a major inspection is required, the jet is launched unmanned to meet customer requirements, and its ultimate demise.[450]

Just as the QF-16 represents the latest in FSAT technology, so do missiles sent against it in testing. On 5 August 2021, an F-15C at Eglin successfully put an Infrared Search-and-Track (IRST) system to work in the destruction of a QF-16. The Eagle pilot used IRST along with radar to lock onto the drone prior to it being destroyed by an AIM-120.[451] Less than a year later, the AIM-120D3, with beyond-visual-range capability said to exceed 85 miles, made its test debut successfully against a QF-16 over the Gulf of Mexico on 30 June 2022. The distance flown by the test missile was not revealed by the USAF.[452]

Boeing opened a QF-16 conversion line at Cecil Field in Jacksonville, Florida, for initial deliveries. A second QF-16 modification line was set up at Davis-Monthan, with Boeing collaborating with the 309th AMARG to deliver the first Arizona QF-16 in July 2020.[453] Then, on 29 July 2022, the original Boeing QF-16 line in Florida delivered its last 'Zombie Viper', leaving the Davis-Monthan centre to finish future drones for the USAF.

A black funeral pyre cast a shadow in the New Mexico desert as it marked the impact location of the first QF-16 drone downed by an AIM-9X missile on 24 April 2019. *USAF*

American military prognosticators have always acknowledged the QF-16 as a viable, yet transitory, drone. It represents fourth-generation fighters ably, but by the age of its design, it misses the mark for serious use as a fifth-generation opponent. As potential adversary nations continue to develop and deploy fifth-generation warplanes, the need to test advanced missiles against aircraft of such calibre becomes ever more acute. With US fifth-generation Lockheed Martin F-35 Lightning IIs forecast to be in service for at least a half-century, the likelihood of a drone gap between 'Zombie Vipers' and a fifth-generation FSAT is a real concern.

In the summer of 2022, the USAF announced a request for information from potential contractors for the Next Generation Aerial Target (NGAT). The design needs to be supersonic and 'threat representative', says the USAF. This suggests a new airframe will be expected that can produce a realistic signature for discovery and target acquisition indistinguishable from an adversary's fifth-generation aircraft. Examples of such types to be emulated cited in the request include the Chinese Chengdu J-20 and Russian Sukhoi Su-57 fifth-generation fighters. The USAF's request for information says the NGAT 'should be capable of supporting representative (J-20, Su-57, etc.) RF [Radio Frequency] and EA [Electronic Attack] emissions while maintaining an appropriate RCS [Radar Cross Section], IR [Infrared] signature or both for a given test scenario.'[454]

On several occasions in the non-binding request for information, the intent to create an affordable NGAT is emphasised. While purpose-built aircraft like a clean-sheet NGAT have some costs not associated with converted existing airframes, the fact that the early NGAT notions are based on pure drones without cockpits for pilots could represent a saving since no expensive life-support or egress systems would be required. A notional early view of what the NGAT could be is also detailed in the request for information:

> 'The NGAT solution is envisioned with flexibility and growth capability to adapt to new technologies for future threat representation, leverage technologies and design/manufacturing practices to give the vehicle the ability to grow with future technologies, and enable modifications to the system in order to keep up with emerging threats. The Air Force is interested in developing and demonstrating technologies that could enable highly affordable and capable vehicles.'[455]

Fighting Falcons recently pulled out of storage are restored to airworthiness at Davis-Monthan prior to being flown to Cecil Field for conversion into drones. This photograph was taken on 1 August 2017. *USAF*

Civilian contractors overhaul the undercarriage of an F-16C. Drone conversion for a long-stored Fighting Falcon can take several years to complete. *USAF*

The emphasis on initial NGAT discussions is for a new pilotless airframe that can adapt to represent emerging fifth-generation threats. Drones that could be recovered by parachute instead of landing gear are given consideration. Will that mean the end of America's decades-old creation of drones from formerly-piloted aircraft? Is the QF-16 the end of the line for the family tree of historic piloted aircraft as drones, some still carrying vestiges of paint and markings from their heyday? Or will the skies over Holloman and Eglin one day reverberate with the roar of remotely-piloted QF-35s?

A QF-16 Full Scale Aerial target takes off from Holloman on a piloted flight for a rehearsal of a missile test. *USAF*

Endnotes

[1] Duncan Curtis, *The QF-86 Sabre* manuscript shared with the author.

[2] Gordon Swanborough and Peter M Bowers, *United States Military Aircraft Since 1908*, Putnam, London, 1971.

[3] Ibid.

[4] Jay Womack and Arthur Steczkowski, 'Review of Past and Current Trials and Uses of Unmanned Vehicles', Report HSD-TR-87-011, Dayton, Ohio (USAF).

[5] Joseph P Juptner, *U.S. Civil Aircraft – ATC Numbers 601 to 700, Volume 7,* Aero Publishers, Fallbrook, California, 1978.

[6] Jay Womack and Arthur Steczkowski, 'Review of Past and Current Trials and Uses of Unmanned Vehicles', Report HSD-TR-87-011, Dayton, Ohio (USAF).

[7] Ibid.

[8] Gordon Swanborough and Peter M Bowers, *United States Military Aircraft Since 1908*, Putnam, London, 1971.

[9] Peter M Bowers, *Boeing Aircraft Since 1916*, Aero Publishers, Fallbrook, California, 1966.

[10] Ibid.

[11] 'Location of U.S. Naval Aircraft', 25 September 1942, Copy 9 of 25 in US Naval History and Heritage Command (NHHC) collection.

[12] Subject: Final Report on *Aphrodite* Project, from Headquarters 3rd Air Division to Commanding General, Eighth Air Force, 20 January 1945. (This report, archived at the Air Force Historical Research Agency under microfilm reel B5529, includes many attachments and supporting documents referenced in this narrative. All of those documents are intended to be covered with this endnote citation).

[13] Ibid.

[14] Ibid.

[15] Ibid.

[16] Ibid.

[17] Ibid.

[18] Ibid.

[19] Ibid.

[20] Ibid.

[21] Ibid.

[22] Ibid.

[23] Ibid.

[24] Ibid.

[25] Ibid.

[26] Ibid.

[27] Ibid.

[28] Ibid.

[29] Ibid.

[30] Ibid.

[31] Ibid.

[32] Ibid.

[33] Ibid.

[34] Ibid.

[35] History, 3205th Drone Group, Air Proving Ground Command, January–March 1952 (including supporting documents all located in Air Force Historical Research Agency (AFHRA) microfilm reel M0212).

[36] Subject: Final Report on *Aphrodite* Project, from Headquarters 3rd Air Division to Commanding General, Eighth Air Force, 20 January 1945. (This report, archived at the AFHRA under microfilm reel B5529, includes many attachments and supporting documents referenced in this narrative. All of those documents are intended to be covered with this endnote citation).

[37] Letter, Lt Gen Barney M Giles to Maj Gen Carl A Spaatz, 27 April 1945.

[38] Letter, Maj Gen J E Hull, Assistant Chief of Staff, OPD, Memorandum for the Commanding General, U.S. Forces in the European Theater of Operations, Subject: Employment of War-Weary U.S. Bombers Against Large Industrial Target Areas in Germany, 28 February 1945.

[39] Letter, Maj Gen Carl Spaatz to Lt Gen Ira Eaker, 3 May 1945.

[40] Letter, Brig Gen Grandison Gardner to Maj Gen Carl Spaatz, February (date obscured) 1945.

[41] Letter, United States Army Air Forces in Europe, to Commanding General, Army Air Forces, Subject: *Willie Orphan* Weekly Progress Report, 26 January 1945.

[42] Memo, Col Alfred R Maxwell, untitled, dealing with *Aphrodite* and *Willie Orphan*, 19 January 1945.

[43] Memo, United States Army Air Forces in Europe, Col Alfred R Maxwell, Subject: Implementation of *Willie Orphan* Project, 17 January 1945.

[44] Ibid.

[45] Ibid.

[46] Ibid.

[47] Memo, Col Robert M Lee, Headquarters, Ninth Air Force, Advanced, to Commanding General, US Strategic Air Forces in Europe. Subject: Utilization of *Willie Orphan* in the Tactical Area, 7 January 1945.

[48] Ibid.

[49] Subject: Final Report on *Aphrodite* Project, from Headquarters 3rd Air Division to Commanding General, Eighth Air Force, 20 January 1945. (This report, archived at the AFHRA under microfilm reel B5529, includes many attachments and supporting documents referenced in this narrative. All of those documents are intended to be covered with this endnote citation).

[50] Ibid.

[51] Ibid.

[52] Ibid.

[53] Ibid.

[54] Ibid.

[55] Ibid.

[56] Ibid.

[57] Ibid.

[58] 'Personal Narrative', Capt Arthur G Phillips, Heavy Bomb Squadron Flight Test Section, Eglin Field, Florida, 17 April 1946.

[59] Ibid.

[60] Ibid.

[61] Notes from interview by the author with Bell Muroc technician Don Thomson.

[62] 'Pushbutton Pilots' by Louis Bruchiss, *Air News With Air Tech,* 15 March 1946.

[63] 'Safe Testing of Supersonic Planes Seen in New Radio Control Device', *Aviation News*, 19 November 1945.

[64] 'Drones Fly in Cloud Column of Atom Bomb', *Naval Aviation News,* September 1946.

[65] Report on Atomic Bomb Tests *Able* and *Baker* (Operation *Crossroads*), Volume I, Commander, Joint Task Force One, Part VII, Special Reports, (E) Air Operations.

[66] 'Drones Fly in Cloud Column of Atom Bomb', *Naval Aviation News,* September 1946.

[67] Final Report for Tests *Able* and *Baker*, Bureau of Aeronautics Group, Director of Ship Material – Joint Task Force 1, J E Dodson, Capt, US Navy, 18 October 1946.

[68] Operation *Crossroads* Official Report, Task Unit 1.52. Authors not attributed and publication undated, but presumed to be contemporary with 1946.

[69] Ibid.

[70] Final Report for Tests *Able* and *Baker*, Bureau of Aeronautics Group, Director of Ship Material – Joint Task Force 1, J E Dodson, Capt, US Navy, 18 October 1946.

[71] Ibid.

[72] Historical Report – Atomic Bomb Tests *Able* and *Baker* – Operation *Crossroads*, Volume 1 of 3, Director of Ship Material, Joint Task Force 1, History of Director of Ship Material.

[73] Ibid.

[74] Ibid.

[75] Ibid.

[76] Report on Atomic Bomb Tests *Able* and *Baker* (Operation *Crossroads*), Volume I, Commander, Joint Task Force One, Part VII, Special Reports, (E) Air Operations.

[77] Historical Report – Atomic Bomb Tests *Able* and *Baker* – Operation *Crossroads*, Volume 1 of 3, Director of Ship Material, Joint Task Force 1, History of Director of Ship Material.

[78] Report on Atomic Bomb Tests *Able* and *Baker* (Operation *Crossroads*), Volume I, Commander, Joint Task Force One, Part VII, Special Reports, (E) Air Operations.

[79] Ibid.

[80] Ibid.

[81] Ibid.

[82] Ibid.
[83] Ibid.
[84] Ibid.
[85] Ibid.
[86] Ibid.
[87] Report on Atomic Bomb Tests *Able* and *Baker* (Operation *Crossroads*), Commander, Joint Task Force One, Part VII, Special Reports, (G) Photographic.
[88] Operation *Sandstone*: 1948 (Report DNA 6033F), United States Atmospheric Nuclear Weapons Tests – Nuclear Test Personnel Review, Prepared by the Defense Nuclear Agency as Executive Agency for the Department of Defense, 19 December 1983.
[89] Ibid.
[90] Ibid.
[91] History of Project 1, 1st Experimental Guided Missiles Group, July 1947 through May 1948 (including supporting documents all located in AFHRA microfilm reel B0745).
[92] Ibid.
[93] Operation *Sandstone*: 1948 (Report DNA 6033F), United States Atmospheric Nuclear Weapons Tests – Nuclear Test Personnel Review, Prepared by the Defense Nuclear Agency as Executive Agency for the Department of Defense, 19 December 1983.
[94] History of Project 1, 1st Experimental Guided Missiles Group, July 1947 through May 1948 (including supporting documents all located in AFHRA microfilm reel B0745).
[95] Ibid.
[96] History of Project 1, 1st Experimental Guided Missiles Group, July 1948 through December 1948 (including supporting documents all located in AFHRA microfilm reel B0745).
[97] Operation *Greenhouse*: 1951 (Report DNA 6034F), United States Atmospheric Nuclear Weapons Tests – Nuclear Test Personnel Review, Prepared by the Defense Nuclear Agency as Executive Agency for the Department of Defense, 15 June 1983.
[98] Ibid.
[99] Ibid.
[100] Ibid.
[101] Ibid.
[102] Ibid.
[103] Ibid.
[104] Ibid.
[105] Ibid.
[106] Ibid.
[107] Ibid.
[108] Ibid.
[109] Operation *Upshot–Knothole* – Nevada Proving Grounds, March–June 1953, Project 5.1, Atomic Weapon Effects on AD Type Aircraft in Flight.
[110] *Ibid.*
[111] Operation *Upshot–Knothole* – Report to the Test Director – Aircraft Participation, WT-825 (EX) Extracted Version, Nevada Proving Grounds March–June 1953, Air Force Special Weapons Center Kirtland Air Force Base Albuquerque, New Mexico, November 1955.
[112] Operation *Upshot–Knothole* – Nevada Proving Grounds, March–June 1953, Project 5.1, Atomic Weapon Effects on AD Type Aircraft in Flight.
[113] *Ibid.*
[114] *Ibid.*
[115] *Ibid.*
[116] Operation *Upshot–Knothole* – Nevada Proving Grounds, March-June 1953, Project 5.1, Atomic Weapon Effects on AD Type Aircraft in Flight.
[117] Operation *Upshot–Knothole* – Report to the Test Director – Aircraft Participation, WT-825 (EX) Extracted Version, Nevada Proving Grounds March–June 1953, Air Force Special Weapons Center Kirtland Air Force Base Albuquerque, New Mexico, November 1955.
[118] *Ibid.*
[119] *Ibid.*
[120] *Ibid.*
[121] *Ibid.*
[122] Operation *Upshot–Knothole* – Nevada Proving Grounds, March–June 1953, Project 5.1, Atomic Weapon Effects on AD Type Aircraft in Flight.
[123] Operation *Upshot–Knothole* – Project 4.1 – The Radiation Hazards to Personnel Within an Atomic Cloud, WT-743 (EX) Extracted Version, Nevada Proving Grounds March–June 1953, Headquarters Field Command, Armed Forces Special Weapons Project, Sandia, Base Albuquerque, New Mexico. Extracted version prepared for Director, Defense Nuclear Agency, Washington, D.C. 20305, 1 August 1983.
[124] Bert W Adams, 'They Might Be Giants: Small-Scale RPAs as a Threat to Air Base Defense and Air Power Projection', Thesis, School of Advanced Air and Space Studies, Maxwell AFB, Alabama, June 2014.
[125] Action Report for the period 23 August through 6 September 1952, USS *Boxer* (CV-21), 8 September 1952.
[126] Ibid.
[127] Ibid.
[128] Ibid.
[129] *Korean War: Chronology of US Pacific Fleet Operations, May–August 1952,* NHHC website.
[130] 'Effectiveness of Small Arms Incendiary Ammunition at High Altitudes (U), Project TS1-47, Report R-1392, D Jacobs, chemical engineer and J J Caven, chemist, for Col James A Richardson III, Ordnance Corps, circa June 1957.
[131] Ibid.
[132] Ibid.
[133] Ibid.
[134] 'F6F Commits Hari Kari', *Naval Aviation News,* July 1950.
[135] 'Effectiveness of Small Arms Incendiary Ammunition at High Altitudes (U), Project TS1-47, Report R-1392, D Jacobs, chemical engineer and J J Caven, chemist, for Col James A Richardson III, Ordnance Corps, circa June 1957.
[136] 'Genesis of Infrared Decoy Flares, The early years from 1950 into the 1970s', Naval Surface Warfare Center, 26 January 2009.
[137] Ibid.
[138] 'All The Missiles Work – Technological Dislocations And Military Innovation: A Case Study in US Air Force Air-To-Air Armament, post-World War II through Operation *Rolling Thunder*' by Steven A Fino, thesis for School of Advanced Air and Space Studies, Air University, Maxwell AFB, Alabama, June 2010.
[139] 'Last F6F-5K is Converted', *Naval Aviation News,* January 1958.
[140] 'Privateer Navy's Newest Drone', Lt Cdr B F Emge, NADC Johnsville, *Naval Aviation News,* March 1953.
[141] Ibid.
[142] Ibid.
[143] Ibid.
[144] Ibid.
[145] Ibid.
[146] Ibid.
[147] Frederick A Johnsen, *Consolidated B-24 Liberator, Volume 1, Warbird Tech Series,* Specialty Press, North Branch, Minnesota, 1996 and 2001.
[148] Frederick A Johnsen, *Bombers in Blue – PB4Y-2 Privateers and PB4Y-1 Liberators,* Bomber Books, Tacoma, Washington, 1979.
[149] Frederick A Johnsen, *Consolidated B-24 Liberator, Volume 1, Warbird Tech Series,* Specialty Press, North Branch, Minnesota, 1996 and 2001.
[150] Ibid.
[151] History, 3205th Drone Group, Air Proving Ground Command, January–March 1952 (including supporting documents all located in AFHRA microfilm reel M0212).
[152] *History of the 1st Experimental Guided Missiles Group,* July–December 1947.
[153] *History of the 1st Experimental Guided Missiles Group,* January–June 1947.
[154] Ibid.
[155] *History of the 1st Experimental Guided Missiles Group*, January–June 1949 (including supporting documents all located in AFHRA microfilm reel B0745).
[156] *History of the 1st Experimental Guided Missiles Group*, July–December 1948 (including supporting documents all located in AFHRA microfilm reel B0745).

[157] 'Ditching of B-17s', from Headquarters, 1st Experimental Guided Missiles Group, 25 June 1947, included as a supporting document in *History of the 1st Experimental Guided Missiles Group,* January–June 1947.

[158] Ibid.

[159] Ibid.

[160] From supporting documents with *History of the 1st Experimental Guided Missiles Group,* July–December 1947.

[161] Ibid.

[162] *History of the 1st Experimental Guided Missiles Group*, January–June 1949 (including supporting documents all located in AFHRA microfilm reel B0745).

[163] Ibid.

[164] Ibid.

[165] History, 3205th Drone Group, Air Proving Ground Command, October–December 1951 (including supporting documents all located in AFHRA microfilm reel M0212).

[166] Ibid.

[167] 'Nike: Air Defense's First Flight' by Capt Peter Mitchell, *Fires, ADA 50th Anniversary Issue,* undated.

[168] Ibid.

[169] History, 3205th Drone Group, Air Proving Ground Command, October–December 1951 (including supporting documents all located in AFHRA microfilm reel M0212).

[170] Ibid.

[171] Ibid.

[172] History, 3205th Drone Group, Air Proving Ground Command, January–March 1952 (including supporting documents all located in AFHRA microfilm reel M0212).

[173] History, 3205th Drone Group, Air Proving Ground Command, Oct-Dec 1951 (including supporting documents all located in AFHRA microfilm reel M0212).

[174] Ibid.

[175] Ibid.

[176] Ibid.

[177] Ibid.

[178] Ibid.

[179] Ibid.

[180] Ibid.

[181] Ibid.

[182] Ibid.

[183] Ibid.

[184] Excerpted from Supplemental Handbook Maintenance Instructions, USAF Model QB-17 Aircraft, 1 May 1955 and revised 15 June 1957.

[185] History, 3205th Drone Group, Air Proving Ground Command, January–March 1952 (including supporting documents all located in AFHRA microfilm reel M0212).

[186] Ibid.

[187] Ibid.

[188] Ibid.

[189] Ibid.

[190] Ibid.

[191] Ibid.

[192] Ibid.

[193] Ibid.

[194] Ibid.

[195] Ibid.

[196] Film, 'USAF Falcon Missile Tests 8/1951', USAF 21440, National Archives and Records Administration.

[197] History, 3205th Drone Group, Air Proving Ground Command, January–March 1952 (including supporting documents all located in AFHRA microfilm reel M0212).

[198] History, 3205th Drone Group, Air Proving Ground Command, April–June 1952 (including supporting documents all located in AFHRA microfilm reel M0212).

[199] Ibid.

[200] Ibid.

[201] Ibid.

[202] Ibid.

[203] Ibid.

[204] Ibid.

[205] Ibid.

[206] History, 3205th Drone Group, Air Proving Ground Command, July–December 1952 (including supporting documents all located in AFHRA microfilm reel M0212).

[207] Ibid.

[208] Ibid.

[209] Ibid.

[210] Ibid.

[211] Ibid.

[212] Ibid.

[213] Ibid.

[214] Ibid.

[215] Ibid.

[216] History, 3205th Drone Group, Air Proving Ground Command, July–December 1952 (including supporting documents all located in AFHRA microfilm reel M0212).

[217] Ibid.

[218] Ibid.

[219] Ibid.

[220] Ibid.

[221] History, 3205th Drone Group, Air Proving Ground Command, April–June 1952 (including supporting documents all located in AFHRA microfilm reel M0212).

[222] Ibid.

[223] History, 3205th Drone Group, Air Proving Ground Command, January–March 1952 (including supporting documents all located in AFHRA microfilm reel M0212).

[224] Ibid.

[225] History, 3205th Drone Group, Air Proving Ground Command, January–June 1953 (including supporting documents all located in AFHRA microfilm reel M0212).

[226] Ibid.

[227] Ibid.

[228] Ibid.

[229] Ibid.

[230] Ibid.

[231] Ibid.

[232] Ibid.

[233] Ibid.

[234] Ibid.

[235] History, 3205th Drone Group, Air Proving Ground Command, July–December 1953

[236] Ibid.

[237] Ibid.

[238] Ibid.

[239] Ibid.

[240] Ibid.

[241] History, 3205th Drone Group, Air Proving Ground Command, January–March 1952 (including supporting documents all located in AFHRA microfilm reel M0212).

[242] History, 3205th Drone Group, Air Proving Ground Command, July–December 1952 (including supporting documents all located in AFHRA microfilm reel M0212).

[243] History, 3205th Drone Group, Air Proving Ground Command, July–December 1955 (including supporting documents all located in AFHRA microfilm reel M0213 [poor quality of copy inhibits usefulness of this source]).

[244] History, 3205th Drone Group, Air Proving Ground Command, July–December 1952 (including supporting documents all located in AFHRA microfilm reel M0212).

[245] Ibid.

[246] History, 3205th Drone Group, Air Proving Ground Command, January–June 1953 (including supporting documents all located in AFHRA microfilm reel M0212).

[247] Ibid.

[248] Ibid.

[249] History, 3205th Drone Group, Air Proving Ground Command, July–December 1953.

[250] History, 3205th Drone Group, Air Proving Ground Command, January–June 1954 (including supporting documents all located in AFHRA files).

[251] Ibid.

[252] Ibid.

[253] History, 3205th Drone Group, Air Proving Ground Command, January–June 1954 (including supporting documents all located in AFHRA files).

[254] History, 3205th Drone Group, Air Proving Ground Command, January–June 1955 (including supporting documents all located in AFHRA microfilm reel M0213 [poor quality of copy inhibits usefulness of this source]).

[255] Ibid.

[256] Ibid.

[257] Ibid.

[258] Ibid.

[259] Ibid.

[260] Ibid.

[261] Ibid.

[262] Background, US Army Redeye Programme on US Army website https://history.redstone.army.mil/miss-redeye.html at the time of this writing.

[263] History, 3205th Drone Group, Air Proving Ground Command, January–June 1955 (including supporting documents all located in AFHRA microfilm reel M0213 [poor quality of copy inhibits usefulness of this source]).

[264] Ibid.

[265] Ibid.

[266] Ibid.

[267] Ibid.

[268] History, 3205th Drone Group, Air Proving Ground Command, July–December 1955 (including supporting documents all located in AFHRA microfilm reel M0213 [poor quality of copy inhibits usefulness of this source]).

[269] Ibid.

[270] Ibid.

[271] Ibid.

[272] Ibid.

[273] Ibid.

[274] 'Douglas Develops Camera System To Record Accuracy of Missiles', *Aviation Week,* 5 March 1956.

[275] Ibid.

[276] Excerpted from Supplemental Handbook Maintenance Instructions, USAF Model QB-17 Aircraft, 1 May 1955, Revised 15 June 1957.

[277] Ibid.

[278] 'Douglas Develops Camera System To Record Accuracy of Missiles', *Aviation Week,* 5 March 1956.

[279] 'Air Force Orders 100 BOMARC IM-99s', *Aviation Week,* 27 January 1958.

[280] Duncan Curtis, QF-80 manuscript shared with the author.

[281] Ibid.

[282] History, 3205th Drone Group, Air Proving Ground Command, October–December 1951 (including supporting documents all located in AFHRA microfilm reel M0212).

[283] 'Operation *Teapot* Nevada Test Site February–May 1955, Project 5.1 Destructive Loads on Aircraft in Flight, Issuance Date January 31, 1958', Headquarters Field Command, Armed Forces Special Weapons Project, Sandia Base, Albuquerque, New Mexico.

[284] Ibid.

[285] Ibid.

[286] Ibid.

[287] Ibid.

[288] Ibid.

[289] Ibid.

[290] Ibid.

[291] Ibid.

[292] Ibid.

[293] Ibid.

[294] Ibid.

[295] Ibid.

[296] History, 3205th Drone Group, Air Proving Ground Command, July–December 1952 (including supporting documents all located in AFHRA microfilm reel M0212).

[297] Ibid.

[298] History, 3205th Drone Group, Air Proving Ground Command, January–June 1953 (including supporting documents all located in AFHRA microfilm reel M0212).

[299] History, 3205th Drone Group, Air Proving Ground Command, July–December 1953.

[300] History, 3205th Drone Group, Air Proving Ground Command, July–December 1955 (including supporting documents all located in AFHRA microfilm reel M0213 [poor quality of copy inhibits usefulness of this source]).

[301] Ibid.

[302] 'Drone Control Improved', *Naval Aviation News,* May 1955.

[303] At the time this is written, information on the FSI QF-86E programme is found at: https://aviationarchives.net/Flight%20Systems%20Sabres.htm

[304] Ibid.

[305] 'Manned Aircraft Provide RPV Source', *Aviation Week and Space Technology*, 22 January 1973.

[306] 'QF/PQM-102 Target System, Project *Pave Deuce*', PQM-102 System Program Office, May 1975 – Final Report: March 1973 – April 1975, Deputy for Armament Systems, Armament Development and Test Center, Air Force Systems Command, United States Air Force, Eglin Air Force Base, Florida. (ADTC-TR-75-20)

[307] Ibid.

[308] Ibid.

[309] Ibid.

[310] Ibid.

[311] Ibid.

[312] Ibid.

[313] Ibid.

[314] 'Developmental Verification of Flight Termination System for Proposed PQM-102 Drone', abstract from final report, November 1973 by John M Hill, Air Force Special Weapons Center, Kirtland AFB, New Mexico, Defense Technical Information Center (DTIC) accession number AD0770562.

[315] 'QF/PQM-102 Target System, Project *Pave Deuce*', PQM-102 System Program Office, May 1975 – Final Report: March 1973 – April 1975, Deputy for Armament Systems, Armament Development and Test Center, Air Force Systems Command, United States Air Force, Eglin Air Force Base, Florida. (ADTC-TR-75-20)

[316] Ibid.

[317] Ibid.

[318] Ibid.

[319] Ibid.

[320] 'USAF Expands Weapons Center Effort', *Aviation Week and Space Technology*, 15 July 1974.

[321] 'QF/PQM-102 Target System, Project *Pave Deuce*', PQM-102 System Program Office, May 1975 – Final Report: March 1973 – April 1975, Deputy for Armament Systems, Armament Development and Test Center, Air Force Systems Command, United States Air Force, Eglin Air Force Base, Florida. (ADTC-TR-75-20)

[322] Ibid.

[323] Ibid.

[324] News Release 770409A, 'PQM-102 Drones', 25 April 1977, United States Air Force, Headquarters Aerospace Defense Command Directorate of Information, Peterson AFB, Colorado.

[325] 'QF-16 Full Scale Aerial Target' page from F-16.net website.

[326] 'F-100s Set to Become Target Drones' by David M North, *Aviation Week and Space Technology,* 28 September 1981.

[327] '309 AMARG', Ogden Air Logistics Center, 309th Maintenance Wing, computer presentation by Jeff Peterson, circa 2011 from DTIC online holdings.

[328] 'Drone Wars: QF-100 Super Sabre' by Aaron Hutchins, 12 May 2021, Blind Bat News website.

[329] 'AMRAAM Successful in Key Test: GAO Calls for Halting Production' by William B Scott and John D Morrocco, *Aviation Week and Space Technology*, 14 May 1990.

[330] Ibid.

[331] '309 AMARG', Ogden Air Logistics Center, 309th Maintenance Wing, computer presentation by Jeff Peterson, circa 2011 from DTIC online holdings.

[332] More QF-106 details were available at the time of this writing at: https://f-106deltadart.com/drones.htm

[333] 'Cost-Benefit Comparison of Alternative Configurations for QF-4B Target System' by ARINC Research Corporation, prepared for US Naval Missile Center, Point Mugu, California, under Contract F09603-73-A-4392-0010, Publication 1250-01-1-1321, September 1974.

[334] '309 AMARG', Ogden Air Logistics Center, 309th Maintenance Wing, computer presentation by Jeff Peterson, circa 2011 from DTIC online holdings.

[335] US Air Force Fact Sheet, 'QF-4 Aerial Target', at af.mil.

[336] Aviation Safety Network online report listed as ASN Wikibase Occurrence #225322.

[337] 'Drone crashes on take-off from Holloman', news release by Arlan Ponder, 49th Fighter Wing Public Affairs, 28 August 2006.

[338] 'Report of the Defense Science Board Task Force on Aerial Targets', Office of the Under Secretary of Defense for Acquisition, Technology, and Logistics, Washington, D.C., October 2005.

[339] Ibid.

[340] Ibid.

[341] 'BAE Systems Delivers Its 300th F-4 Flying Drone for U.S. Air Force', BAE press release, 12 November 2012.

[342] 'Phantom Pharewell: The Last Flight of the QF-4 at Holloman AFB' by Steven Valinski, *Aviation Photography* Digest, 6 January 2017.

[343] 'New Development at Mugu', *Naval Aviation News,* February 1965.

[344] Ibid.

[345] Report, 'Review of Past and Current Trials and Uses of Unmanned Vehicles', Jay Womack and Arthur Steczkowski, HSD-TR-87-011, September 1986–May 1987, Quest Research Corporation, Dayton, Ohio.

[346] 'Drone Establishes Records', *Naval Aviation News,* March 1964.

[347]Abstract, 'QT-33A Flight Termination System Development', Naval Weapons Center, China Lake, California, October 1971. DTIC accession number AD0888663.

[348] Ibid.

[349] Abstract, 'QT-33A Aerial Target Smoke-Generating Systems (Mineral Oil and JP-4 Aircraft Fuel)', Naval Weapons Center, China Lake, California, October 1970. DTIC accession number AD0876825.

[350] Camera Pod in Production",' *Naval Aviation News,* May 1957.

[351] Ibid.

[352] Jay Womack and Arthur Steczkowski, 'Review of Past and Current Trials and Uses of Unmanned Vehicles', Report HSD-TR-87-011, Dayton, Ohio, United States Air Force.

[353] Duncan Curtis, *The QF-86 Sabre,* manuscript shared with the author.

[354] Ibid.

[355] Ibid.

[356] Ibid.

[357] Ibid.

[358] Ibid.

[359] Ibid.

[360] Ibid.

[361] Ibid.

[362] Ibid.

[363] Ibid.

[364] Ibid.

[365] Ibid.

[366] Ibid.

[367] Ibid.

[368] 'QB-47 Improves BOMARC Targeting Ability' by Erwin J Bulban, *Aviation Week,* 5 September 1960.

[369] Ibid.

[370] Ibid.

[371] 'Operational Analysis Report of the Microwave Command Guidance System', prepared for Aeronautical Systems Division, Air Force Systems Command, United States Air Force, Wright-Patterson AFB, Dayton, Ohio, circa May 1962.

[372] Ibid.

[373] Ibid.

[374] Ibid.

[375] Excerpted from interview transcript, Lockheed test pilot Jim Eastham with Dana Kilanowski, 26 September 2003, in the holdings of the Society of Experimental Test Pilots.

[376] Ibid.

[377] Peter M Bowers, *Boeing Aircraft Since 1916,* Aero Publishers, Fallbrook, California, 1966.

[378] Ibid.

[379] Fred Anderson, *Northrop – An Aeronautical History,* Northrop Corporation, Los Angeles, California, 1976.

[380] Gordon Swanborough and Peter M Bowers, *United States Military Aircraft Since 1908,* Putnam, London, 1971.

[381] Howard L. Turner, John S. White and Rudolph D. VanDyke, Jr, 'Flight Testing by Radio Remote Control – Flight Evaluation of a Beep Control System', NACA TN 3496, March 1955. (dates in the report suggest the testing was done circa 1951–52).

[382] Ibid.

[383] Ibid.

[384] Gordon Swanborough and Peter M Bowers, *United States Military Aircraft Since 1908,* Putnam, London, 1971.

[385] 'USASC-USAAS-USAAC-USAAF-USAF Military Aircraft Serial Numbers – 1908 to Present' by Joe Baugher, online website.

[386] TSENG Report No 3, Formerly Report TSEST-A3, 'Characteristics of Experimental Airplanes (& Missiles) – short title 'Green Book', 9th Edition, 1 January 1948.

[387] Ibid.

[388] Ibid.

[389] History of 1st Experimental Guided Missiles Group, Eglin Air Force Base, Florida – 1 July–31 December 1948.

[390] Office of the Operations Officer, 1st Experimental Air Service Squadron, Eglin Air Force Base, Florida, to Commanding Officer, 1st XGM Group, Eglin Air Force Base, Florida. Subject: Banshee Training Flights to Hawaii, 7 December 1948 (included as attachment to History of 1st Experimental Guided Missiles Group for 1 July–1 December 1948).

[391] History of 1st Experimental Guided Missiles Group, Eglin Air Force Base, Florida – 1 July–31 December 1948.

[392] History of 1st Experimental Guided Missiles Group, Eglin Air Force Base, Florida – 1 January–30 June 1949.

[393] Ibid.

[394] Air Proving Ground Termination Report, Project No 12481–5, Subject: Operational Potentialities of Banshee Systems and Techniques, 19 July 1950.

[395] Ibid.

[396] Ibid.

[397] Ibid.

[398] Ibid.

[399] Ibid.

[400] 'Cruise Missiles for the U.S. Navy: An Exemplar of Innovation in a Military Organization' by Capt Philip W Signor, Naval War College paper, June 1994.

[401] 'QF-104 drones' by Charles Dildine, International F-104 Society website.

[402] 'Partial Flight Manual, USAF Series QF-104A Aircraft', 30 June 1966.

[403] Ibid.

[404] 'QF-104 drones' by Charles Dildine, International F-104 Society website.

[405] Ibid.

[406] Ibid.

[407] 'Remote Control Recovery System Flight Test Plan for Air Force Flight Test Center' Abstract by Sperry Phoenix Company, Arizona, 18 November 1963.

[408] Summary Report – Full-Scale Transport Controlled Impact Demonstration Program, DOT/FAA/CT-87/10, US Department of Transportation, Federal Aviation Administration, September 1987.

[409] 'Remote Control of an Impact Demonstration Vehicle', NASA Technical Memorandum 85925, April 1985, by Paul F Harney, James B Craft, Jr and Richard G Johnson.

[410] Summary Report – Full-Scale Transport Controlled Impact Demonstration Program, DOT/FAA/CT-87/10, US Department of Transportation, Federal Aviation Administration, September 1987.

[411] Ibid.

[412] 'Remote Control of an Impact Demonstration Vehicle', NASA Technical Memorandum 85925, April 1985, by Paul F Harney, James B Craft, Jr and Richard G Johnson.

[413] Summary Report – Full-Scale Transport Controlled Impact Demonstration Program, DOT/FAA/CT-87/10, US Department of Transportation, Federal Aviation Administration, September 1987.

[414] Ibid.

[415] Ibid.

[416] From information provided by the National Museum of the United States Air Force.

[417] 'Effectiveness of Small Arms Incendiary Ammunition at High Altitudes (U), Project TS1-47, Report R-1392 by D Jacobs, chemical engineer and J J Caven, chemist, for Col James A Richardson III, Ordnance Corps, circa June 1957.

[418] History of 1st Experimental Guided Missiles Group, January–June 1949 (including supporting documents all located in AFHRA microfilm reel B0745).

[419] 'Effectiveness of Incendiary Ammunition at High Altitude', HQ Air Materiel Command, Wright-Patterson Air Force Base Engineering Division, Memorandum Report, 21 August 1950 (at AFHRA).

[420] Ibid.

[421] Ibid.

[422] 'Effectiveness of Small Arms Incendiary Ammunition at High Altitudes (U), Project TS1-47, Report R-1392 by D Jacobs, chemical engineer and J J Caven, chemist, for Col James A Richardson III, Ordnance Corps, circa June 1957.

[423] Ibid.

[424] Gordon Swanborough and Peter M. Bowers, *United States Navy Aircraft Since 1911,* Putnam, London, 1976.

[425] 'Jet Vortices Present Light Plane Hazard' by Claude Witze, *Aviation Week,* 17 December 1956.

[426] Ibid.

[427] 'Wingtip Vortices Menace Light Planes', *Aviation Week*, 24 June 1957.

[428] Jet Vortices Present Light Plane Hazard' by Claude Witze, *Aviation Week*, 17 December 1956.

[429] 'HTK-1 Remotely Controlled', *Naval Aviation News,* April 1955.

[430] 'Remote-Controlled 'Copter', *Naval Aviation News,* September 1956.

[431] 'Kaman's External Control System', *Naval Aviation News,* May 1957.

[432] Ibid.

[433] Ibid.

[434] 'Electric 'Copter Flown', *Naval Aviation News,* November 1958.

[435] 'Less Than a Year After his Death, Charlie Kaman's Helicopters Achieve Another First' by Robert F Dorr, *Defense Media Network*, 19 January 2012.

[436] 'Marines get "hot hookup", pioneer new technique' by Cpl Lisa Tourtelot, US Marine Corps, 29 May 2012, via Defense Visual Information Distribution System.

[437] 'Boeing AH-6', Wikipedia as of 25 March 2023.

[438] Ibid.

[439] 'Report of the Defense Science Board Task Force on Aerial Targets', Office of the Under Secretary of Defense for Acquisition, Technology and Logistics, Washington, D.C., October 2005.

[440] Ibid.

[441] Ibid.

[442] 'First unmanned QF-16 flight takes place' by 2Lt Andrea Valencia, 325th Fighter Wing Public Affairs.

[443] 'QF-16' online fact sheet, *Air and Space Forces Magazine.*

[444] Interview, Steve Rainey with the author, 16 July 2023.

[445] Ibid.

[446] Ibid.

[447] Ibid.

[448] Ibid.

[449] From observations made by Steve Rainey to the author, August 2023.

[450] E-mail, QF-16 pilot Gregg Welling to the author, 22 July 2023.

[451] 'F-15 puts tracking-system-assisted missile on target', 11 August 2021, Eglin Air Force Base, Florida.

[452] '53rd Wing completes first-ever guided launch of AIM-120D3' by 1Lt Lindsey Heflin, 53rd Wing, Eglin Air Force Base.

[453] 'Boeing, U.S. Air Force public-private partnership Yields First QF-16 Full-Scale Aerial Target', Defense Advancement web page.

[454] 'Request for Information for Next Generation Aerial Target', Version 1 dated 19 August 2022.

[455] Ibid.

APPENDIX 1

List of B-17 Flying Fortresses converted into Drones and Drone Directors

The scope of droned B-17 Flying Fortress operations, tests and training from the Second World War to 1960 consumed many airframes considered expendable, and led to the preservation of others when director aircraft outlived the last of the QB-17 drones. This listing, while not exhaustive, nonetheless collates details from USAAF/USAF records plus photographs from many sources to provide an idea of the magnitude of the B-17s' contributions to remotely-piloted technology. Comments show details like service and disposal where known – some of these aircraft may have had longer and more varied service in the drone and director community than the sometimes-anecdotal tables in USAF reports indicate.

Aircraft	Drone or Director	Year(s)	Comments
41-24639	Drone	1944	*Aphrodite*; B-17F *Careful Virgin* lost on mission 4/8/44
42-3438	Drone	1944	*Aphrodite*; B-17F lost on mission 31/10/44
42-3461	Drone	1944	*Aphrodite*; B-17F lost on mission 4/8/44
42-5484	Drone	1945	Project *Hermit*; B-17F deliberately flown into mountain after remote control take-off 11/45
42-30039	Drone	1944	*Aphrodite*; B-17F *Liberty Belle* lost on mission 15/10/44
42-30066	Drone	1944	*Aphrodite*; B-17F *Mugwump* lost on mission 31/10/44
42-30178	Drone	1944–45	*Aphrodite*; B-17F *Darlin' Dolly* lost on mission 1/1/45
42-30180	Drone	1944	*Aphrodite*; B-17F *Black Hawk* lost on mission 11/9/44
42-30212	Drone	1944	*Aphrodite*; B-17F *Quarterback* lost on mission 6/8/44
42-30237	Drone	1944–45	*Aphrodite*; B-17F *Stump Jumper* lost on mission 1/1/45
42-30342	Drone	1944	*Aphrodite*; B-17F *T'aint A Bird II* lost on mission 4/8/44
42-30353	Drone	1944	*Aphrodite*; B-17F *TEN KNIGHTS IN A BAR ROOM* lost on mission 5/12/44
42-30363	Drone	1944	*Aphrodite*; B-17F *Ruth L III* lost on mission 14/9/44
42-30595	Drone Trainer	1944	*Aphrodite*; B-17F *GREMLIN GUS II* with cut-down open cockpit; intended bomber used as *Aphrodite* trainer
42-31394	Drone	1944	*Aphrodite*; B-17G lost on mission 6/8/44
42-37743	Drone	1944	*Aphrodite*; B-17G *Yankee Doodle Dandy* lost on mission 15/10/44
42-39824	Drone	1944	*Aphrodite*; B-17G lost on mission 5/12/44
42-39827	Drone	1944	*Aphrodite*; B-17G lost on mission 14/9/44
42-39835	Drone	1944	*Aphrodite*; B-17G lost over Britain on mission 4/8/44
43-37652	Drone	1954	B-17G Holloman, destroyed 10/6/54
43-37793	Director	1944–45	*Aphrodite*; B-17G
43-37946	Director/Navigation	1944–45	*Aphrodite*; B-17G sold for scrap, Kingman, 11/45
43-37953	Director/Control	1944–45	*Aphrodite*; B-17G sold for scrap, Kingman, 11/45
43-37962	Director	1944–45	*Aphrodite*; B-17G sold for scrap, Kingman, 12/45
43-38006	Director	1944–45	*Aphrodite*; B-17G sold for scrap, Kingman, 12/45
43-38081	Director	1944–45	*Aphrodite*; B-17G sold for scrap, Kingman, 1/46
43-39021	Drone	1955	B-17G (QB-17L) destroyed 21/11/55
43-39112	Drone	1953	B-17G lost Holloman 4/12/53
43-39362	Drone	1953	B-17G (probably previously SB-17) lost Holloman 21/10/53
43-39499	Drone	1955	B-17G damaged by F6F drone ground collision, Point Mugu, 6/10/55
43-39508	Drone	1956–58	Last Boeing-built B-17G (QB-17N); lost Patrick 21/10/58
44-83388	Drone	1949	B-17G Eglin ditching programme
44-83513	Drone	1949	B-17G Eglin ditching programme
44-83514	Director	1951	B-17G 3205th Drone Squadron Letter J; *Greenhouse*; air tanker; Confederate Air Force *Sentimental Journey*
44-83517	Drone	1955	B-17G 3205th Drone Squadron; Inyokern, lost on desert wheels-up landing 21/1/55
44-83519	Drone	1946	B-17G *Crossroads*; Eglin; scrapped 1949
44-83525	Director	1951	B-17G 3205th Drone Squadron Letter E; *Greenhouse*; Tallmantz Aviation; Junior Burchinal; Kermit Weeks.
44-83528	Drone	1946	B-17G *Crossroads*, then ditching programme at Eglin.
44-83533	Drone	?	B-17G

Aircraft	Drone or Director	Year(s)	Comments
44-83537	Drone	?	B-17G *Greenhouse*
44-83542	Director	?	B-17G *Greenhouse*; later Aero Union N9324Z crash; parts source
44-83549	Drone	1951	B-17G 3205th Drone Squadron Letter J; *Greenhouse*
44-83553	Drone	1946	B-17G *Crossroads*; Eglin; scrapped 1950
44-83556	Drone	1955–56	B-17G Point Mugu, Holloman/White Sands
44-83559	Director	1951	B-17G 3205th Drone Squadron; *Greenhouse*; Strategic Aerospace Museum, Nebraska.
44-83560	Drone	1946	B-17G *Crossroads*
44-83565	Drone	1951	B-17G 3205th Drone Squadron Letter B; *Greenhouse*; Holloman, destroyed by Nike 20/4/53
44-83566	Drone	1951	B-17G 3205th Drone Squadron Letter D; *Greenhouse*
44-83588	Drone	1946	B-17G *Crossroads*; Eglin; scrapped 1950
44-83589	Drone	1946–55	B-17G *Crossroads*, *Sandstone*; China Lake, destroyed by Bird Dog, 14/6/55
44-83591	Drone	1946	B-17G *Crossroads*, *Sandstone*
44-83592	Director	1946–48	B-17G *Crossroads*, *Sandstone*; crash B-17 for *Twelve O'Clock High*, 1949
44-83596	Director	1946–48	B-17G *Crossroads*, *Sandstone*
44-83597	?	1948	B-17G *Sandstone*
44-83602	Director	1946–48	B-17G *Crossroads*, *Sandstone*
44-83603	Drone	1946–51	B-17G *Crossroads*; Det 1, Holloman, Falcon tests; crashed 4/12/51
44-83604	Director	1946–48	B-17G *Crossroads*, *Sandstone*
44-83605	Drone	1946–55	B-17G *Crossroads*, *Sandstone*; downed, Project *Porcupine*, China Lake, 17/5/55
44-83606	Drone	1946–48	B-17G *Crossroads*, *Sandstone*
44-83610	Drone	1946–50	B-17G *Crossroads*, *Sandstone*; later shot itself down in altitude fuel test, 24/5/50
44-83612	Director	1946–48	B-17G *Crossroads*, *Sandstone*
44-83613	Drone	1946–48	B-17G *Crossroads*, *Sandstone*
44-83616	Director	1946	B-17G *Crossroads*, *Sandstone*
44-83617	Drone	1951	B-17G 3205th Drone Squadron Letter E; *Greenhouse*
44-83622	Drone	1946–48	B-17G *Crossroads*, *Sandstone*
44-83624	Drone	1946–48	B-17G *Crossroads*, *Sandstone*
44-83635	Drone	1946–48	B-17G *Crossroads*, *Sandstone*
44-83636	Director	1951	B-17G 3205th Drone Squadron; *Greenhouse*
44-83639	Director	1946–48	B-17G *Crossroads*, *Sandstone*
44-83641	Director	1946	B-17G *Crossroads*, *Sandstone*; squared numeral 9 on vertical fin circa 1949
44-83644	Drone	1951	B-17G 3205th Drone Squadron Letter G; *Greenhouse*; downed by F-86D Eglin 3/4/53
44-83645	Drone	1946	B-17G *Crossroads*, *Sandstone*
44-83646	Director	1946–48	B-17G *Crossroads Super Mother* tail numeral VI; *Sandstone;* Eglin; scrapped 1950
44-83649	Drone	1951–54	B-17G 3205th Drone Squadron Letter I; *Greenhouse*; Inyokern, destroyed by Sidewinder 18/2/54
44-83652	Drone	1951	B-17G 3205th Drone Group Letter L; *Greenhouse*
44-83654	Director	?	B-17G *Greenhouse*; Holloman
44-83656	Drone	1951–54	B-17G 3205th Drone Squadron Letter A; *Greenhouse*; Holloman, destroyed by Falcon 12/3/54
44-83657	Director	1951	B-17G Letter A, 3205th Drone Squadron
44-83658	Drone	1951–52	B-17G *Greenhouse*; Det 1, Holloman, destroyed by Nike 10/4/52
44-83660	Director	1946–48	B-17G *Crossroads*, *Sandstone*
44-83662	Drone	1946–48	B-17G *Crossroads*, *Sandstone*
44-83664	Drone	1946–48	B-17G Crossroads, *Sandstone*; out of control loops and crash during *Sandstone* 15/4/48
44-83665	Drone	1952	B-17G Det 1, Holloman; Talos test
44-83666	Drone	?	B-17G *Greenhouse*
44-83669	Drone	1951	B-17G 3205th Drone Squadron Letter C; *Greenhouse*

Aircraft	Drone or Director	Year(s)	Comments
44-83674	Drone	1951–54	B-17G 3205th Drone Squadron Letter K; *Greenhouse*; Inyokern, destroyed by Terrier 18/5/54
44-83678	Director	1946	B-17G *Crossroads*, *Sandstone*
44-83679	Drone	1951	B-17G 3200th Drone Squadron; *Greenhouse*
44-83680	Director	1951	B-17G 3205th Drone Squadron Letter L; shot down in error by F-86D at Eglin 25/8/52
44-83683	Director	1951	B-17G 3205th Drone Squadron Letter K; *Greenhouse*
44-83684	Director	1951–59	B-17G 3205th Drone Squadron; *Greenhouse*; N3713G, Ed Maloney, Planes of Fame
44-83687	Director	1951	B-17G 3205th Drone Squadron Letter I; *Greenhouse*
44-83689	Director	1951	B-17G 3205th Drone Squadron Letter D; *Greenhouse*
44-83690	Director	1951	B-17G 3205th Drone Squadron Letter H; *Greenhouse*; Grissom AFB; Robins AFB museum
44-83692	Drone	1951	B-17G 3205th Drone Squadron Letter F; *Greenhouse*
44-83694	Director	1951	B-17G 3205th Drone Squadron; *Greenhouse*
44-83695	Drone/Monitor	1952	B-17G Det 1, Holloman for Falcon tests; destroyed by Falcon 1952
44-83697	Drone	1951–52	B-17G *Greenhouse*; Det 2 Point Mugu
44-83704	Drone	1955	B-17G (ex-SB-17); believed lost in China Lake Bird Dog test 25/6/55
44-83715	Director	?	B-17G *Greenhouse*
44-83717	Drone	1959	B-17G Holloman, destroyed by Falcon from F-101 6/8/59
44-83725	Drone	1953	B-17G Holloman
44-83738	Drone	1951–52	B-17G *Greenhouse*; Det 1, Holloman for missile tests, destroyed by Nike 24/4/52
44-83756	Drone	1953	B-17G Holloman
44-83766	Drone	1955	B-17G destroyed China Lake by Bird Dog 12/4/55
44-83777	Drone	1954	B-17G destroyed Holloman by Talos 27/5/54
44-83782	Drone	1955	B-17G (QB-17L) Point Mugu
44-83784	Drone	1955	B-17G (QB-17L) destroyed 5/12/55
44-83791	Drone	?	B-17G
44-85499	Drone	1955	B-17G destroyed by Bird Dog 16/3/55
44-85504	Drone	1946–47	B-17G *Crossroads*, Eglin ditching programme
44-85546	Drone	?	B-17G Eglin ditching programme
44-85569	Drone	1952	B-17G Det 1, Holloman for Nike tests
44-85573	Drone	1951–52	B-17G Det 1, Holloman for Falcon, Nike tests
44-85575	Drone	1950	B-17G Eglin; scrapped 1951
44-85589	Drone	1952	B-17G Det 1, Holloman for Nike tests
44-85599	Director	1951–52	B-17G Det 1, Holloman, later Dyess AFB display
44-85600	Director	1951–55	B-17G Det 1, Holloman for Falcon tests
44-85612	Drone	1952	B-17G Det 1, Holloman for Nike tests
44-85648	Drone	1947	B-17G Eglin ditching programme (possibly destroyed/salvaged 1949)
44-85690	Director	1946–50	B-17G *Crossroads* tail numeral V; Eglin; scrapped 1950
44-85738	Director	1946–?	B-17G *Crossroads* tail numeral IV; Det 1, Holloman Falcon, Nike; display Tulare
44-85752	Director	1946–50	B-17G *Crossroads* tail numeral III; Eglin; scrapped 1950
44-85815	Director	1946–50	B-17G *Crossroads* tail numeral II; Eglin; scrapped 1950
44-85818	Director	1946–49	B-17G *Crossroads* tail numeral I; Eglin; scrapped 1949
44-85819	Drone	1946	B-17G *Crossroads*; Wright-Patterson; scrapped 1949
44-85820	Drone	1946	B-17G *Crossroads*

APPENDIX 2

Glossary of Terms, Acronyms and Abbreviations

'Air-Beeper' Pilot – Remote pilot of a drone aircraft.

'Beeping' – Flying a droned aircraft by remote control.

DB (as in DB-17) – Director Bomber; mother ship.

DSCE – Drone Stabilisation and Control Equipment.

MB (as in MB-17) – Missile Bomber, an early name for the drone; later nomenclature was QB-17.

Metal Stick – A method of drone control used by the safety pilot for system checkout, training and orientation. Commands are initiated by the safety pilot from the cockpit of the drone. They simulate commands from the guidance radio system and are routed directly to the DSCE.

NOLO or NULLO – Based on 'No Live Operator' or 'Not Under Live Local Operator', this indicates a drone flight with no onboard human.

APPENDIX 3

Select Bibliography

Bell, Dana, *Air Force Colors, Volume 3, Pacific and Home Front, 1942-47,* Squadron/Signal Publications, Carrollton, Texas, 1997.

Bowers, Peter M, *Fortress in the Sky,* Sentry Books, Granada Hills, California, 1976.

Swanborough, Gordon and Bowers, Peter M, *United States Military Aircraft Since 1908,* Putnam, London, 1971.

Swanborough, Gordon and Bowers, Peter M, *United States Navy Aircraft Since 1911,* Putnam, London, 1968.

Thompson, Scott A, *Final Cut, The Post-War B-17 Flying Fortress – The Survivors,* Pictorial Histories Publishing Co, Missoula, Montana, 1995.

Index

Ferret!

USAAF Airborne Signals Intelligence Development and Operations 1942-1945

William M Cahill

The design and production of the airborne signals intelligence (SIGINT) aircraft of the USAAF during World War Two was a story of rapid wartime evolution. In three short years, the USAAF went from hand-built prototypes to full scale production of an aircraft type that had not previously existed in the US inventory. Government partnered with universities to form research laboratories focused on radar countermeasures (RCM) while US airline maintenance facilities were requisitioned to form production centres for modifications to allow rapid insertion of the technology. The USAAF pushed the bounds of systems integration and programme management, learning how to rapidly develop, field and operate aircraft in the ever-evolving signals war.

This new study of the origins of US SIGINT operations is profusely illustrated with expansive captions, maps, and operational details. William Cahill, a former USAF officer with a reconnaissance background, offers unique historical insights into the development and operation of these vital airborne signals intelligence assets.

ISBN: 9781800352971

Price: £34.95

Order at **crecy.co.uk**

Aeronautica Macchi Fighters

Mc.200 Saetta – Mc.202 Folgore – Mc.205 Veltro

Luigino Caliaro

In this thoroughly researched, detailed and indeed exhaustive study, aviation historian Luigino Caliaro tells the story of the three main World War II fighters produced by the Varese-based Aeronautica Macchi.

Drawing on company and military archive reports, the author traces the origins of Aeronautica Macchi before examining the design and development of each type, as well as, in each case, production, prototypes and technical aspects. Also covered in this profusely-illustrated volume are details of the operational variants and project designs, along with a detailed narrative covering the history of each aircraft in service with the Regia Aeronautica, the Aviazione Nazionale Repubblicana, the Luftwaffe and Croatian Air Legion. Additionally, post-war service with the Aeronautica Militare and the Royal Egyptian Air Force is explored, as well as camouflage, markings, heraldry and insignia.

With hundreds of photographs, technical drawings and colour artwork, this book is an important addition to the 'Classic' series and forms the most comprehensive and informative account of this trio of aircraft in the English language.

ISBN: 9781800352803

Price: £40.00

Order at **crecy.co.uk**

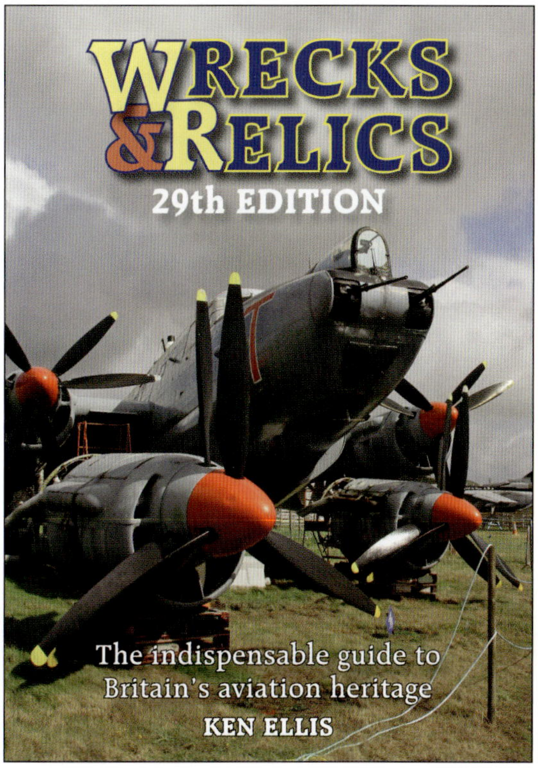

Wrecks & Relics 29th Edition

The indispensable guide to Britain's aviation heritage

Ken Ellis

Now remarkably in its 29th edition, since it was first published in the 1960s every edition of Wrecks & Relics has been eagerly sought after by aviation enthusiasts, historians, restorers and curators alike. Through five decades of publication under the authorship of Ken Ellis, 'W&R' has become renowned as the go-to source charting the highlights, changes and trends in the preservation of the aviation heritage of the British Isles. With in-depth coverage of more than 700 locations across the UK and Ireland, it lists more than 4,000 aircraft including their potted histories, previous identities and arrival dates.

Wrecks & Relics remains the only publication required to discover the incredible aeronautical treasures found across the United Kingdom and Ireland. It provides a trusted, comprehensive rundown of museums and collections and their exhibits – static or flying – together with workshops, military 'gate guardians', stored and instructional airframes, etc. It also reveals redundant and even derelict airframes being used for the most unlikely of purposes, including 'glamping' and at paint-ball sites.

ISBN: 9781800353046

Price: £19.95

Order at **crecy.co.uk**

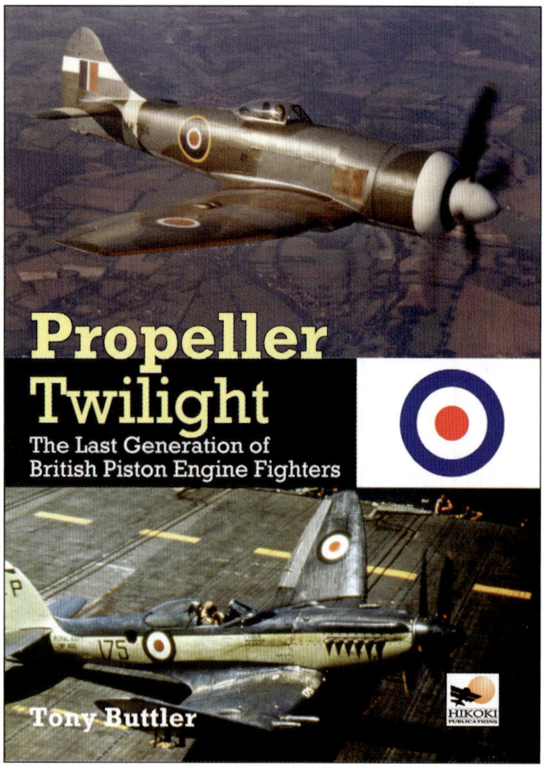

Propeller Twilight

The Last Generation of British Piston Engine Fighters

Tony buttler

This book examines the last generation of high-performance British propeller-driven fighters, types such as the Firecrest, late mark Spitfires and Seafires, Spiteful and Seafang, Sea Fury, late mark Tempests, Hornet and Sea Hornet, M.B.5 and Wyvern. From about 1942 onwards these extraordinary and very complex aeroplanes brought British piston fighter development to its zenith, but then in a very short space of time the new jet engine wiped this generation away. Perhaps it would not have been possible to take piston power any further anyway but the turboprop might have been a longer-term alternative, though in the end the only British type with this form of powerplant would be the Westland Wyvern naval strike fighter.

Chapters look at the engines involved including the Rolls-Royce Merlin 130 series, Griffon and Eagle, Napier Sabre and Bristol Centaurus, propeller developments (contra-rotating) and then take each fighter type in turn. The coverage describes their development and testing and includes quotes and passes from flight test reports.

ISBN: 9781800352735

Price: £34.95

Order at **crecy.co.uk**